JOHN AND SALLY McKEN[...] [...] [GU]IDE TO
IRELAND IS RECOGNISED [...] [CLA]SSIC GUIDE TO THE BEST PLACES FOR
VEGETARIANS TO EAT AND STAY IN IRELAND.

" THIS ESSENTIAL GASTRONOMIC GUIDE TO THE COUNTRY FEATURES A

WIDE RANGE OF VEGETARIAN RESTAURANTS, HOTELS, B&B'S AND

SHOPS WITH SOMETHING FOR EVERYONE FROM POVERTY-STRICKEN

BACKPACKERS TO THE DISCERNING VEGETARIAN CONNOISSEUR.

THE AUTHORS' DISTINCTIVE PROSE STYLE VIVIDLY CONVEYS THEIR

LOVE OF THE COUNTRY AND THE CULINARY HEIGHTS ITS CHEFS CAN

ACHIEVE. EVEN IF YOU DIDN'T WANT TO GO TO IRELAND BEFORE

READING THIS BOOK,

YOU'LL BE BUYING A TICKET BEFORE YOU TURN THE LAST PAGE "

BBC VEGETARIAN GOOD FOOD

THE BRIDGESTONE VEGETARIAN GUIDE TO IRELAND

FIRST PUBLISHED IN 1996 BY ESTRAGON PRESS, DURRUS, CO. CORK

© ESTRAGON PRESS

TEXT © JOHN AND SALLY McKENNA

THE MORAL RIGHT OF THE AUTHORS HAS BEEN ASSERTED

ISBN 1 874076 19 7

DESIGNED BY NICK CANN

COVER PHOTOGRAPH BY MIKE O'TOOLE

FOOD STYLING BY CONRAD GALLAGHER & ANN MARIE TOBIN

LOCATION: PEACOCK ALLEY, DUBLIN

PRINTED BY COLOUR BOOKS LTD

■ COVER PHOTO:
Shows Conrad Gallagher's Pumpkin Risotto with Grilled Vegetables and Chilli Aïoli. See page 191 for recipe.

■ Whilst every effort has been made to ensure that the information given in this book is accurate, the publishers and authors do not accept responsibility for any errors or omissions or for any change in the circumstances of any of the entries.

THE BRIDGESTONE

VEGETARIAN GUIDE TO IRELAND

BY JOHN & SALLY McKENNA

ESTRAGON PRESS

FOR DR DENIS COTTER

WITH THANKS TO:

Des Collins, Colm Conyngham, Eddie, Nick Cann, Pat Young,
Mike O'Toole, Ann Marie Tobin, Maureen Daly, Maria McCarthy,
Colette Tobin, Paula, Kevin and Ana, Pat Ruane.

JOHN McKENNA was born in Belfast and educated there and in Dublin, where he practiced as a barrister before turning to writing in 1989. He has won three Glenfiddich Awards, as Regional Writer, Radio Broadcaster and Restaurant Writer, in 1993, 1994 and 1995.

SALLY McKENNA was born in Kenya, and brought up on the Pacific island of Fiji before coming to Ireland in 1982. She cooked professionally before turning to writing about cookery and food.

CONTENTS

BRIDGESTONE

BRIDGESTONE is Japan's largest tyre manufacturer and the world's largest producer of rubber products.

Founded in 1931, it currently employs over 95,000 people in Europe, Asia and America and its products are sold in more than 150 countries. Its European plants are situated in France, Spain and Italy.

■ Bridgestone manufacture tyres for a wide variety of vehicles from passenger cars and motorcycles, trucks and buses to giant earthmovers and aircraft.

■ Many Japanese cars sold in Ireland have been fitted with Bridgestone tyres during manufacture and a host of exotic sports cars including Ferrari, Lamborghini, Porsche and Jaguar are fitted with Bridgestone performance tyres as original equipment.

■ Bridgestone commercial vehicle tyres enjoy a worldwide reputation for superior cost per kilometre performance and its aircraft tyres are used by more than 100 airlines.

■ In 1988 Bridgestone acquired the Firestone Tyre and Rubber Company combining the resources of both companies under one umbrella. This coupled with an intensive research and development programme has enabled Bridgestone to remain the world's most technologically advanced tyre company with testing centres in Japan, USA, Mexico and Italy.

■ Bridgestone tyres are distributed in Ireland by Bridgestone/Firestone Ireland Limited, a subsidiary of the multinational Bridgestone Corporation. A wide range of tyres are stocked in its central warehouse and staff provide sales, technical and delivery services all over the country.

■ Bridgestone tyres are available from tyre dealers throughout Ireland.

For further information:
BRIDGESTONE/FIRESTONE IRELAND LTD
Unit 4
Leopardstown Office Park,
Dublin 18
Tel: (01) 295 2844
Fax: (01) 295 2858

34 Hillsborough Road,
Lisburn
BT28 1AQ
Tel: (01 846) 678331
Fax: (01 846) 673235

HOW TO USE THIS BOOK

This Vegetarian Guide is arranged **ALPHABETICALLY**, firstly into the four provinces of Ireland – Connaught, Leinster, Munster and Ulster – and then into the individual counties within the provinces. Within the counties, the arrangement of the entries again follow alphabetically.

■ Entries in Northern Ireland, though part of the Ulster section, are itemised at the end of the book.

■ The contents of the Bridgestone Vegetarian Guide are exclusively the result of the authors' deliberations. All meals and accommodation were paid for and any offers of discounts or gifts were refused.

■ In a number of cases, where we have encountered a restaurateur or producer whose work represents a special and unique effort in terms of Irish food, we have awarded these people a star and marked these entries thus: ✪
These people are, simply, the very best at what they do.

■ In other cases where we felt the food was of special interest we have marked the entry with a ➔, meaning that the entry is worthy of making a special detour to enjoy the food.

■ Many of the Country Houses and B&Bs featured in this book are only open during the summer season, which means that they can be closed for any given length of time between October and March. Many others change their opening times during the winter. Even though opening times are given for restaurants it is always advisable in Ireland to telephone in advance and check opening times when booking.

PRICES All prices and details are correct at the time of going to press. Should the circumstances of any of the entries change, however, we are unable to accept any responsibility.

■ Finally, we greatly appreciate receiving reports, suggestions and criticisms from readers, and would like to thank those who have written in the past, whose opinions are of enormous assistance to us.

KEY: Restaurant ⓡ Accommodation ⓐ Food ⓕ Pub ⓟ Shop ⓢ

THE BRIDGESTONE AWARDS

THE BRIDGESTONE AWARDS are unique, inasmuch as we give awards not only to people who cook food – the normal recipients of gongs and what-have-yous in guide books – but also to people who produce the food which the cooks use.

■ We do this because as far as the Bridgestone Guides are concerned, we feel that it is not only important to reward creativity wherever we find it, but also because we feel it is vitally important to embrace and applaud the entire food culture.

■ Without an appreciation of where food comes from and how it is produced, without a concern as to the dedication and devotion of growers and cheesemakers and bakers, we cannot properly understand why we eat the food we eat.

■ It is for these reasons that we use books such as the Bridgestone Vegetarian Guide to single out the most committed and consummate food producers, as well as those cooks who convert their basic ingredients into culinary magnificence.

■ Of course, it is very often the case that the ability of the best chefs is explained by their appreciation of, and determination to find and use, the very best produce. When this delicious duality occurs, one enjoys food of unimpeachable splendour, food which is produced in harmony with nature and then cooked with true sympathy for its nature.

■ This is what we seek when we research and write the Bridgestone Guides. Happily, for us and for those who use these books, this situation is becoming ever more common. Ireland is daily building an ever richer, more pluralist and more enjoyable food culture. The people who practice this at its height are those who are described in the following pages.

■ The Bridgestone Awards are a celebration of creativity, of that spark of hunger and devotion which we praise in whatever circumstance we happen to find it. Unlike other guides, we hold no torch for grandeur or for slickness. Good food, and good hospitality, are best enjoyed in their simple, unpretentious glory.

✪ BRIDGESTONE AWARD - THE VERY BEST

ARDRAHAN CHEESE Kanturk, Co Cork

CAFÉ PARADISO Cork, Co Cork

DRIMCONG HOUSE Moycullen, Co Galway

DURRUS FARMHOUSE CHEESE Durrus, Co Cork

EDEN PLANTS Rossinver, Co Leitrim

INAGH FARMHOUSE CHEESE Inagh, Co Clare

THE IVORY TOWER Cork, Co Cork

PENNY & UDO LANGE Ballineen, Co Wicklow

LETTERCOLLUM HOUSE Timoleague, Co Cork

LISSARD LAKE LODGE Skibbereen, Co Cork

MANCH ESTATE Dunmanway, Co Cork

ORGANIC LIFE Kilpedder, Co Wicklow

TIR NA NOG Sligo, Co Sligo

TRUFFLES Sligo, Co Sligo

WEST CORK NATURAL CHEESE Schull, Co Cork

⊕ WORTHY OF A DETOUR

AVOCA HANDWEAVERS Kilmacanogue, Co Wicklow

AYUMI-YA Blackrock, Co Dublin

AYUMI-YA Baggot Street, Dublin

THE IONA Holywood, Co Down

THE OLD RECTORY Wicklow, Co Wicklow

QUAY CO-OP Cork, Co Cork

RAJDOOT TANDOORI Dublin

SAAGAR RESTAURANT Dublin

WEST CORK HERB FARM Skibbereen, Co Cork

INTRODUCTION

This latest edition of the BRIDGESTONE VEGETARIAN GUIDE TO IRELAND continues our policy of seeking out the most creative and accomplished vegetarian cooking, and describing the most exciting and original food producers, involved in the food chains of Ireland.

Once again, we have not limited our choices to restaurants and places to stay which cater solely for vegetarians. We have instead explored a broader field, looking also for cooks who are fired by the challenge of vegetarian cooking, but who also cater for the general market.

Indeed, this field of creative vegetarian cooking which is emerging from the mainstream restaurants, may very well be the most exciting thing happening in contemporary Irish cooking.

Inspired by many diverse factors, the great cooks of Ireland are increasingly turning towards a style of cooking which cannot be described as strictly "vegetarian" or "non-vegetarian". It is, rather, simply good cooking, with ingredients used to obtain maximum deliciousness in any given dish.

One could explain this new direction by pointing to many factors which have led to increasing suspicion amongst people regarding the food they eat.

But the truth of the matter is that the drive towards an accomplished, original and exciting vegetarian cooking is simply part of a greater confidence and self-consciousness about their work which one finds amongst the great cooks.

Their ambition now derives not from the hierarchical style with which French cuisine swaddled the world for so long, but on a style which is inclusive, democratic, individual and, ultimately, devoted to enjoyment.

This may seem like an obvious thing to state - for what other reason could a restaurant or a place to stay exist? - but in the past too many restaurateurs have felt that we should worship at the feet of their skills, rather than concentrate on having a good time.

For the younger generation of chefs, the stale concept of veneration is anathema to the very idea of their work. They want us to share their food, not merely spectate it. They see their work as part of the dynamic of a society, as part of the culture of a society, and have no wish to be applauded for virtuosity which does not ultimately serve the noble cause of having one hell of a good time.

This book is dedicated to the pursuit of pleasure, and its central focus is a respect for pleasure. This is why we eat, and it is why we should enjoy eating. When that enjoyment is placed within the context of a food culture which is respectful, caring and animated, there is no higher pinnacle onto which we can place the simple, essential act of cooking and eating.

JOHN AND SALLY McKENNA
DURRUS,
COUNTY CORK

CONNAUGHT

INCLUDING THE COUNTIES OF

GALWAY

LEITRIM

MAYO

SLIGO

COUNTY GALWAY

CONNEMARA – A SERENE DREAMSCAPE

CLIFDEN

THE CONNEMARA KITCHEN Ⓢ
Lyle McElderry & Connie Menezes
Clifden
Tel: (095) 21054
Kitchen Tel: (095) 43475

"It's like walking into someone's larder" is how Connie and Lyle's Connemara Kitchen has been described. The wooden shelves are laden with their own-label chutneys, marmalades, vinaigrettes and flavoured oils. There is honey, local bread, de Cecco pasta, wholefoods and fresh organic herbs. The cold cabinet stores their own pakoras, tortillas and arancini rice balls.

But the stars of this operation are their frozen curries and casseroles. You might find cauliflower and pea curry, cabbage with lentils or chilli bean and mixed vegetable casserole, Chinese cauliflower and broccoli in a lemon sauce, and Mexican style vegetable and bean stew. (All gluten free).

Connie hails originally from Burma - via Brighton, Lyle is from Antrim so authenticity and an understanding of many culinary cultures is evident, making choices all the more difficult.

● **OPEN:** 10am-6pm Mon-Sun.

ERRISEASKE HOUSE Ⓡ Ⓐ
Christian & Stefan Matz
Ballyconneely, nr Clifden
Tel: (095) 23553, Fax: 23639

Stefan Matz is a dazzlingly talented cook, a man who uses all his ability to make his food delicious. His vegetarian dishes such as watercress soup, or his ravioli, stuffed with a variety of fillings and pooled in a cream mushroom sauce, or his gratinated courgette in a tomato and olive coulis, show all of his skills at work, flavours precisely summoned, finishing stunningly achieved.

This is cookery built around essentials and essences. The essential things are assembled on the plate, the essences are the pure flavours which Stefan Matz extracts from each ingredient, with his skills subjugated in the cause of flavour

Modesty and a lack of display are major factors of the success of the Erriseaske. It is a small, quiet restaurant with rooms in a lonely and lovely spot on the coastline.

● **OPEN:** 6.30pm-9.30pm Mon-Sun.
High season lunches by reservation.
Closed 1 Nov-1 Apr.
● **AVERAGE PRICE:** Dinner over £20.
B&B over £25.
Visa, Access/Master, Amex, Diners.
Take the coast road from Clifden to Ballyconneely, then follow the signposts.

HIGH MOORS RESTAURANT ®
Hugh & Eileen Griffin
Dooneen
Clifden
Tel: (095) 21342

Hugh Griffin begins any conversation about his garden with the words "It may seem ordinary, but..." but a few seconds into the dialogue his speech becomes more and more enthusiastic and animated.

"We have really concentrated on Variety – we have five different types of beans, thin and thick green ones, long yellow ones, we also have cardoon, and at least thirty types of lettuces!"

With these wonderful varieties of organic vegetables Eileen Griffin makes vegetarian choices such as twice baked St Tola goat's cheese soufflé; baked potato gnocchi with tomato ragout; cannelloni with pine nuts and "our cabbage and nutmeg just walks out the door".

Vegetarians are advised to give notice, as extra time allows Eileen to put a lot of thought into the menu.

The restaurant is one of a small number in Ireland which are located in people's houses. As evening sets across the high moor from which the Griffins' house takes its title, there are few places indeed where one would rather be. Smashing food, unabashed friendliness, unforgettable.

● **OPEN:** 6.30pm-9.30pm Wed-Sun. Closed Oct-May.
● **AVERAGE PRICE:** Dinner under £20. Visa, Access/Master, Amex.
Look for the sign, 1km from Clifden on the Ballyconneely road.

KILLE HOUSE Ⓐ
Anya Brand Vermoolen
Kingstown, Clifden
Tel: (095) 21849

Kille is a house of sumptuous, pristine elegance. You would be happy to be here in its elegant embrace even if the views were deathly dull, or breakfasts were boring.

But, of course, the location of the house near to the arching Sky Road allows for vistas of endless fascination in every direction, and Anya herself not only gives the house great good cheer, she is also a splendid cook with a very true touch and a very spontaneous style.

She scrambles fresh eggs to a rich and velvety emulsion, organises an array of fine cheeses, and there is crumbly, warm bread and excellent coffee.

Upstairs, meanwhile, the housekeeping in the four rooms is of such an extraordinary standard that there are few other places in the country to which Kille can be compared.

This means that you fold yourself into a big, snowy-white duvet, in a big beautiful bed, in a big handsome room, after a big, lazy soak in a big deep bath, and thank the stars you are in Connemara, and here in Kille.

● **OPEN:** 1 Apr-31 Oct.
● **AVERAGE PRICE:** B&B under £25. Dinner under £20.
No Credit Cards.
Ask directions for the Sky Road, and from this you will see the small hand-written sign directing you to the house.

ROUNDSTONE

ANGLER'S RETURN Ⓐ
Lynn Hill
Toombeola, Roundstone
Tel: (095) 31091

The Angler's Return, once part of the Ballynahinch estate, enjoys a superb location for exploring this most indomitable, mysterious part of Connemara: close to Roundstone, close to Clifden, a scoot away from Maam, adjacent to the severe waters of Leenane. And, you don't need a full length Barbour and an Ena Sharples' hairnet to stay here, despite the name of this 18th century sporting lodge.

The house is a quiet, peaceably run and simply furnished in muted pastels that show happy signs of maturity. The beds are high and soft, the rooms places in which to sleep deeply and Lynn Hill looks on breakfast as a deliciously wholesome experience, offering free-range eggs, homemade muesli and granola, yogurt and local cheeses.

● **OPEN:** May-end Oct (out of season by arrangement).
● **AVERAGE PRICE:** Under £25.
No Credit Cards.
Four miles down the Ballynahinch - Roundstone road.

O'DOWD'S Ⓟ
Margaret Griffin
Roundstone, Tel: (095) 35809

There could scarcely be a more beautiful site for a country pub on the sloping village of Roundstone, overlooking the sea. The pub is snuggy and smoky, the bar food simple and agreeable, and nicely, slightly spruced up in the restaurant at evening time. It is a pub that can be hard to leave.

● **OPEN:** Pub hours, bar food served noon-9.30pm Mon-Sun.
Restaurant closed mid-Oct-Feb.
● **AVERAGE PRICE:** Bar food under £5.
Restaurant under £10.

CREESHLA FARM Ⓕ
Josie Monks
Cushatrower
nr Roundstone
Tel: (095) 35814

Working patiently and productively over the last ten years, Josie Monks and her family have expanded their little farm shop to include a dizzying range of goodies.

There are porter cakes, madeira cakes, gateaux, chutneys, jams and marmalades. But, extra-special are the foods made from their herd of thirty goats: a clever variety of cheeses, including a goat's cheddar (mature and mild), cheese in oil, soft fromage frais, yogurt, and a feta. From these they make a memorable salad dip and, when they have enough cheese, a snap-upable cheesecake.

● **OPEN:** 9.30am-8pm Mon-Sun high season.
(Limited hours and limited foods available throughout the winter).
Look for signs about two-and-a-half miles from Roundstone.

GALWAY CITY

GALWAY RESTAURANTS

CAFÉ DU JOURNAL ®
Chris Terry
Quay Street, Galway
Tel: (091) 568426

A friendly and popular café in which vegetarians can order omelettes and filled croissants; Chris Terry also serves Emer Murray's wonderful cakes and desserts from Goya's.

● **OPEN:** 9am-9pm Mon-Sun.
● **AVERAGE PRICE:** Under £5.
Galway city centre.

CREATIVE CUISINE ®
Michael O'Grady
Kirwin's Lane
Galway
Tel: (091) 568 266

The modern decor and funky ambience of Kirwin's Lane Creative Cuisine has quickly built a lively following for its modern food.

Vegetarian dishes such as Summer Salad and deep-fried vegetable cutlet are typical offerings.

Staff are lively and helpful

● **OPEN:** 12.30pm-2.30pm Mon-Sat. 6pm-10.15pm.
● **AVERAGE PRICE:** Dinner under £20.
Visa, Access/Master.
Galway city centre.

FAT FREDDIE'S ®
Deirdre Coin
The Halls, Quay Street, Galway
Tel: (091) 567279

Freddie's is such a well-known pizza parlour, with a buzzy atmosphere and cheerful food, that it seems an integral part of the city. At summertime weekends the crack in the place will be cranked up to 90, like the city itself.

Deirdre Coin, the new owner, has worked in Freddie's for some time, so the beat goes ever on.

● **OPEN:** 11am-10.30pm Mon-Sun.
● **AVERAGE PRICE:** Pizzas under £10.
Visa, Access/Master.
Galway city centre.

LE GRAAL ®
Sean Connolly & Alex Company
Dominick Street, Galway
Tel: (091) 567614

Adopted by Galwegians almost the instant it opened, thanks perhaps to its relaxed and enlightened policy of serving good wine by the glass late into the evening, Le Graal also serves more-than-decent food with a number of vegetarian alternatives, usually including quiches and various salads.

● **OPEN:** 9.30am-12.30am Mon-Sun.
● **AVERAGE PRICE:** Lunch under £5.

Dinner under £10-under £15.
Visa, Access/Master, Amex, Diners.
Galway city centre.

KASHMIR ®
Arun Bhan
3 Mary Street, Galway
Tel: (091) 566674

Kashmir is a well loved and
genuinely authentic Indian restaurant. The use of fresh herbs in the
cooking, the exquisite naan bread,
and the thoughtful advice of
manager Mr Kumar are just some of
the reasons why this restaurant is so
valued.

A tv muttering away in the corner
lets you know you are in a family
restaurant, with no pretensions other
than to serve good, simple Indian
food. Do note that they also do
takeaways.

● **OPEN:** Noon-2.30pm, 5pm-midnight
Tue-Fri, 2.30pm-12.30am Sat-Sun.
● **AVERAGE PRICE:** Lunch under £10.
Dinner under £15.
Visa, Access/Master, Amex.

ROYAL VILLA ®
Charlie Chan
13 Shop Street
Galway
Tel: (091) 563450

The cooking is excellent in Charles
Chan's Royal Villa, and the
thoughtfulness of the enterprise
makes certain that there are good

dishes and good cooking for
vegetarians to enjoy. Overall, however, it is the untramelled
friendliness and helpfulness of the
staff which makes it special. Kids, of
all ages, simply adore it.

● **OPEN:** 12.30pm-2.30pm, 6pm-midnight
Mon-Sat (Fri & Sat 'till 12.30am), 1pm-
midnight Sun.
● **AVERAGE PRICE:** Lunch under £10.
Dinner under £20.
Visa, Access/Master, Amex, Diners.
Galway city centre.

TULSI ®
Shamsul Huque & MD Mostofa
3 Buttermilk Walk
Middle Street
Galway
Tel: (091) 564831
Fax: 569518

Messrs. Huque and Mostofa have a
successful background serving
populist Indian cooking to an Irish
audience – they have worked in
management of the successful
Eastern Tandoori trio of restaurants
in Dublin and, more recently, in the
Tulsi's sister restaurant in Baggot
Street in the capital. They bring to
Galway a sure confidence and a sure
knowledge of accessible and exceed-
ingly agreeable Indian cooking.

● **OPEN:** Noon-2.30pm Mon-Fri
(Sat lunch if pre booked).
6pm-11.30pm Mon-Sun.
● **AVERAGE PRICE:**
Lunch under £10.
Dinner under £15.
Visa, Access/Master.
Galway city centre.

GALWAY SHOPS

EVERGREEN ⓢ
Kieron & Aideen Hurley
1 Mainguard St & High St
Tel: (091) 564215

The Galway Shopping Centre
Headford Road
Tel: (091) 564550

Not just your average corner healthfood shop, Evergreen sells vegetarian samosas, pakoras and spring rolls to take away, the wholesome Galway cheeses from Brekish Dairy, bread from Moyglass, the organic, locally-produced Avallo pure apple juice, fresh orange juice, and all the necessary dried goods: lexia raisins, Californian sultanas, oats, flours and porridges.

And the good news for discerning shoppers is that they have recently opened a new branch in the busy shopping centre on the Headford Road.

● **OPEN:** 9am-5pm Mon-Sat in the city centre.
9am-6.30pm Mon-Sat (Wed-Fri 'till 9pm) in the Shopping Centre.

GOYA'S ⓢ ⓡ
Emer Murray
19 Quay Street, Galway
Tel: (091) 567010

Emer Murray is the best baker in the country, and she is the best baker in the country for a very simple reason.

Where Irish baking tends to the domestic and the obvious, and disdains the intricacies and artfulness of true patisserie, Ms Murray fuses the two skills in her magical pair of hands.

Her soda bread, for example, is not made as others make it, in the rustic, ruddy style with little time for finesse. Her soda bread is richly flavourful and considered, elegant in appearance, shining brown in colour, a cross between the Irish staple and the involved tastes of a porter cake.

If this makes it sound like an experiment, it is no such thing. The taste is sweet and yielding, perfectly constructed, and you could eat it every day of your life.

This ability to find an intersection between the simple and the special makes Ms Murray's baking unique. She can deliver the powerful flavours which Irish people seek in cakes and breads, but she can also take these staples forward into a more achieved, artistic dimension. And, unlike a lot of over-involved patisserie, there is nothing flootery about her work, she never shows off. The ideal, the intention, is to make sure each invention is a sure-fire success.

The cakes are best enjoyed with the wonderful coffee in the restaurant, and there are well considered lunches which show the same care as everything else.

Wonderful baking, wonderful food, wonderful artistry in every bite, every morsel.

● **OPEN:** 9.30am-6pm Mon-Sat.
● **AVERAGE PRICE:** Lunch under £15.
Visa, Access/Master.
Galway city centre.

McCAMBRIDGE'S ⑤
Pat McCambridge
38/39 Shop Street, Galway
Tel: (091) 562259

The cheese counter in McCambridge's is one of the very finest in the country.

But the shop is not merely selective, it is selectively local. Vitally, you will also find in here the fine local Brekish dairy products, and much else that is produced around, about and adjacent to the city.

This, however, is but one of the charms of McCambridge's. As well as selling local foods, it has all the necessary stuff you expect to find in a good delicatessen – herbs, patisserie, a good wine selection, groovy chocolates – and all the stuff you expect to find in a good supermarket, a fact which makes it someplace special.

Service is charming, and it is someplace where they manage to make everything seem a little bit special.

● **OPEN:** 9am-6pm Mon-Fri.
Sat 9am-5.30pm.

MERCHANTS WINE CLUB ⑤
Noel O'Loughlen
The Cornstore
Middle St
Galway
Tel: (091) 561833, Fax: 569216

As you might expect from a Galway wine merchant, the selection in Noel O'Loughlen's shop is splendidly idiosyncratic and appealing, very much a Galway list in a Galway shop.

France is Mr O'Loughlen's main area of expertise, but new arrivals all share careful sourcing and selection, and there are many wines here which cannot be found in any other shop: good Aussies with lots of character, good Africans with plenty of charm, smashing sherries and slurpsome ports

In addition to the business of buying and selling, Noel also hosts many tastings with visiting winemakers, and members receive a regular Newsletter which is sparky and engaging.

● **OPEN:** 9.15am-7pm Mon-Sat.

SILKE & DAUGHTERS ⑤
Brian Silke & Scott Ishmael
Munster Avenue, Galway
Tel: (091) 561048

Silke's has evolved, with typical Galway restlessness, from its earlier days when it was a conventional fruit 'n' veg operation, into a full-blown delicatessen with lots of interesting artisan foods.

In recent times they have augmented this core business by introducing a fine range of prepared foods cooked by themselves. It is a clever, thoughtful shop, especially valuable for those times when you suddenly realise that you have no time to cook but want something delicious for dinner.

● **OPEN:** 8.30am-6pm Mon-Sat.
On the Strandhill side of the river on the edge of Galway city centre.

Galway Saturday Market

The Galway Saturday morning market is not just the best street market in the country, it is also an aleph of this crazy city and this extraordinary county. Stroll around on a Saturday morning and you get a glimpse of everything Galway has to offer.

The wild, willing energy of the city is on show, the cosmopolis of language and love of life is at its pulsating best, and the plum-rich pickings of good food are all around. It can seem less like a market and more like a stage set, but it is for real. For the market shares with the city a vital secret which keeps it alive: this glorious invention exists for the people of Galway, by the people of Galway.

It is not a fake tourist trap. It is not artificial, though it can seem so vivacious and splendid that you might imagine it is imaginary. It has been created – organically, logically, patiently – by the people of Galway, beginning from an ass-and-cart market decades ago and evolving slowly into the food-and-arts-and-crafts jamboree it is today.

This quiet evolution is the secret of its strength. Stallholders may come and go, but the central core of those who arrive here in the early hours of Saturday morning remains consistent.

Walk past the flower stall and you hit the Northern European Strip: Joachim Hess has smashing breads and great vegetables. Dirk and Hella Flak grow their produce right out on Aughinish – next stop

New York! – and don't doubt that it is just your culinary imagination which suggests that there is a wild seaspray richness of taste from their outstanding organic produce: it's real alright. A little further along the rails, Hugo Zyderlann will be behind the Brekish Dairy stall, laden with big truckles of cheese and big tubs of yogurt.

In between and round and about will be Babs McMullen with wonderful organic vegetables picked that morning, and every Saturday sees a changing chorus of others, with hallucinogenically coloured candles and crafts, with pure-coloured flowers and fantastically flootery hats, with delicate water colours propped against the church railing, or spindly, curling jewellery affixed to boards.

There may be rarities to buy such as samphire collected from the shoreline. There are local cakes and hand-churned butter, sprays of herbs, jars of preserves, sacks of spuds and fluster-topped squadrons of carrots, eggs sold from the boots of people's cars.

And there is the babble and the babel of a thriving market, a market where people simply love shopping. Indeed, there is nowhere else in the country where it is so much fun to shop, to buy, to wander from stall to stall, enjoying not just the finest food you can imagine, but also seeing in microcosm this tumultuous city and its people at their very best.

WALL'S FARM
Zara Brady
Rinnaknock, Headford
Co Galway, Tel: (093) 35661

As well as breeding pedigree goats on the family farm, just by the shores of Lough Corrib, Zara Brady organises the maintenance of her self-catering cottage with relentless energy.

The cottage sleeps approximately five people. There is one double bedroom with en suite bathroom, two single rooms with their own bathroom, and a small bunk room. For families, this is an ideal place, as there are ponies to ride and boats to mess about in.

Vegetables, eggs and milk are available to buy direct from the farm.

● **OPEN:** All year round
● **AVERAGE PRICE:** £250-£400 per week. No Credit Cards.
6 miles due west of Headford, on the shores of Lough Corrib.

enterprise culture

"Commercial Organic Horticulture and Enterprise" is how Dolores Keegan describes her six-month courses in organic market gardening. "There is no point in teaching people how to grow organic vegetables commercially if you don't give them the marketing side of it, so I teach a course for people who want to grow and make an enterprise of making and selling organic produce".

Dolores Keegan learned her considerable skills during the years she spent both growing and marketing organic foods with both Eden Plants and the Co-Op shop in Leitrim.

Her courses usually last approximately six months, but Dolores will also travel to advise individuals on a one-session basis. Previous courses have spawned lustrous vegetables on the Aran islands, a walled garden in Enniscoe House in Mayo which was organised for a community development group, and a Horizon project to teach students how to cultivate vegetables and herbs in inner city Dublin.

Most courses are commercial, but a recent course in Moycullen taught students simply to grow and store food for home consumption.

"Even if just one person's life and livelihood is transformed by a course, then it's worth it" says Dolores.

DOLORES KEEGAN
30a Ashleigh Gr., Knocknacarra
Tel: (091) 590157
● **OPEN:** Groups arranging a course should contact Dolores for advice on funding, which can come from EU and government sources. Individuals can also arrange advisory sessions.

much of the history of Eden Plants, who also continues this vital work in her role as an educator and consultant, as an enlightener.

"Over the years many hundreds of people have visited Eden Plants – a number of thousands, I suppose", he writes. "Some have made flattering comments to the effect that it is something special, different. Some seem to find real stimulation or enjoyment here. This is quite as important as the money for the sale of vegetables and herbs".

This sense of vision, this grasp of the essentials of what truly makes for the good life, has been revolutionary. In a quiet way, of course, for some revolutions work slowly, patiently, and Mr Alston's quest has been one of those.

But his importance and his influence have extended even farther than those lucky areas of the north west, where you can actually find and buy his staggeringly taste-filled food.

His establishment of The Organic Centre, in Sraud, is the latest move to make organics accessible, to demonstrate the logic and construct the legacy of this important work.

This trio of the theoretical, the practical and the professional, amount to a great testament to one man's work. The Organic Centre promises to be another splendid late Twentieth Century Folly and, like the extraordinary folly which has been Eden Plants in the last two decades, it will surely be successful, influential, inspirational, and invaluable.

● **OPEN:** The herb nursery garden is open every afternoon from 2pm-6pm.

Eden Plants is 7 miles north of Manorhamilton: take the road to Rossinver and Garrison, in Rossinver go past the post office and shop, turn right immediately after the convent, where there is a sign to the herb farm. Eden Plants is the first turning on the left. Herbs can also be bought by mail order: ring or write for their catalogue.

THE ORGANIC CENTRE ❻
Norita Clesham
Sraud
Rossinver
Tel: (072)54338/54397

Set at the foot of limestone hills beside Lough Melvin, this is an ambitious project, hugely ambitious.

Designed to meet the growing demand for information on organic gardening and farming, it plans to offer courses and workshops, and will itself have two acres of display gardens alongside fruit gardens and herb gardens.

By mid-1996, the first building on the site had been erected, and the first polytunnel had joined it. Short courses and an open day were held, including novel courses such as "Growing for Restaurants".

● **OPEN:** For details of courses, write to the Secretary. The Organic centre invites applications from interested parties to become friends of the Centre. To find the centre, coming from Manorhamilton - Rossinver direction heading towards Garrison, take a left turn marked Kinlough. Continue on the road, cross the bridge and take a left turn directly beside a house on the left side. The centre is at the end of this road.

COUNTY MAYO

ETHEL'S HOMEMADE **F**
PRESERVES

Ethel Walker
Ballyholan House
Downhill Road
Ballina
Tel: (096) 21853

Ethel Walker was amongst the first of that hardy band of devotees who have re-awakened our taste buds with their authentic, correctly made and sublimely delicious jams and preserves.

And she is still continually experimenting and innovating, taking advantage of the arrival of new fruits to create new combinations.

Recent arrivals include Damson jam – increasingly a rarity, sadly – and both a fine Apple and Ginger and a sharply-accented Rhubarb and Fig jam. There is more than an echo of the kitchen table and the kitchen sink to be enjoyed in these splendid concoctions, which maybe the real secret of their special allure.

● **OPEN:** Ethel's Preserves are found in the Supervalu stores in Clifden, Westport and Castlebar and in Kate's Kitchen in Sligo.

T MCGRATH **S**

Mr McGrath
O'Rahilly Street, Ballina
Tel: (096) 22198

McGrath's is a true country town shop, packed higgledy piggledy with good deli selections and with a good cheese counter.

● **OPEN:** 9am-8pm Mon-Sat. (Winter times 'till 7.30pm). 10am-2pm, 5pm-8pm Sun.

FLAVOUR OF INDIA **R**

Main Street, Castlebar
Tel: (094) 25738

The dishes on offer in Flavour of India are a fairly typical Indian tandoori restaurant selection, with a small array that are suitable for vegetarians: vegetable samosa or pakora to begin, and an array of vegetable entrées: lentils with aromatic spices; chickpeas cooked with potatoes; cottage cheese in a spinach sauce, and various vegetable stews. The food may be familiar tandoori cuisine, but it's genuine, which makes this a welcome place.

● **OPEN:** 5.30pm-12.30am Mon-Thur, 5.30pm-1.30am Fri & Sat, 5pm-12.30am Sun.
● **AVERAGE PRICE:** Dinner under £15. No Credit Cards.

CROSSMOLINA

ENNISCOE HOUSE Ⓐ
Susan Kellett
Castlehill, nr Crossmolina
Tel: (096) 31112, Fax: (096) 31773

It may seem somewhat oxymoronic to suggest that any substantial old pile of a country house, set fast in its own substantial grounds, could be accurately described as "modest". Yet, that is the description that most comes to mind when one thinks of Susan Kellett's Enniscoe House.

Appositely, this element of under-statement, of a Puritanical plainness and abstinence from any style of frivolity, rather suits a part of the country which is, likewise, modest and under-celebrated. Enniscoe couldn't be anywhere but Mayo.

Mrs Kellett is slowly doing her best to awaken the house from a lengthy slumber, and careful renovation is re-energising the landings and common rooms of the house. Those bedrooms at the front of the house, overlooking the grounds, are truly the ones you want to reserve when staying, and their quirky four posters and big lazy canopy beds are great fun.

Quiches, tarts, gratins and salads are all vegetarian friendly, all part of solid country house cooking, and the food feels just right, friendly food within a friendly house.

● **OPEN:** For dinner if pre-booked.
Closed mid Oct-Apr.
● **AVERAGE PRICE:** Dinner under £25.
B&B over £30. Visa, Access/Master, Amex.
Two miles south of Crossmolina on the road to Castlebar.

CONG

ECHOES Ⓡ
Siobhan Ryan
Main Street
Cong
Tel: (092) 46059

Siobhan Ryan is a good cook, with a style that embraces happily a culinary vocabulary of lusty, trusty tastes. Vegetarians, especially those who can give a little notice, will discover a very personal, un-complicated and unpretentious style of cooking, food that is exactly what you want. Desserts are big, lush, lascivious affairs, with the brown bread ice cream something of a local legend.

This deeply comforting food, rich with goodness, comes in grandly generous portions, and the happy family affair of Echoes is a haven of simplicity, decency and delight.

● **OPEN:** 5pm-10pm Mon-Sun.
(7pm-10pm Thur-Sun during winter season).
Open for breakfast and lunch during very high season (ring to check).
Open on Xmas day lunch.
● **AVERAGE PRICE:** Dinner under £20.
Visa, Access/Master, Amex.
Right in the centre of Cong.

WESTPORT

BERNIE'S HIGH ST. CAFÉ Ⓡ
Bernadette Hoban
High Street, Westport
Tel: (098) 27797

For a long time associated with the well-known Quay Cottage, Bernie's eponymous, welcoming café in the middle of Westport is almost all things to all men and women. Along with breakfasts and high teas for those who want the traditional tastes of the past, you will find omelettes, pastas, stirfries and pancakes with imaginative stuffing – sweet and sour, Chinese Vegetable or broccoli and cauliflower florettes. There are even Pacific rim specialities such as Mexican dip with tortilla chips and the all-day breakfast includes boxty.

● **OPEN:** 10am-10pm Mon-Sat.
1pm-10pm Sun. (Limited hours off season).
● **AVERAGE PRICE:** Lunch under £10.
Dinner under £15. Visa, Access/Master.

THE CORK ®
Willie & Jutta Kirkham
The Octagon, Westport
Tel: (098) 26929

Willie and Jutta moved their restaurant from the Westport hills, where it was housed in their house and known as The Ceili House, to a location hard by the Octagon in the centre of town.

The menu fuses both obvious and charmingly surprising choices – there are few places which include heart of palm as a vegetable – and they cleverly include dishes created especially for both vegetarians and vegans, including the rather ominously named Healthy Heaps.

● **OPEN:** 6pm-10pm Wed-Sun.
● **AVERAGE PRICE:** Dinner under £15.
Visa, Access/Master.
Near the Octagon in Westport.

CARROWHOLLY CHEESE ❺
Irma van Baalen
Kilmeenacoff
Westport
Tel: (098) 26762

The West is, for some inexplicable reason, rather denuded of cheesemakers, so the weekly presence of Irma van Baalen, with her own lovely, richly savoury Gouda-type cheeses, is a valuable, vital staple of the bubbly Thursday market in the Octagon in Westport.

Irma's plain gouda is offered alongside cheeses flavoured with nettles and with garlic.

During the busy tourist rush of the summer Irma can be found in the centre of town on both Fridays and Saturdays also, with both cow's milk and goat's milk cheeses, as well as some yummy freshly made cheeses, all for sale.

● **OPEN:** Market-day is Thursday.

CONTINENTAL CAFÉ ®
Wendy Stringer
High Street, Westport
Tel: (098) 26679

The Continental has long been one of Westport's landmark places, and Wendy Stringer has maintained the old style of the old favourite, and many of the old favourites of the Continental Café – pitta sandwiches, warming soups and wholesome cakes.

● **OPEN:** Tues-Sat 9.30am-6pm.
(Shorter hours off season).
Westport town centre.

COUNTRY FRESH Ⓢ
Sean Langan
Shop Street
Westport
Tel: (098) 25377

Sean Langan's shop is a fine general
greengrocer, which has already
celebrated twenty years of business.
Keep an eye out for organic herbs
and vegetables grown by Chris
Smith of Clogher.

● **OPEN:** 8am-6.30pm Mon-Sat
('till 7pm Fri & Sat).
Westport town Centre.

CIRCE'S Ⓡ
Antoinette Turpin & Corry
O'Reilly
1 Bridge Street, Westport
Tel: (098) 27096

Circe's is a fine example of the
zeitgeist of Westport and Westport's
restaurants, being a buzzy, bubbly,
easy-going place.

It's a winning formula, whether
you have a troupe of kids in tow or
are on a romantic fling with a
significant other.

Good breads, good salads and
clever use of many local foods gives
Circe's a bit of an edge on other
places in town, and it is very, very
easy to enjoy yourself in here.

● **OPEN:** 10am-10pm Mon-Sat, 7pm-
10pm Sun. (Limited hours off season).
● **AVERAGE PRICE:** Breakfast & lunch
under £5.
Dinner under £15.
Visa, Access/Master.

QUAY COTTAGE RESTAURANT Ⓡ
Peter & Kirstin McDonagh
The Harbour, Westport
Tel: (098) 26412

An intimate and pleasingly simple
restaurant, the Quay Cottage is one
of the most enduring of Westport's
eating houses.

● **OPEN:** Noon-10pm Mon-Sat, 1pm-
10pm Sun. Closed Xmas and Jan.
● **AVERAGE PRICE:** Lunch & dinner
under £15.
Visa, Access/Master, Amex.
Down on the quays.

WESTERN HERBS AND Ⓕ VEGETABLES
Chris & Brid Smith
Westport
Tel: (098) 26409

If cheesemakers are scarce in the far
north west, then so, likewise, are
those devoted pioneers who farm
organically. This scarcity makes the
efforts of Chris and Brid Smith even
more welcome.

Farming only half an acre, they
nevertheless produce almost fifty
types of herbs and you can find them
for sale at the Thursday market at
the Octagon in Westport as well as
in Country Fresh greengrocers in the
town and their salad leaves are used
by some local restaurants.

● **OPEN:** 2pm-6pm May-Sept.
From Westport take the Castlebar road
turn left at the sign for Fahy, travel until
you see the sign for Clogher and the farm
is at the end of the road at the T-junction.

COUNTY SLIGO

TEMPLE HOUSE Ⓐ
Sandy & Deb Perceval
Ballymote
Tel: (071) 83329
Fax: (071) 83808

"The food was absolutely delicious. The vegetables were an orgasm of organicness whose high note was the slinky, sinuous, scrumptious spinach, which brought oohs and aahs from around the table", wrote one guest, attempting to describe Deb Perceval's fine cooking. But the understated, flavourful food – the spinach, like most of the vegetables, will have travelled only a few hundred yards from the Percevals's organic walled garden – is only one attraction.

The dinner party atmosphere, the whacky rooms, the friendship which emerges amongst the guests and the Percevals' ability to remove any strain of preciousness or pretension means that Temple House is all things to all men and women, and all these things spell happiness.

● **OPEN:** For dinner for guests only. Closed Dec-Mar.
● **AVERAGE PRICE:** Dinner under £20. B&B over £40.
Visa, Access/Master, Amex, Diners.
Temple House is signposted from the N17.

CLIFFONEY CHEESE Ⓕ
Hans & Gaby Wieland
Ballincastle, Cliffoney
Tel: (071) 66399

If the very best food that you can eat is food that is prepared with love, then the breads, cheeses, quark and cut herbs produced by Hans and Gaby Wieland will hit home in your heart with the accuracy of Cupid's arrow.

These are foods – all of them organic – conjured out of the veritable goodness of people's hearts, painstakingly and perfectly prepared, rich with the blessing of inherent, natural, pristine flavours.

Hans' goat's and cow's milk cheeses are petulantly herbaceous, The sourdough breads baked by Gaby are truly stuff which can be called the staff of life, and if you can get your hands and then a fork onto a slice of their baked cheesecake, it is something you will remember.

But all of their foods are filled with joie de vivre, with a gracious goodness, which makes them irresistible.

● **OPEN:** Telephone first if you want to order from the house, otherwise the cheeses and bread are available in Tir na nOg in Sligo town.

COLLOONEY

GLEBE HOUSE ℝ 𝔸
Brid & Marc Torrades
Collooney
Tel: (071) 67787

Brid Torrades is a fine, thoughtful cook, a chef who works to produce the most delicious food she can manage.

Producing many of the vegetables used in her own garden helps this quest for taste, and gifts her food with a purity and directness which is enchanting. This is very nimble cooking, always well balanced, always involving for all the senses.

She does quite lovely vegetarian dishes: a filo of vegetables hollandaise; escalopes of chickpeas with tomato and garlic; good crisp tabouleh; a bright, baked baby squash; an excellent warm goat's cheese salad, and there are good breakfast choices as well: compote of seasonal fruits; potato cakes with mushrooms on toast; pancakes in lemon syrup. It is soulful food, always a delight to the appetite.

Glebe House itself is a modest, simple, shoe-string operation, but the homeliness and the sense of care evident in both the house and the food make for memories that remain for a very long time indeed.

● **OPEN:** 6.30pm-9.30pm Feb-Dec.
● **AVERAGE PRICE:** Dinner under £20.
B&B under £30.
Visa, Access/Master.
Signposted from Collooney, just before the railway bridge as you drive out of the village heading towards Sligo.

INNISCRONE

CARRAIG FHADA SEA WEED 𝔽
Frank & Betty Melvin
Cabra, Rathlee, Inniscrone
Tel: (096) 49042

SEA WEED BATH HOUSE 𝕊 ℝ
Edward Kilcullen
Pier Road, Inniscrone
Tel: (096) 36238

Over 500 different varieties of seaweed grow wild in Ireland. Of these a dozen are harvested, ten of which are edible. All the seaweed harvested for sale in Ireland is wild.

Frank Melvin's wonderful dried dilisk, carrageen, Kombu, Wakame, Kombu Royale and Spaghetti Demer seaweeds are the purest, finest seaweeds you can buy in Ireland, sold under the Carraig Fhada label and available in good shops in their nifty little packets.

Near to Frank's base in western Sligo, Edward Kilcullen operates the splendid old Victorian seaweed baths at Enniscrone. He uses hot sea water and into this places a bucket of washed Fucas Serratus (or toothed rack) to prepare the bath. The combination of weightlessness gifted by the sea water and the unctuous, sublime oils gifted by the seaweed make for one of the most lascivious, sensuous things it is legal to enjoy. It is legal, isn't it?

● **OPEN:** Carraig Fhada seaweeds are available in healthfood shops.
Baths open noon-8.30pm Mon-Sun. Closed weekdays in Oct, and from Nov-St Patrick's Day weekend.

SLIGO

COSGROVE'S Ⓢ

The Cosgrove Family
32 Market Street, Sligo
Tel: (071) 42809

Cosgrove's is a most wonderful shop, a fabulous trove of good things which, if it was in almost any other town in Ireland, would be celebrated as a classic example of just what a country grocery store can aspire to. In Sligo, where standards are high, they almost take it for granted. Outsiders, however, are bowled over by it.

The distinctiveness of the shop, with its craftsmanship in the art of selling, and its pleasure in painstaking service, makes it a joy to visit. Kevin and Michael Cosgrove have the ability to make everything seem special: the welter of Xmas fruits in season; a bucket of new dilisk at the front door; the wafting smell of bread and baking. It is a storybook place which recaptures a childish innocence, to return to a time when shops were part and parcel of a community, and not just part and parcel of commerce.

● **OPEN:** 9.30am-9pm Mon-Sat, 11.30am-1.30pm, 5.30pm-8pm Sun.

HARGADON'S Ⓟ

Pat Leigh Doyle
O'Connell Street, Sligo
Tel: (071) 42974

This magnificent palace of porter and other choice drinks is one of the finest pubs anywhere in Ireland. The arrival of Tim Boland and his astute people-pleasing cooking adds a further blissful complexion to a happy place.

Mr Boland, as one can see from his smashing recipe for mungbean and aubergine casserole in the recipe section at the back of the book, is on first name terms with deliciousness.

● **OPEN:** Regular pub hours.

THE GOURMET PARLOUR Ⓢ

Annette Burke & Catherine Farrell
Bridge Street, Sligo
Tel: (071) 44617

The Gourmet Parlour is one of the great success stories of Sligo in recent years, its success founded on Annette and Catherine's baking, which is expertly elegant in execution and yet which never loses touch of those comfortingly rustic, real flavours we savour. Invaluable at Xmas time, indispensable for parties and entertaining.

● **OPEN:** 9.30am-6pm Mon-Sat.

KATE'S KITCHEN Ⓢ

Kate Pettit & Frank Hopper
24 Market Street, Sligo
Tel: (071) 43022

A great delicatessen, and a whole lot more beside. Kate and Frank have a sure touch with their cooked foods, and perfect discrimination with the other lines they sell.

● **OPEN:** 9am-6.30pm Mon-Sat.

SARU Ⓐ
Maureen Quinn
Tonadhuble lane, Sligo
Tel: (071) 70518

Maureen Quinn has been contributing to people's knowledge of vegetarian and vegan food for over twenty years in Sligo with her cookery classes which she runs at her home two to three nights a week from October to Easter.

Last year saw her open three rooms to provide vegetarian accommodation for guests. Breakfasts come in the form of apricot and prune compote with natural yogurt, tofu burgers for vegans, free range eggs and potato cakes, mushrooms, spiced lentils and, occasionally, home made muffins. "I am interested in food that provides you with energy. There are various foods I don't cook with, like tomatoes – Eating for Good Health is the title of the cookery classes and that's what I practice".

Do note that Maureen is also happy to accommodate pets.

● **OPEN:** All year.
Cookery classes from Oct-Easter.
● **AVERAGE PRICE:** Under £20 per person sharing.
Visa, Access/Master.

TIR NA NOG Ⓢ ✪
Mary, John & Norah McDonnell
Grattan Street
Sligo
Tel: (071) 62752

One of the secrets of Sligo food people is that they not only talk about doing things, they make sure that the things they talk about get done. Things happen here, people evolve their businesses, they get better and better, and there is no better example of this knack of progress in action than Tir na nOg.

The McDonnells simply get better and better. Patiently, painstakingly, they continually examine what the shop is doing and wonder if it could be done better. If it can be done better, then they set about finding the right way to do it.

What this means is a commitment to local people and producers. Tir na nOg is a magnet for the fine food in the county, but the traffic between shop and supplier is two way: the skill in selling which Mary, John and Norah McDonnell exhibit helps their suppliers, but it is their encouragement and their determination to keep things local which is most impressive.

So, if the McDonnells are concerned about a dull sounding topic like import substitution, they set about counteracting it. Use local seaweeds, not imported ones. Use local breads, not some junk shipped in overnight from France. Use local vegetables, not rubbish grown in water on the continent. Sell local cheeses, not dodgy, pasteurised gunk.

It sounds easy, but of course if it was, then everyone would do it. The McDonnells were amongst the first to do it, and they have kept on doing it, and doing it better every time. Slowly, surely, their plans are realised, and the quality of life in Sligo is improved by their efforts.

● **OPEN:** 9am-6pm Mon-Sat.

TRUFFLES ® ✪
Bernadette O'Shea
11 The Mall
Sligo
Tel: (071) 44226

Truffles is a groovy, happening place, simply but soulfully decorated, with an urgent, up-for-it buzz which is irresistible.

Its achievement lies not only with Bernadette O'Shea's sensational cooking, but with the fact that it is an oasis of pleasure. It does just exactly what you want it to do, becomes just what you want it to be.

How do they manage this? In truth, Truffles' ambience is founded on the basis of respect: the staff take themselves just as seriously as they need to, the customers take their own desires seriously, and everyone takes the food seriously.

And what food! Truffles is known mostly for Bernadette's pizza cookery, but everything she touches is graced with culinary magic.

The remarkable salads confected from Rod Alston's extraordinary leaves and herbs and served with roasted red pepper crostini and Wieland's goats' cheese; brilliant polenta baked with gorgonzola; the fantastic foccaccia baked with oregano, garlic, fresh tomatoes, and Parmesan; the brilliant dessert cookery, and of course those stupendous tablets of dough decorated with exotic ingredients: the Truffles's Best; the Chilli Pizza; Milleens Pizza with fresh herbs.

Very few other restaurants in Ireland manage to offer all of the features we find in this unique restaurant, but in Truffles you find a place where everything is at all times striving to be the very best it can be.

● **OPEN:** 5pm-10.30pm Tue-Sat
● **AVERAGE PRICE:** Pizza over £10.
No credit cards.
The Mall is on the main road to Enniskillen going in the direction of the hospital.

THE WINDING STAIR ⑤ ®
Kevin Connolly
Street, Sligo
Tel: (071) 41244, Fax (071) 41299

Book-selling mogul Kevin Connolly's Winding Stair has been a colossal success since opening. A brilliant mixture of books, music and super soup and sandwiches is irresistible.

● **OPEN:** 10pm-6pm Mon-Sat.

THE WINE BARREL ⑤
Michael Gramsch
Johnston Court, Sligo
Tel: (071) 71730

Michael Gramsch actually made wine when he lived in Germany, and the influence of his homeland remains strong, for he has the finest array of German wines sold in Ireland, alongside great wines from all over the world. 40% of what Michael stocks is imported by himself, and if you can make it to the shop, you will enjoy the wise advice of a wine seller with an accurate and undogmatic palate.

● **OPEN:** 10.30am-7pm Mon-Sat, 'till 8pm Fri & Sat. (Extended hours during high summer and festive seasons).

LEINSTER

INCLUDING THE COUNTIES OF

CARLOW

DUBLIN

KILDARE

KILKENNY

LAOIS

LONGFORD

LOUTH

MEATH

WESTMEATH

WEXFORD

WICKLOW

COUNTY CARLOW

KILGRANEY COUNTRY HOUSE Ⓐ
Bryan Leech & Martin Marley
Bagenalstown
Co Carlow
Tel & Fax: (0503) 75283

Bryan Leech is destined to become a celebrated B&B keeper, for he is that character most beloved of guide-books: a charming host.

The prudish, Presbyterian poise of Kilgraney is cunningly offset by the furnishings which Bryan and Martin Marley have culled from their travels: bright mirrors ringed in beaten stainless steel, chairs in imitation of the female form, artful concoctions of coconut shell.

The house not only scores high in the World of Interiors stakes, for Mr Leech can cook, helped by the deliciousness of vegetables and herbs from their own garden. Desserts are purest, giggly, fun food.

In the warm womb of the dining room, with its cheeky, fluttering cherubs, it is hard to believe Dublin is only an hour away, so expert is the feeling of away-from-it-all.

● **OPEN:** Feb-Oct.
● **AVERAGE PRICE:** B&B over £30.
Dinner over £15.
Visa, Access/Master.
3.5m from Bagenalstown (Muine Bheag) on the Borris road. Turn right at Kilgraney X.

DANETTE'S FEAST Ⓡ
Danette O'Connell
& David Milne
Urglin Glebe
Bennekerry
Co Carlow

"We consider vegetarians an asset, not a nuisance", writes Danette O'Connell, a proud boast which her eponymous restaurant consummately achieves.

For a start, she sources her vegetables from Penny Lange's Ballinroan farm in Wicklow, the most marvellous bio-dynamically grown vegetables one can find.

So scrumptious tomatoes will be filled with feta cheese, basil and lemon, or those vegetables may be served as crudités, paired with a spicy dipping sauce

Then, she prepares all her soups with vegetables, using no meat stocks at all, so we can happily agonise over whether we should choose Jerusalem artichoke soup, or a brewy minestrone with fresh pesto, or a spicy red lentil, tomato and coriander, or a zingy beetroot soup.

And then, there are truly imaginative choices for main courses: roast pepper and cheese filled enchiladas show her Mexican influences; vegetarian felafel with a soured cream and onion sauce takes us to the Middle East; a tort wherein cheeses are layered with sautéed vegetables and enclosed with puff pastry is finished with a mustard and soured cream sauce; or that tort might be in the shape of a yummy meld of organic tomatoes, roasted peppers and ricotta cheese with pesto, or we could have something Italianate such as home-made ravioli with a shiitake and oyster mushroom filling.

This imagination dresses each detail: fine breads such as rye and coriander or a rye with pecans and garlic, perhaps olive bread or tomato and fennel.

Indeed, we should point out that Ms O'Connell is a musician, and there is more than a touch of symphonic collection and harmonious searching in her food. They do occasionally organise evenings of music and food, but the real melody here is in the cooking.

● **OPEN:** 7pm-10pm Wed-Sat,
7pm-9pm Sun.
NB Booking essential.
● **AVERAGE PRICE:** Dinner over £20.
Visa, Access/Master.
Leave Carlow on the Blessington road, two miles out of town turn left after the Dolmen Service Station.

OTTERHOLT RIVERSIDE LODGE Ⓐ
Dot or Suzanne
Kilkenny Road, Carlow
Tel: (0503) Fax: 41318

A hostel which offers "Creative Breaks" and whose workshops include a course on Vegetarian and Herb Cookery given by Danette O'Connell of Danette's Feast. Other courses include silver jewellery making, spring gardening, interior design and Canadian canoeing.

● **OPEN:** Courses run throughout the summer. Phone for their brochure.

THE LORD BAGENAL INN Ⓡ
James Kehoe
Leighlinbridge, Co Carlow
Tel: (0503) 21668

"First and foremost, wine is made to be enjoyed" writes James Kehoe, the mastermind proprietor behind the fabulous wine list of the Lord Bagenal Inn. "I say you drink what you like, and that is what is important".

The greatest of Mr Kehoe's achievements is not just his wine list, but the fact that such a spiffing piece of work is put to play in the friendly, sociable and enjoyable bar and restaurant which is The Lord Bagenal Inn.

His menus are typically thoughtful, with good vegetarian choices: pineapple and almond pilaff; savoury quiche with coleslaw; a stir-fry of seasonal vegetables.

● **OPEN:** 12.30pm-2.15pm Mon-Sun,
6pm-10.30pm Mon-Sat, 6pm-9pm Sun.
● **AVERAGE PRICE:** Lunch under £15.
Dinner over £15.
Visa, Access/Master.
The Lord Bagenal Inn is signposted from the N9 Dublin/Carlow road, south of Carlow town.

DUBLIN CITY

Dublin is divided as follows:

Heart of the City page 46

Temple Bar page 63

The Villages page 81

COUNTY DUBLIN

DUBLIN – HEART OF THE CITY

ASIA MARKET ⓢ
Helen Pau
18 Drury Street
Dublin 2
Tel: (01) 677 9764

Helen Pau's shop has increased enormously in size with its move further back up Drury Street, and whilst the extra space may have robbed the Asia Market of that old cluttered charm which was such an attractive feature, the new space has allowed them to offer many more good things for sale, including char sui buns, kilo bags of chillies, and more woks, steamers and canvas shoes than you can shake a stick at.

● **OPEN:** 10am-7pm Mon-Fri,
11am-6pm Sat & Sun.
Stretches between George's St & Drury St.

AYUMI-YA JAPANESE STEAKHOUSE ⓡ⊙
Yoichi Hoashi
132 Lower Baggot Street
Dublin 2
Tel: (01) 662 0233

The title of the Ayumi-Ya is something of a joke, for it refers to teppan-yaki steaks, rather than some thing simply carnivorous, and it is deeply ironic inasmuch as it is the title of the restaurant which may serve the most exciting vegetarian dishes in town.

Japanese cooking, like Indian, cuisines, has deep respect for vegetarianism ingrained in its strictures, and the deft execution of the Steakhouse shows this at its best: slender vegetable tempura; deep fried soba noodles wrapped with nori; deep fried aubergine with sweetened miso paste; grilled shiitake; tempura soba, dishes which are thrillingly revitalising and exciting. Service is sublime, and the Ayumi-Ya is only brilliant.

● **OPEN:** 12.30pm-2.30pm Mon-Fri,
6pm-11.30pm Mon-Thur.
('till 12.30am Fri & Sat).
● **AVERAGE PRICE:** Lunch and early evening menu under £15.
Dinner under £20.
Visa, Access/Master, Amex.
At the corner of Baggot St/Pembroke St.

THE BIG CHEESE Co ⓢ
David Brown & Sonia Bradford
Trinity Street
Tel: (01) 671 1399

Alongside a fine selection of cheeses – including the Dublin-made cheese Dunbarra, which wings across the Liffey from North King Street where Barra McFeely produces it – there are quality comestibles from France, Italy and the US – lots of good bottles from Fauchon alongside the Hershey bars.

● **OPEN:** 10am-6pm Mon-Sat.

BLAZING SALADS II ⓢ
Lorraine Fitzmaurice
Powerscourt Townhouse Centre
Clarendon Street
Dublin 2
Tel: (01) 671 9552

The Salads is a thoughtful place, with gluten-, sugar-, dairy- and yeast-free dishes on offer. The food is imaginative, yet still manages to satisfy the conservative callings of the customers who have been filling the place for years. To get the best out of Blazing Salads, it's an idea to choose the more imaginative special dishes made each day.

● **OPEN:** 9.30am-6pm Mon-Sat.
● **AVERAGE PRICE:** Meal under £10.
No Credit Cards.
Top of Powerscourt Townhouse Centre.

BROWN'S BAR ⓡ
Paul Kelly
Brown Thomas
Grafton St
Dublin 2
Tel: (01) 679 5666

The chic Brown's Bar is an arm of the Masarella Catering Group, offering a menu of soups, groovy sarnies, salads and drinks devised in collaboration with the caterer Lorna Wing. They don't actually call any of their creations "sandwiches", so foccaccia and crostini are the order of the day.

● **OPEN:** 9am-6pm Mon-Sat.
('till 8pm Thur).
● **AVERAGE PRICE:** Lunch under £10.
Visa, Access/Master, Amex, Diners.

RISTORANTE BUCCI ⓡ
Eoin Doyle
7 Lower Camden Street, Dublin 2
Tel: (01) 475 1020

One of the more confident, assured, funky places to open in the city in recent years. Bucci's roll-call of pasta and pizzas is well executed, another fashionable variation on that grab-bag modern style of food that has little time for authenticity, but is rather good at delivering food with savour.

● **OPEN:** 12.30pm-2.30pm Mon-Fri,
6pm-11.30pm Mon-Sun.
● **AVERAGE PRICE:** Lunch under £10.
Dinner over £10.
Visa, Access/Master, Amex, Diners.
Halfway up Camden Street.

CAFÉ JAVA ⓡ
Kieran Mulligan
145 Upr Leeson Street, Dublin 4
Tel: (01) 660 0675

5 South Anne Street, Dublin 2
Tel: (01) 660 8899

The Javas are extremely popular breakfast, lunchtime and coffeetime places, and their clever mix of light foods is confidently handled. Good coffee, and a selection of wines.

● **OPEN:** LEESON ST – 8am-6pm Mon-Fri, 9am-5pm Sat, 11am-5pm Sun.
SOUTH ANNE ST – 7.45am-7pm Mon-Fri ('till 8pm Thurs), 9am-6pm Sat, 10am-6pm Sun.
● **AVERAGE PRICE:** Meals under £5.
Visa, Access/Master.

CANALETTO'S ®
Terry Sheeran
69 Mespil Road
Dublin 4
Tel: (01) 678 5084

They cook good, punchy, soulful food in Canaletto's, and it has considerably greater imagination than many other Dublin eateries. Lunchtime sees speedy counter service – good sandwiches and bakes, lively salads – which transforms into calmer evening service – pasta with chillies or maybe pesto, friendly vegetarian dishes.

● **OPEN:** 8am-late Mon-Sat,
11am-4.30pm, 7pm-late Sun.
● **AVERAGE PRICE:** Lunch under £10.
Dinner under £20.
Visa, Access/Master, Amex.

LA CAVE ®
Margaret Beskri
28 Sth Anne Street
Dublin 2
Tel: (01) 679 4409

The basement Cave remains an enigmatic, thoroughly enjoyable space, nostalgically decorated, and with cleverly agreeable bistro dishes such as couscous aux sept legumes.

Upstairs is an airy new grill bar on the first floor, which has allowed the formula of La Cave to expand into somewhat more ambitious cooking.

● **OPEN:** 12.30pm-2am Mon-Sun.
● **AVERAGE PRICE:** Lunch under £10.
Dinner under £15.
Visa, Access/Master, Amex.
Just past the post office on Sth Anne St.

THE CEDAR TREE ®
Ismail Sarhan
11 St Andrew's Street, Dublin 2
Tel: (01) 677 2121

A restaurant popular with a left-field crowd who like its informal way, and with vegetarians who appreciate its clever use of pulses and grains.

● **OPEN:** Noon-5pm Mon-Sun,
5.30pm-midnight Mon-Sat ('till 11pm Sun).
● **AVERAGE PRICE:** Lunch under £10.
Dinner over £15.
Visa, Access/Master, Amex, Diners.
Beside the Old Stand pub.

CORNUCOPIA ⑤
Deirdre McCafferty
19 Wicklow Street
Dublin 2
Tel: (01) 677 7583

It's an institution now, Cornucopia, but the recent arrival of Eddie Bates has seen this old darling acquire a new lease of life.

Mr Bates is one of the best vegetarian cooks in the city, and has brought with him the sensitive culinary touches which have made his restaurants popular: mushroom and mung bean moussaka; Californian bean stew; red pepper quiche; chick pea salad with red onions, lovely cooking with a true touch and excellent appreciation of flavours.

● **OPEN:** 8am-11pm Mon-Sat.
● **AVERAGE PRICE:** Lunch under £5.
Dinner over £10.
Visa, Access/Master.
Half way up Wicklow Street.

CORA'S ®
Mr and Mrs Basini
1 St Mary's Road, Dublin 4
(Off Lower Baggot Street)
Tel: (01) 660 0585

A darling little Italian family restaurant, which specialises as much in kissing babies as it does in very simple Italian cooking. Great for slow, easy, lazy Sunday lunches.

● **OPEN:** 9am-5pm Mon-Fri, 10am-3pm Sun. (Closed Sat).
● **AVERAGE PRICE:** Lunch under £10. No Credit Cards.
First left after Baggot Street Bridge, heading south towards Ballsbridge.

CHINACO LTD ⓢ
(Just ask for) Rosemary
67 Bride Street, Dublin 8
Tel: (01) 478 4699

A great big barn of a place, with all the charm of a deserted football stadium on a wet Wednesday, Chinaco is nevertheless a good source for exotic vegetables in addition to the other staples of Oriental cookery.

● **OPEN:** 10am-6.30pm Mon-Fri, 11am-6.30pm Sat, 11am-5.30pm Sun.
Just down from the Kevin St Junction.

THE CHOCOLATE BAR ℗
Paul Jackson & Melissa Jones
Upper Hatch Street, Dublin 2
Tel: (01) 478 0166

Possibly the trendiest bar in town, and the food is pretty vogueish also:

strawberry and ricotta bagel; the Ultimate salad sandwich, with the daily bakes less self-conscious.

● **OPEN:** Lunch served 11am-4pm Mon-Sun.
● **AVERAGE PRICE:** Lunch under £10. Visa, Access/Master, Amex.

THE CITY CENTRE ®
Michael Creedon
23-25 Moss Street, Dublin 2
Tel: (01) 671 5907

As you might expect, the City Centre is not in the city centre, but just beside the Liffey in a fast-developing neck of the woods. The sense of humour evident in its name is evident in the room, which is unpretentious and relaxed, and their mix of sandwiches, salads and bakes are fresh and satisfying.

● **OPEN:** 9am-6pm Mon-Fri, 11am-4pm Sat.
● **AVERAGE PRICE:** Lunch under £5. No Credit Cards.
Opposite the Matt Talbot bridge, across from the Custom House.

COOKE'S CAFÉ ®
John Cooke
14 Sth William Street, Dublin 2
Tel: (01) 679 0536/7/8

John Cooke is the Wolfgang Puck of Dublin, as much of a mover, shaker and social staple as he is a chef with a funky restaurant.

In addition to the Café with its cool leanness of design and the cool leanness of the smart set who have been coming here since the day it opened, there is also the shop – just across the street – and the bakery. This diaspora of interests might make one fear for the quality of the cooking, and whilst it can be uneven it can also be fearsomely good and terrifically simple.

● **OPEN:** RESTAURANT – 12.30pm-3.30pm, 6pm-11.30pm.
UPSTAIRS AT COOKE'S – 10am-6pm Mon-Sun.
● **AVERAGE PRICE:**
"Upstairs" under £10.
RESTAURANT – Lunch over £15.
Dinner over £20.
Visa, Access/Master, Amex, Diners.
Rear of Powerscourt Centre.

COOKE'S FOOD HALL ⓢ
John Cooke
Castle Market Street, Dublin 2
Tel: (01) 679 9923
Bakery Tel: (01) 836 5208

John Cooke has always made a feature of selling the things other people don't sell, and so it is with his new shop. Excellent oils, hard-to-find pulses and rices from obscure parts of the globe, and a wide range of their own breads and cakes.

● **OPEN:** 10am-6pm ('till 8pm Thur).

CHAPTER ONE ⓡ
Ross Lewis
18/19 Parnell Square, Dublin 1
Tel: (01) 873 2266

Ross Lewis' food in the Writers' Museum has acquired more confidence and brio of late – a fine

shallot and soya tart tatin with goat's cheese shows the interesting mixture of styles and techniques he employs, and his zest with vegetarian cooking.

● **OPEN:** 12.30pm-2pm, 6pm-11pm Tue-Sat.
● **AVERAGE PRICE:**
Lunch under £15. Dinner over £20.
Visa, Access/Master, Amex, Diners.
In the basement of the Writers' Museum.

THE DUBLIN FOOD CO-OP ⓢ
Pauraic Cannon
St. Andrew's Centre
Pearse Street
Dublin 2
Tel: (01) 872 1191
Fax: (01) 873 5737

This splendidly altruistic organisation has been vital in introducing the concept of a farmers' market – or at least a Dublin version of it – to Saturday morning shoppers, and it has gone some way to filling the enormous gap which exists in the capital city for a true market where one can buy the produce from the people who actually grow it.

Organic and bio-dynamic growers line up and sell alongside the cost-cut dried goods and the agit-prop leaflets. The organisers do like it if you are prepared to lend a hand, for some it becomes a social place.

● **OPEN:** The Dublin Food Co-Op is open from 10.30am-5pm every Sat.
St Andrew's Hall is in the middle of Pearse Street.

L'ECRIVAIN ®
Derry & Sally Anne Clarke
112 Lower Baggot St
Dublin 2
Tel: (01) 661 1919

Derry Clarke's emergence as one of the most distinctive, creative cooks in Dublin has been achieved patiently and precisely, but it was the move to a less formal, more spacious room in 1995 which catalysed the creativity of this kitchen, and since then L'Ecrivain has scarcely put a foot wrong.

It is a very friendly, very real, very genuine place, where spirited, professional people do their best to make sure you have a good time. There is no artifice to L'Ecrivain, no pose. They want you to have the best time.

"Good food, good service, good value" is how Derry and Sally Anne Clarke describe their ambitions, but what is terrific about their restaurant is the fact that they achieve these objectives with such effect. They don't just talk about these ideals; they make sure they happen.

The main banker in Mr Clarke's cooking is a love of pure, generous flavours. Vegetarian dishes are especially inventive, and show a restaurant that caters perfectly for its customers' demands. Derry Clarke's cooking now seems perfectly his own, truly Irish, his culinary signature a high five of flavour.

● **OPEN:** 12.30pm-2pm Mon-Fri, 6.30pm-11pm Mon-Sat.
● **AVERAGE PRICE:** Lunch under £15. Dinner under £30.
Visa, Access/Master, Amex, Diners.
In a courtyard at Lad Lane, on Baggot St.

the Dublin pub

We thought it would never change, and we were wrong.

The old Dublin pub, that meld of nicotined walls, studiously assertive barmen, grand pints, quiet afternoons and boisterous evenings, that fusion of gothic design and middle class style, has fallen out of favour in Dublin.

Nowadays, that style of drinking emporium is the choice in Gothenberg and Dallas, in Paris and Munich, as the concept of the Irish pub is slowly exported to the four corners of the world.

But, back home, the youthful city of Dublin has demanded a change, and the change that has been a long time a comin' has arrived with a rush. The Dublin pub has gone to the Continent, and so the continent has come to the Dublin pub.

Nowadays, young wans can not only be seen through plain glass as they shamelessly sip imported beers from the bottle itself, but they are likely to be munching on a strawberry baguette as they do so. Sacrilege!

And the names of them! Cafe en Seine. The Chocolate Bar. Odessa. The Globe. Not a Maguire's or a Neeson's among them, though there is, merciful Lord, a Hogan's.

Fear not. For they are, all of them, Dublin pubs in Dublin city.

FINDLATER'S ⑤

Nigel Werner
The Harcourt Street Vaults
10 Upper Hatch Street, Dublin 2
Tel: (01) 475 1699, Fax: 475 2530

One of the city's most traditional wine merchants, housed for the last few years in the vaults of Harcourt Street railway station. There is a splendid wine museum tucked away in here, amidst a formidable range of wines from all over the world.

● **OPEN:** 9am-6pm Mon-Fri,
10.30am-6pm Sat.

FITZPATRICK'S ⑤

Philip Fitzpatrick
40a Lwr Camden Street, Dublin 2
Tel: (01) 475 3996

Long the best fruit and vegetable shop in town, Fitzpatrick's is an invaluable source for organic and bio-dyn foods, as well as essential wholefoods and whatnots.

● **OPEN:** 8am-6.30pm Mon-Sat.

THE GALLIC KITCHEN ⑤

Sarah Webb
49 Francis Street, Dublin 8
Tel: (01) 454 4912

Sarah Webb is not only the best baker in the capital, she is effortlessly the most consistent baker, also. You sometimes wonder, munching through a salmon and broccoli plait or dipping a twin-bangered sausage roll into some slurpsome ketchup or chomping your way through a chocolate brownie, if this tenacious young woman has ever baked something that wasn't perfect. Certainly, we have no evidence that her work has ever slipped off that pedestal of pure, pristine flavour which adorns everything she does, and the ruthless quality level of this modest bakery is daunting to contemplate.

For the most part, the baking is relatively simple, playing with the savoury flavours Ms Webb loves.

Pastry is Sarah Webb's canvas, and with it she demonstrates the discipline and confidence of a true artist. But she is a rare artist in that she never disappoints, and never dips below a level of perfection which others can only marvel at.

● **OPEN:** 9am-5pm Tue-Sat.

GIROLLES ⑱

Gary & Helen Morris
64 Sth William Street, Dublin 2
Tel: (01) 679 7699

Gary Morris loves food with big, ruddy flavours, food that is very comforting and elemental, food that calls for an appetite. Parsnip and apple soup; Wicklow mountain goat's cheese with Provençal vegetables; risotto with girolles and Parmesan. Friendly food, friendly place, a favourite of many folk.

● **OPEN:** 12.30pm-2.15pm Tue-Fri, 6pm-11pm Tue-Sat, 5pm-10pm Sun.
● **AVERAGE PRICE:** Lunch under £15.
Dinner under £25.
Visa, Access/Master, Amex, Diners.
Near the corner with Wicklow Street.

GLORIA JEAN'S GOURMET COFFEE Co ⑤Ⓡ
Adrian Keaveney
Powerscourt Centre
Dublin 2
Tel: (01) 679 7772

A new venture which has been imported from the 'States, Gloria Jean's offers an enormous array of coffees, all from Arabica beans, and a broad range of flavoured coffees. You can drink them here, or take them home.

● **OPEN:** 8am-7pm Mon-Sat ('till 8pm Thur). 10am-6pm Sun.

THE GOTHAM CAFÉ Ⓡ
David Barry
5 South Anne Street
Dublin 2
Tel: (01) 679 5266

For many people, the Gotham produces the best pizza in the city, but there are other fine things to be had in here. Their recent emphasis has been in the direction of Cal-Ital food: goat's cheese crostini; penne with chilli. It's a buzzy, funky space, with good vibes.

● **OPEN:** 11am-midnight Tue-Sat. ('till 12.30am Fri & Sat).
● **AVERAGE PRICE:**
Lunch under £10.
Dinner over £10.
Visa, Access/Master.
South Anne Street leads off Grafton Street.

HERE TODAY ⑤
Declan Tiernan
25 Sth Anne Street, Dublin 2 &
Corporation Market, Dublin 7
Tel: (01) 671 1454

The city centre shop has been revised recently, and now offers a smattering of deli goods alongside the familiar fruit and veg. Always a good source for the obscure and for a good range of organically grown foods.

● **OPEN:** SHOP – 6.30am-6.30pm, MARKET – 5am-2.30pm.

IMPERIAL CHINESE REST Ⓡ
Mrs Cheung
12a Wicklow Street, Dublin 2
Tel: (01) 677 2580

Mrs Cheung's restaurant is one of the landmarks of Dublin's restaurant scene. The cooking, for the main part, tends to the familiar and it's best to go on a Sunday lunchtime, for the family meal that is their sublime Dim Sum.

Then, the joyous, dazzling skill of this food and its enchanting flavours reveal the capacious, incisive culinary skills of the Imperial at its very best.

For such fine cooking, prices are tremendously keen, and you can feed the family for half nuthin'. This is probably the best value meal in the city.

● **OPEN:** Noon-midnight. (Dim sum served 12.30pm-5.30pm) Mon-Sun.
● **AVERAGE PRICE:** Lunch under £10. Dinner over £20. Visa, Access/Master, Amex. Half-way down Wicklow Street.

JUICE ®
David Keane
73 South Gt George's Street
Dublin 2
Tel: (01) 475 7856

Juice is a restaurant which positively proselytises on behalf of healthy food, offering a wide range of foods which can be eaten raw and adding a fine fresh juice bar to its roll-call.

Their wines are all organically produced – a smart touch, and proof that organic wines can hold their own – but the cooking perhaps has more ambition on the page than on the plate.

Oftentimes, it seems happy to tread largely familiar vegetarian themes: miso soup with tofu; pinto bean stew with Mediterranean vegetables; penne a la arribiatta; goat's cheese in filo; cashew and hazel-nut roast; vegetable stir-fry with noodles. Service is friendly, the music is proudly ambient and up-to-the-minute.

● **OPEN:** 8am-2.30pm, 6.30pm-10.30pm.
● **AVERAGE PRICE:** Lunch under £10.
Dinner over £10. Visa, Access.
End of George's St near the pedestrian crossing.

KILKENNY DESIGN ⑤ ®
Catherine Curran
6 Nassau Street, Dublin 2
Tel: (01) 677 7066

The Kilkenny shop is a brilliant source of desirable kitchen implements and objects, all of them chosen with great care, but don't overlook the careful and enjoyable cooking in the upstairs restaurant.

● **OPEN:** 9am-9pm Mon-Sat (8pm Thurs).
● **AVERAGE PRICE:** Lunch under £10.
Visa, Access/Master, Amex, Diners.
Overlooks Trinity, over the Kilkenny shop.

LITTLE CAESAR'S PIZZA ®
Adel Samy
Balfe Street
Dublin 2
Tel: (01) 671 8714

A boisterous place that fizzles with gung-ho energy, Little Caesar's specialises in pizzas, and specialises especially in the theatrics of spinning the tablets of dough way up in the air. Fun, especially if you are twelve years old.

● **OPEN:** 12.30pm-12.30am Mon-Sun.
● **AVERAGE PRICE:** Under £15.
Visa, Access/Master, Amex, Diners.
Opposite the Westbury Hotel.

MAGILL'S ⑤
Brendan Condon
14 Clarendon Street
Dublin 2
Tel: (01) 671 3830

One of the great city centre delis, the Condon family's shop has just about everything your heart might desire. Good breads from Wicklow, good cheeses from all over the country, good salads prepared by themselves, good oils and essential jars: you could shop here every week of the year and always come across something new and tempting.

● **OPEN:** 9.30am-5.45pm Mon-Sat.
Opposite Powerscourt Townhouse Centre.

MILANO ®
Russell Daly
38 Dawson Street, Dublin 2
Tel: (01) 670 7744

Milano is a branch of the UK's Pizza Express chain, specialising in pizzas and pastas. It's a cool space, with the food perhaps a little reserved.

● **OPEN:** Noon-midnight Mon-Sun.
● **AVERAGE PRICE:** Lunch under £10. Dinner under £15. Visa, Access/Master. Across from the Mansion House.

MITCHELL'S ®
Peter Dunne
21 Kildare Street, Dublin 2
Tel: (01) 668 0367

Mitchell's is not only a classy, handsome wine shop, but also boasts a simple restaurant in the basement. Peter Dunne and his staff are a finely choreographed operation, and their range is augmented by a good Wine Club which hosts regular tastings of new vintages and organises visits by many of the winemakers whose wines they stock.

● **OPEN:** SHOP – 10.30am-5.30pm Mon-Fri, ('till 8pm Thur), 10.30am-1pm Sat. RESTAURANT – 12.15pm-2.30pm Mon-Sat
● **AVERAGE PRICE:** Lunch under £15. Visa, Access/Master, Amex, Diners. At the side entrance of the Shelbourne.

LA MERE ZOU ®
Eric Tydgat
22 St Stephen's Green, Dublin 2
Tel: (01) 661 6669

The name sounds French, but the orientation of the cooking is actually Belgian. Don't let that put you off, for it is an unpretentious, fun place, and Belgian cooking is often excellent and largely misunderstood.

● **OPEN:** 12.30pm-2.30pm, 6pm-10.30pm. (Open for snacks in the afternoon, no lunch Sat).
● **AVERAGE PRICE:** Lunch under £10. Dinner under £20. Visa, Access/Master, Amex, Diners. In a basement on the north side of the Green.

MOTHER REDCAP'S MARKET ®
Back Lane
Dublin 8
Tel: (01) 454 4655

Useful address at the weekends for browsing and for the work of Lime & Lemongrass who sell their flavoured oils and vinegars here.

● **OPEN:** 10am-5.30pm Fri-Sun.

THE NATIONAL MUSEUM CAFÉ ®
Joe Kerrigan
Kildare Street, Dublin 2
Tel: (01) 662 1269

He cooks good, flavourful, friendly food, does Joe Kerrigan, and his confidence has grown steadily over the years as the Museum Café has become an ever-more popular place.

● **OPEN:** 10am-5pm Mon-Sat, 2pm-5pm Sun.
● **AVERAGE PRICE:** Lunch under £10. Visa, Access. First floor of the National Museum.

ODESSA ℝ
Jonathan Bourke & Eoin Foyle
13/14 Dame Court, Dublin 2
Tel: (01) 670 7634

Odessa's menu is a classic example
of the modern style. "An eclectic
mix of freshly prepared food for
cosmopolitan palates" they promise,
which in practice means ciabatta,
marinated tofu, angel hair with
pesto. There is also a bar.

● **OPEN:** Noon-midnight Mon-Sun.
● **AVERAGE PRICE:**
Lunch under £10.
Dinner under £15.
Visa, Access /Master, Amex, Diners.
Between Dame St and Excheqeur St.

THE OLD DUBLIN ℝ
Eamonn Walsh
90/91 Francis Street
Dublin 8
Tel: (01) 454 2028

Eamonn Walsh's restaurant is one of
the senior citizens of Dublin restaurant life, but the presence in the
kitchen of Neil McFadden has given
the old Dub a powerful lease of life.
Mr McFadden is a gifted cook, and
he makes the eclectic style of the Old
Dub – a strange fusion of Irish food
and Scandinavian themes – a most
agreeable success.

● **OPEN:** 12.30pm-2.15pm Mon-Fri.
7pm-11pm Mon-Sat.
● **AVERAGE PRICE:**
Lunch under £15.
Dinner over £20.
Visa, Access/Master, Amex, Diners.
Halfway down Francis Street.

101 TALBOT ℝ
Margaret Duffy & Pascal Bradley
100-102 Talbot Street, Dublin 1
Tel: (01) 874 5011

There are far, far more than 101
good things about 101. Margaret
and Pascal are a great team, and they
run a happy, charming place: where
vegetarian dishes are treated with
the utmost care – moreish chickpea
casserole, brilliant filled hot pittas.
It's someplace to enjoy a seriously
good long lunch, a grand family
dinner, or to just grab a sandwich,
with everything dist-inguished by the
fact that the food is not so much
bathed in flavour as anointed with
it. As if that wasn't enough, prices
are keen.

● **OPEN:** 10am-3pm Mon.
10am-11pm Tue-Sat.
(Lunch served noon-3pm).
Dinner served 6pm-11pm.
● **AVERAGE PRICE:** Lunch under £10.
Dinner over £15. Visa, Access/Master.
Near the Abbey.

OW VALLEY FARM SHOP Ⓢ
Sean McArdle
Powerscourt Centre, Dublin 2
Tel: (01) 679 4079

Shoehorned into the smallest space
imaginable, the Ow Valley has made
itself an indispensable place for
exotica – smoked garlic, real Turkish
delight, unusual nuts, wild mushrooms – sold alongside the essentials of everyday cooking.

● **OPEN:** 8.30am-6pm Mon-Sat
('till 7pm Thur).

PASTA FRESCA ® ⑤
Mai Frisby
3-4 Chatham Street, Dublin 2
Tel: (01) 679 2402

A decade on from its opening, Pasta Fresca remains a favourite haunt of the style-conscious classes. The shop continues out front, selling fresh pasta, oils and sauces, whilst the restaurant is open all day, selling familiar pastas and Italian dishes.

● **OPEN:** 8am-11.30pm Mon-Sat,
12.30pm-8.30pm Sun.
● **AVERAGE PRICE:** Lunch under £10.
Dinner under £15. Visa, Access/Master.
Top end of Grafton Street.

IL PRIMO ®
Dieter Bergman & William Frisby
16 Montague Street, Dublin 2
Tel: (01) 478 3373

A fine wine list assembled by Dieter Bergman is one of the main attractions of the little Il Primo. The food is familiar modern Italian.

● **OPEN:** Noon-3pm, 6pm-11pm Mon-Sat.
● **AVERAGE PRICE:** Lunch under £10.
Dinner over £15.
Visa, Access/Master, Amex, Diners.
Montague St is a laneway off Harcourt St.

CONRAD GALLAGHER'S PEACOCK ALLEY ®
Conrad Gallagher
47 Sth William Street, Dublin 2
Tel: (01) 662 0760

Peacock Alley has gotten off at such a pace since Conrad Gallagher found his new home that everyone in the city has been either breathlessly trying to get a table in here or else, if you are a chef, breathlessly trying to catch up.

His food is an extraordinary confection, described by himself as "Mediterranean Provincial Cooking", and whilst this gives a clue to his intentions, for he loves extracting the inherent sweetness of foods, he loves unveiling the sunshine – it gives little or no idea of food which is a total thrill to the senses.

He loves multiple flavours on the plate, but cleverly finds alliances and sympathies in everything he cooks: wild greens with baked tomato, pumpkin seeds and baby asparagus; canneloni stuffed with organic greens, shaved artichokes, baked tomato and Parmesan; confit of tomato and basil soup with capelletti and guacamole.

But the Peacock Alley story is not merely founded on audacious cooking. Mr Gallagher's staff are superb, the music is super-cool, the ambience oftentimes almost electrified. Youth, ambition, talent, skill, and precise judgement all coincide here in an extraordinary place.

● **OPEN:**
12.30pm-2.30pm Mon-Fri,
6pm-10.30pm Mon-Sat.
● **AVERAGE PRICE:**
Lunch under £15.
Dinner under £30.
Visa, Access/Master, Amex, Diners.
Half way down Sth William Street.

QV2 ®

John & Sylvia McCormac
14/15 St Andrew's St, Dublin 2
Tel: (01) 677 3363

The most modish of the cluster of restaurants on St. Andrew's Street, QV2 is an efficient operation with vogue-ish Italian food.

● **OPEN:** Noon-3pm,
6pm-12.30am Mon-Sat.
● **AVERAGE PRICE:** Lunch under £15.
Dinner over £15.
Visa, Access/Master, Amex, Diners.
Near the Dublin Tourism Office.

CAFÉ ROUGE ®

Bronwyn Bailey
1 St Andrew's Street, Dublin 2
Tel: (01) 679 1357

Café Rouge tends to get referred to as an "empire" these days, and certainly it has become a mega-buck operation, attracting more attention on the financial pages than the culinary pages.

But it is a very clever empire, clever enough to get the brilliant Dublin designer David Collins to polish up their faux French style, and clever enough to know that food need only play a supporting role when style, ambience and value are as perceptively understood as they are here.

● **OPEN:** 9am-11pm Mon-Sat. 10am-10.30pm Sun.
● **AVERAGE PRICE:** Lunch £6.95.
Dinner over £10.00.
Visa, Access/Master, Amex, Diners.
Beside the Dublin Tourism Office.

THE RAJDOOT TANDOORI ® ⊖

Ricky Singh
26-28 Clarendon Street, Dublin 2
Tel: (01) 679 4274

Steady as a rock, and as reliable as the rain in Mayo, the Rajdoot has offered seamlessly successful cooking for a decade now, its Moghul richness expertly conceived and executed.

It belongs to that time when Indian restaurants aimed at the upper-end of the restaurant market, before the Balti craze introduced simple food, low prices and a canteen ethic. So, the Rajdoot is plush, cool, almost like a dining room in one of the posh hotels in India.

Yet what the Rajdoot offers, as well as dedicated, authoritative cooking, is very keen prices. Vegetarian choices are particularly excellent, and throughout many visits since the Rajdoot opened, the standards have never dipped. Service is a by-word for professionalism, and a fine meal here is not easily forgotten.

● **OPEN:** Noon-2.30pm, 6.30pm-11.30pm
Mon-Sat.
● **AVERAGE PRICE:** Lunch under £15.
Dinner over £20.
Visa, Access/Master, Amex, Diners.
At the rear of the Westbury Hotel.

THE REAL OLIVE Co ⑤

Toby Simmonds
George's Street Arcade
Tel: (021) 270842 (Cork market)

Toby Simmonds can be found in markets all over the country, selling his multifarious and magnificent wares – the olives and the oils, the marinated feta, the sun-dried tomatoes, the breads and herbs. He is a perfectly brilliant originator, full of life and energy, revelling in what he does, and shopping at any of the stalls is a joyful, delightful practice.

● **OPEN:** 9am-5.30pm Wed-Sat.

SAAGAR ® ⊝
Sunil & Meera Kumar
16 Harcourt Street
Dublin 2
Tel: (01) 475 5060

Sunil and Meera Kumar have run the celebrated Indian restaurant, Little India, in Mullingar since 1992, and the Saagar has benefited enormously from their experience.

It is a sleek, pristine operation, housed in a basement on Harcourt Street, and the attention to detail is dazzling: crisp blue-white linen, gleaming glasses, sparkling cutlery, and the deft assurance of Nisheeth Tak, the manager.

The menu is extensive, with plenty of vegetarian choices: vegetable Hazari (with yellow lentils and vegetables); Dhingri Palak (mushrooms and spinach); Badal Jaam (aubergine with coriander and yogurt) or Bombay Aloo (potatoes with cumin and tomatoes).

The wine list is good, and whilst some may find the presence of fine wines on the list of an Indian restaurant rather strange, the temperateness of most of the dishes in the Saagar makes them suitable partners for a good bottle.

"I got the impression that the wine, like ourselves, was in good hands" said a friend. Prices, for such fine service and food, are enjoyably modest.

● **OPEN:** 12.30pm-3pm Mon-Fri,
6pm-11.30pm Mon-Sun.
● **AVERAGE PRICE:** Lunch under £10.
Dinner over £15.
Visa, Access/Master, Amex, Diners.
Half way up Harcourt Street.

SENOR SASSI'S ®
Ray & Janice Smith
146 Upper Leeson St
Dublin 4
Tel: (01) 668 4544

Sassi's has always struggled to acquire consistency as various cooks have come and gone from its kitchens. This has led to a long search for their own personality, something which chef-proprietors take for granted, but Sassi's has shown that, when on form, it can produce food which has its own style and confidence. They describe it as a "Mediterranean Restaurant and Brasserie", and indeed the modern mania for things from the Med dominates.

● **OPEN:** Noon-2.30pm Tue-Fri,
6pm-11.30pm Mon-Thur,
6.30pm-midnight Fri,
7pm-midnight Sat,
12.30pm-4pm,
6.30pm-10.30pm Sun.
● **AVERAGE PRICE:** Lunch over £10.
Dinner over £20.
Visa, Access/Master, Amex, Diners.
Corner of Leeson St, near the Burlington.

THE SHALIMAR ⓢⓡ
Anwar Azziz
17 South Gt George's Street
Dublin 2
Tel: (01) 671 0738

The opening of their Balti House downstairs in the Shalimar offers another variant on the Pakistani Punjab cuisine in which the restaurant specialises.

This allows the restaurant to offer the simple Balti dishes alongside the more formal food of the restaurant – tandoori specialities, a variety of Punjabi dishes, a range of biryanis.

● **OPEN:** Noon-2.30pm Mon-Sat, 6pm-midnight Mon-Thurs & Sun, to 1am Fri-Sat.
● **AVERAGE PRICE:** Lunch under £10.
Dinner over £15.
Visa, Access/Master, Amex, Diners.
On the corner with Exchequer Street.

SMYTH'S ON THE GREEN ⓡ
Patrick McGinn
Habitat
St Stephen's Green
Dublin 2
Tel: (01) 677 1058

Smyth's is a stylish showcase for the stylish tableware of the shop in which it is housed, but it is rather more than a mere mannequin for Habitat's kitchenware. There is ambition in the cooking – pumpkin soup, vegetable risottos – and whilst the ambition is sometimes greater than the execution, they are to be applauded for striving to achieve more than bland catering.

● **OPEN:** 10am-5.30pm Mon-Sat ('till 7.30pm Thur).
Noon-5.30pm Sun.
● **AVERAGE PRICE:**
Lunch under £10. Dinner over £10.
Visa, Access/Master.
South side of St Stepehen's Green.

LA STAMPA ⓡ
Paul Flynn
35 Dawson Street
Dublin 2
Tel: (01) 677 8611/677 3336

He is an original talent, Paul Flynn, and his food, at its best, is easily the match of any other chef in the city. Working in the grand culinary engine room which is La Stampa has probably denied him some due recognition, for his creativity is suited best to having his own place, and not having to produce the huge number of meals served in the gorgeous dining room of La Stampa every day.

But, when the kitchen in here is humming, the food has a great proudness and a pleasure principle all its own: roast vegetables with lemon and couscous; rigatoni with four cheeses; feuillette of seared spring vegetables, food that is fizzy with flavour, and confident in its embrace of tastes.

● **OPEN:**
12.30pm-2.30pm Mon-Fri,
6.30pm-11.15pm Mon-Sun
('till 11.45pm Fri & Sat).
● **AVERAGE PRICE:**
Lunch under £20. Dinner over £20.
Visa, Access/Master, Amex, Diners.
Opposite the Mansion House.

TOSCA ®
Norman Hewson
20 Suffolk Street
Dublin 2
Tel: (01) 679 6744

The good humour of Tosca, and the smart, peppy Italian-style cooking, have established it as a popular, reliable restaurant. There are lots of vegetarian dishes, a range of sauces to mix with the different pastas, and they don't roam all over the culinary globe.

● **OPEN:**
12.30pm-3.30pm, 6.30pm-11pm Mon-Sun.
● **AVERAGE PRICE:**
Lunch over £10.
Dinner over £20.
Visa, Access/Master, Amex, Diners.
Half-way up Suffolk Street.

TROCADERO ®
Rhona Teehan
3 St Andrew's Street
Dublin 2
Tel: (01) 677 5545

The Troc doesn't have customers it has disciples, folk who have eyes only for its magical, lovely charms. It's a smashing room, the food is straight out of the 1970s, but who cares? Certainly not the thespians, hacks and media-movers who nightly sail into the small hours on a raft of booze and crack.

● **OPEN:** 6pm-12.15am Mon-Sat,
6pm-11.30pm Sun.
● **AVERAGE PRICE:** Dinner over £20.
Visa, Access/Master, Amex, Diners.
Between Wicklow and Suffolk Streets.

UNICORN RESTAURANT ®
Giorgio Casari
Merrion Court
Merrion Row
Dublin 2
Tel: (01) 676 2182

People come to the Unicorn because it is somewhere to be seen, and the mix of media folk, glad-handling politicos and aspiring actor-types who fill its ageless banquettes are, truth be told, the main action, a vigorous social and political whirl which takes place against the backdrop of familiar, but enjoyable cooking.

● **OPEN:** 12.30pm-3pm,
6pm-11.30pm Mon-Sat
('till midnight Fri & Sat)
● **AVERAGE PRICE:**
Lunch under £15.
Dinner over £20.
Visa, Access/Master.
In a courtyard just off Merrion Row.

THE WINDING STAIR BOOKSHOP & CAFÉ ®
Kevin Connolly
40 Lower Ormond Quay
Dublin 1
Tel: (01) 873 3292

The Winding Stair is easily, gloriously, the loveliest, most lingerable bookshop in Dublin. Arcing and swanning over three floors, its zillions of miles of books are a chamber of delights, with everything from hot-from-the reviewers-hands preview copies at knockdown prices to the trusted, dusted-down contents of treasured personal libraries for sale.

That alone would be enough to be going on with, but there is much more to the Winding Stair than just leafing through leafy pages.

Eileen Connolly has offered cracking lunchtime food for years now, really good sandwiches of door stopping grandeur, soulful brewey soups which fortify and inspire.

The soups and sandwiches draw in an assortment of office types who pack the place out at lunchtime, and set up lengthy queues, but, truth be told, to get the best out of the Winding Stair, you should arrive at about 11am.

Then, slowly, browse the shelves and sip some coffee, check out the cool sounds on the stereo which have always been a major attraction, have some lunch with the office set, buy some books, and wonder, and wonder, just what on earth happened to that young, idealistic person you used to be. Blissful.

Do note, for anyone heading westwards, that there is now a sister-ship - or should that be sister-shop? - in Sligo town, where this inimitable formula is brilliantly replicated, which suggest it is not inimitable, but it is, for sure, unique. Mind you, how on earth can you have two unique places?

Answers on a postcard, please.

● **OPEN:** 10.30am-6pm Mon-Sat.
Soup served from noon.
Coffee, cake and rolls and sandwiches available all day.
● **AVERAGE PRICE:** Under £5.
No Credit Cards.
North side of the Ha'penny Bridge.

YAMAMORI NOODLES ®
Yoshi Iwasaki
71 South Gt George's Street,
Dublin 2
Tel: (01) 475 5001

Whilst there are certain discordant notes in the scheme of things that is the Yamamori – an awkward mix of designs, the awkwardness of some of the staff – there are more than enough good things to compensate, and which work together to create an enjoyable noodle house.

The music is fabulous - good cool school and classic Blue Note jazz amongst other sounds - the Japanese waitresses are truly splendid - funny, droll, whacky, witty - and Yoshi Iwasaki's cooking is buzzy with flavour in dishes such as udon noodles with seaweed and vegetables.

This is good, punchy cooking, and if it isn't the best bowl of noodles in town, it certainly comes in in second place.

The sushi is good, and the food suits a lively, youthful place, looked into stylishness and street-savvy, where it is easy to have a fine old time, even if you are no longer nineteen.

● **OPEN:**
12.30pm-2.30pm, 5.30pm-11pm,
Mon-Sat (Fri & Sat 'till 11.30pm).
Sun 2pm-10pm.
● **AVERAGE PRICE:**
Lunch under £10.
Dinner over £10.
Visa, Access/Master, Amex.
Opposite George's St Arcade.

T E M P L E B A R

CHAMELEON ®
Carol Walshe & Vincent Vis
1 Fownes Street Lower
Dublin 2
Tel: (01) 671 0362

Chameleon is the antithesis of the self-conscious coolness and the flash money of Temple Bar.

An improvised, shoestring operation which is patiently being smartened up all the time, it is dominated by the vivacious bonhomie of Carol Walshe and has Vincent Vis in firm control of the cooking. As such, it is Temple Bar's Mom'n'Pop place, a shrine devoted to the caring work of these two people.

Walk in the door and you get character and charm, sit down and you get a sassy style of Indonesian cooking which Mr Vis understands implicitly: butter beans and long beans cooked in coconut milk and spices, fine gado gado, sate of vegetables, alongside an ever-increasing variety of rijstafel. Excellent value, excellent fun, and deserving winner of the first Taste of Temple Bar Award.

● **OPEN:**
5pm-11pm Wed-Sun
('till 10pm Sun).
● **AVERAGE PRICE:**
Dinner under £20.
Visa, Access/Master.
Fownes Street runs onto the Quays.

THE CLARENCE HOTEL ® Ⓐ
Michael Martin
6-8 Wellington Quay, Dublin 2
Tel: (01) 670 9000
Fax: (01) 670 7800

It is an ambitious place, the Clarence. The hotel is already celebrated for its cutting edge stylishness, the happy recipient of lots and lots of money, whilst in the hotel's restaurant, The Tea Rooms, Michael Martin is back in the saddle with an ambitious menu.

If it is ambitious, it is also thoughtful, with good vegetarian choices: a soufflé of Swiss cheeses roasted in cream, an involved salad Parmesan, with main courses such as fettuccine with asparagus, plum tomato and basil, or a risotto of cepes, or a lasagne of aubergine and tomato with pickled mushrooms.

The room itself is ultra-stylish, and service is svelte. If there is still a sense of balance to be found in some of the food, one doesn't doubt that they will find it as they power up to top gear. The music, curiously, is rather poorly chosen and adds nothing to the dining room.

● **OPEN:** RESTAURANT – noon-2.30pm,
6pm-10.45pm Mon-Sun.
BAR – 11am-11pm Mon-Sun.
● **AVERAGE PRICE:** Lunch under £15.
Dinner under £30.
Visa, Access/Master, Amex, Diners.
Overlooking the river Liffey.

ELEPHANT & CASTLE ®
Liz Mee & John Hayes
18 Temple Bar
Dublin 2
Tel: (01) 679 3121

If there is one restaurant which embodies and articulates the dreams invested in the great experiment in living which is Temple Bar, then that restaurant is the Elephant and Castle.

Why? Well, because day after day it achieves a synthesis of quality, accessibility and affordability, the very things which underpin the hopes of the developers of this little bit of Left Bank living. The E&C is funky, cool, hip – no one plays better music in a restaurant than they do here – and, best of all and something which should not be forgotten, Liz Mee can do food which competes with the Gods.

The system they operate is extremely clever. The basic menu remains unaltered but, then, they have different special dishes every day, which allows the cooks to flex their creativity. When that cook is Liz Mee, then brother are you in for some seriously soulful food. This woman can make mashed potatoes a thrill. With John Hayes, Ms Mee has driven this restaurant with determination right from the day it opened, and its influence has been profound, its success richly deserved.

● **OPEN:** 8am-11.30pm Mon-Fri, 10.30am-midnight Sat, noon-11.30pm Sun.
● **AVERAGE PRICE:** Lunch under £10. Dinner over £15.
Visa, Access/Master, Amex, Diners.
In Temple Bar, south of the River Liffey.

THE MERMAID CAFÉ ®
Ben Gorman & Mark Harrell
69-70 Dame Street, Dublin 2
Tel: (01) 670 8236

Ben Gorman and Mark Harrell's restaurant has been the most happening space in Temple Bar in recent times, its scrubbed tables, ladderback chairs and army of Dublin socialites proving an almost instantaneous success.

Vegetarian choices are small, but it's typical of the unpretentiousness of this restaurant that they are flexible and helpful: the Mermaid antipasti allows them to concoct something friendly, and other ideas such as rolled aubergine with herbs and nuts, served with spiced yogurt and three rices, show the modish, flavoursome style of the food.

● **OPEN:** 8am-11.30pm Mon-Fri, 10.30am-midnight Sat, noon-11.30pm Sun.
● **AVERAGE PRICE:** Lunch under £10. Dinner over £15.
Visa, Access/Master, Amex, Diners.

NICO'S ®
Emilio Graziano
53 Dame Street
Temple Bar, Dublin 2
Tel: (01) 677 3062

Beloved of lovers, post-theatre parties, innocents on a first date, your auntie and, it seems, everyone else, Nico's is ageless, and for everyman.

The food is enjoyable trattoria stuff but the theatre of the evening is what really counts. When it gets late enough, the wonky piano playing, the stage-chauvinism of the waiters, the flaming sambuccas, all conspire to create a magical illusion, and you fall for it every time, every time.

● **OPEN:** 12.30pm-2.30pm Mon-Fri, 6pm-12.30am Mon-Sat.
● **AVERAGE PRICE:** Lunch under £10. Dinner over £15.
Visa, Access/Master, Amex, Diners.

THE OLD MILL ®
Lahcen Iouani
14 Temple Bar, Merchant's Arch
Temple Bar, Dublin 2
Tel: (01) 671 9262

Though Lahcen Iouani changed both the focus and the name of his restaurant – for many years it was the very successful Pigalle – the man himself remains a fine cook, with a very true grasp of the fundamentals of simple French cooking.

● **OPEN:** Noon-4am Mon-Sun.
● **AVERAGE PRICE:** Lunch under £10. Dinner over £15.
Visa, Access/Master.
On the first floor over Merchant's Arch.

OMAR KHAYYAM ®
George Sabongi
51 Wellington Quay,
Temple Bar Dublin 2
Tel: (01) 677 5758

Khayyam is very popular with vegetarians, and the cooking with grains and pulses can be imaginative and enjoyable. It's a youthful, relaxed place which you don't need to take too seriously.

● **OPEN:** Noon-midnight Mon-Sat.
● **AVERAGE PRICE:** Lunch under £10. Dinner over £15.
Visa, Access/Master, Amex, Diners.
A few yards down from the Ha'penny bridge, on the south side of the Liffey.

PADANIA Ⓢ
Pier Fabrizio & Fulvia
Spranger's Yard, Temple Bar,
Dublin 2
Tel: (01) 679 2458

Padania is one of the best shops in Dublin, a mustn't miss for anyone who wants true Italian artisan foodstuffs and not the commercialised, compromised stuff you find everywhere else.

The extra virgin olive oils they sell are superb, the Parmesan the best in the country, and there is a trueness and meticulousness to everything on the shelves.

● **OPEN:** 10.30am-6pm Mon-Sat.

SINNERS ®
Gerry Salam
12 Parliament St,
Temple Bar, Dublin 2
Tel: (01) 671 9345

Sinners produces good, middle eastern cooking – the mezzes are a speciality – and a good time. A little more experience should cure the hesitant nature of the service.

● **OPEN:** 5.30pm-midnight Mon-Sun.
● **AVERAGE PRICE:** Dinner under £20.
Visa, Access/Master, Amex, Diners.
In the centre of Parliament Street.

TANTE ZOE'S ®
Robbie Fox
1 Crow Street
Temple Bar
Dublin 2
Tel: (01) 679 4407

One of the Bar's oldest residents at this stage, the Tante Zoe mixture of Creole cooking for Irish tastes has proved enduringly popular, thanks to its accessibility and their emphasis on fun.

● **OPEN:** Noon-3pm Mon-Sat,
6pm-midnight Mon-Sun.
● **AVERAGE PRICE:** Lunch under £10.
Dinner under £20.
Visa, Access/Master, Amex, Diners.
Centre of Crow Street.

THOMAS READ'S BAR ●
Martin Conroy, Hugh O'Reagan
Parliament St
Temple Bar
Dublin 2
Tel: (01) 677 1487

Friendly service and smart, modern food, not to mention a pretty hip crowd, are the attractions of this groovily designed bar, just across from Dublin castle and right on the corner. Whether for a bit of breakfast, a blow-out brunch or a quick lunch, Read's fits the bill.

● **OPEN:** 10am-11pm, food available –
breakfast 10am-noon.
Lunch noon-4pm Mon-Sat,
('till 3.30pm Fri & Sat).
Sun brunch 11am-3pm.
● **AVERAGE PRICE:**
Breakfast under £5. Lunch under £10.

TRASTEVERE ®
Giovanni Cafolla
Temple Bar Square
Dublin 2
Tel: (01) 670 8343

The Cafolla family have recently opened this groovy goldfish-bowl of a place, with Italian food right in the centre of Temple Bar. It's slick and fun, with the sort of common-place Italian-style food - some pastas, some pizzas, some special dishes – which is now so popular.

● **OPEN:**
12.30pm-11pm Mon-Sun.
● **AVERAGE PRICE:**
Lunch under £10.
Dinner under £15.

THE WELL FED CAFÉ ®
Resource Centre
Crow St
Dublin 2
Tel: (01) 677 1974

Even though it is run by a worker's co-op, it's not necessary to have an agit-prop attitude to enjoy the simple cooking here in the Well Fed. This is a long-established, harmonious organisation, and happily there is nothing but harmony in the good, simple vegetarian food which is often very scrummy indeed. The centre also houses a bookshop, a bike park and various other capacities.

● **OPEN:** 10.30am-8.30pm Mon-Sat.
● **AVERAGE PRICE:** Lunch under £5.
No Cards.
Parallel to Fownes Street.

VILLAGES OF DUBLIN

SOUTH DUBLIN

BALLSBRIDGE

EXPRESSO BAR ®
Ann Marie Nohl
47 Shelbourne Road
Ballsbridge
Dublin 4
Tel: (01) 660 8632

A chic, lifestyle little space with very colourful, well-considered food, and lots of interesting varieties of coffee.

● **OPEN:** 7.30am-5pm Mon-Fri,
10am-5pm Sat-Sun, 7pm-10pm Sat.
(Opening Thu & Fri evening high season,
booking advisable).
● **AVERAGE PRICE:** Lunch under £10.
Dinner under £20.
Visa, Access/Master.

FITZERS CAFÉ ®
Frank Fitzpatrick
RDS, Ballsbridge
Dublin 4
Tel: (01) 667 1301
Dawson Street,
Dublin 2
Tel: (01) 677 1155

Fitzers at the RDS enjoys a gracious, elegant, high-ceilinged room, a counterpoint to the funky space on Dawson Street in the city.

The cooking culls influences from all over the globe, and produces food which is unpretentious and enjoyable. Indeed, a pervasive simplicity is as much a culinary theme of the Fitzer's organisation as the internationalism of the food, and their ambition is to offer the best food at the best value.

● **OPEN:** DAWSON ST – 9am-11.30pm.
RDS – Noon-3pm, 6pm-11pm Mon-Sun
('till 10.30pm Sun).
● **AVERAGE PRICE:** DAWSON ST –
Lunch under £10. Dinner over £10.
RDS – Lunch over £10.
Dinner over £20.
Visa, Access/Master, Amex.

MARRAKESH ®
Margaret & Akim Beskri
11 Ballsbridge Terrace
Ballsbridge
Dublin 4
Tel: (01) 660 5539

Akim Beskri's restaurant is a simple, casual place, with fine Moroccan cooking, a lot of it very vegetarian friendly: harira; tabouleh; grilled salad; tagine of mixed vegetables; couscous with seven vegetables; dolmas. It's friendly and good value.

● **OPEN:** Noon-2.30pm, 6pm-11pm Mon-Sun ('till 11.30pm Fri & Sat).
● **AVERAGE PRICE:** Lunch under £10.
Dinner over £15.
Visa, Access/Master, Amex, Diners.
At the bridge in Ballsbridge.

ROLY'S BISTRO ®
Roly Saul
7 Ballsbridge Terrace, Dublin 4
Tel: (01) 668 261

As important a part of the city as a Joycean Tower or The International Bar, Roly Saul's elegant, smart brasserie is a continual wondershow, packed to the rafters every day, firing away with a relentless ability to deliver a good time.

Colin O'Daly's cooking is assured, flavourful, and terrific value, and amidst the original dishes of the day there are always vegetarian choices: tian of avocado and celeriac with a mustard and garlic mayonnaise; crepe of spinach, oyster mushrooms, Swiss cheese and sesame seeds; deep fried crusted brie with coriander and yogurt; pasta arrabbiata. It is a glorious restaurant, always a joy to return to.

● **OPEN:** Noon-4pm, 6pm-11pm Mon-Sun.
● **AVERAGE PRICE:** Lunch over £10.
Dinner under £20.
Visa, Access/Master, Amex.
On corner between Ballsbridge and Herbert Park.

BLACKROCK

AYUMI-YA ® ⓢ ⟶
Yoichi Hoashi
Newpark Centre
Newtownpark Avenue, Blackrock
Tel: (01) 283 1767

The Ayumi-Ya restaurants have prospered over the years thanks to excellent cooking, a commodious atmosphere, steady adaptation to change, and continual improvement, but the keynote of their success rests almost as much with the confidence and calmness of the service.

This has allowed Yoichi Hoashi to introduce the delicately delicious strictures of Japanese food to a public who might otherwise have been rather suspicious. But, when you encounter the charming service of the Ayumis, service with grace and control, then the introduction to Japanese food becomes an immersion into its delights.

The restaurant has teppan-yaki tables and conventional and cushioned seating areas, and perhaps the most rigorous and delightful vegetarian cooking in the suburbs: vegetable tempura; tofu steak in Japanese style; soba noodles wrapped with nori; grilled shiitake, cooking which is beautifully soulful and satisfying

There is also a shop, open in the evenings and Saturday afternoon.

● **OPEN:** 5pm-7pm Mon-Sat (Sat 1pm-5pm).

BUTLER'S PANTRY ⓢ
Eileen Bergin
53 Mount Merrion Avenue,
Blackrock
Tel: (01) 288 3443

(Also at 97b Morehampton Road Donnybrook, Dublin 4)
Tel: (01) 660 8490, Fax: 660 8490)

The Butler's Pantrys led the way in traiteur food – cooked, ready to carry home dishes – which has become increasingly important in Dublin in recent years. By this stage, their confidence and expertise is one's guarantee of quality, right throughout a very extensive range of foods from finger foods, to salads, to pastas, to ice creams and desserts.

● **OPEN:**
9.30am-9pm Mon-Sat, 11am-3pm Sun.
Halfway down Mt Merrion Ave.

EASTERN TANDOORI ®

Faroze Khan
34-35 South William Street
Dublin 2
Tel: (01) 671 0428

The Old Parish Hall, Kill Lane,
Deansgrange, Blackrock
Tel: (01) 289 2856

1 New Street, Malahide
Tel: (01) 845 4155

The Eastern has mushroomed into an empire of restaurants now, with a branch in Cork city as well as the trio of Dublin restaurants. The vision of the owners is one of comfortable surroundings, and comfortable, comfortingly rich food which can please almost everyone, so an evening here mixes the modus of the western restaurant with the food of the east in an easy-going embrace.

● **OPEN:** WILLIAM ST – noon-2.30pm,
6pm-midnight, Mon-Sat, 6pm-11.30pm Sun.
BLACKROCK – noon-2.30pm, 6pm-
11.30pm Mon-Sat, 1pm-11pm Sun.
MALAHIDE – 6pm-11.30pm Mon-Sat
('till midnight Fri & Sat), 1pm-11pm Sun.
● **AVERAGE PRICE:** Lunch under £10.
Dinner under £20.
Visa, Access/Master, Amex, Diners.

McCABE'S ⑤

Jim McCabe
51-55 Mount Merrion Avenue
Blackrock
Tel: (01) 288 2037

(Also at Vernon Avenue, Clontarf
Dublin 3, Tel: (01) 335277)

Jim McCabe runs two excellent wine shops, places which are testament to his good taste, his hunger to improve his list and to hunt down exciting new wines.

The range is strong in every part of the globe, and McCabe's are very good at demystifying wine; no high-falutin' nonsense here, as demonstrated by their regular tastings which always aim to reveal quality and value for money. Their annual Wine Festival in November is great crack.

● **OPEN:** 10.30am-10pm Mon-Sat,
12.30pm-2pm, 4pm-10pm Sun.

THE VINTAGE ⑤

Newtownpark Avenue, Blackrock
Tel: (01) 283 1664

(also at 149 Upper Rathmines
Road Dublin 6
Tel: (01) 967811)

The Ecock brothers like to introduce new wines very gradually to their list, so the Vintages have patiently built their list and built their business, into a position where they are major suppliers to the restaurant trade in addition to the shops.

● **OPEN:** 10.30am-10pm Mon-Sat,
12.30pm-2pm, 4pm-10pm Sun.

BOOTERSTOWN

LA TAVOLA ®
Bahaa Jaafai
114 Rock Road
Booterstown
Tel: (01) 283 5101

The pizza and pasta recipe familiar from so many places is rather better executed in La Tavola than elsewhere, and its continuing success in an uninspiring site on the main road is testament to their care with staples such as penne all'arrabbiatta, or tomato and mozzarella salad.

They succeed by regarding the menu as a series of challenges to be delivered with control and precision. Usually, they achieve their ambitions, and the relaxed room is very enjoyable.

● **OPEN:** 5pm-11.30pm Tue-Sat
● **AVERAGE PRICE:** Dinner under £20.
Visa, Access/Master.
Opposite Booterstown DART station.

DALKEY

AL MINAR ®
Mr Rahman
21 Castle Street
Dalkey
Tel: (01) 285 0552

A quiet little restaurant on the main street of Dalkey, quietly lit, with quiet service, the Al Minar makes up for this deference by enjoying the demands of customers who ask for dishes to be prepared in the way the staff eat them. So, chilli fiends, ask for pungency and you will receive it.

And how! As you would expect from an Indian restaurant, vegetarian choices are plentiful.

● **OPEN:** Noon-2.30pm, 6pm-midnight Mon-Sun.
● **AVERAGE PRICE:** Lunch under £10. Dinner under £15.
Visa, Access/Master, Amex, Diners.
On Dalkey's Main Street.

LA ROMANA ® ℗
Maura Mulhare
The Queen's
Castle Street, Dalkey
Tel: (01) 285 4569

A room in the big, plush pub that is The Queen's, La Romana offers pasta and pizzas in that style which owes rather more to Ireland than Italy. But the room is bright and busy, and a dinner of simple foods, and a brace of pints, can be fun.

● **OPEN:** 5.30pm-11.30pm Mon-Sat, 12.30pm-10pm Sun.
● **AVERAGE PRICE:**
Under £15.
Visa, Access/Master.

DONNYBROOK

DOUGLAS FOOD Co ⓢ
Richard Douglas
53 Donnybrook Road
Donnybrook, Dublin 4
Tel: (01) 269 4066

Richard Douglas' shop has always been the swishest and most stylish of the Dublin trâiteurs, with the most personal and innovative cooking.

Their list of dishes is, happily, not a compendium of everything that can be cooked, but rather a choice selection which plays to their strengths. They are happy to discuss menu ideas for parties and gatherings, and the shop also sells a small selection of fine packets, oils and cheeses

● **OPEN:**
10am-7.30pm Mon-Fri, 9am-6pm Sat.

FURAMA CHINESE RESTAURANT ®
Rodney Mak
88 Donnybrook Road
Dublin 4
Tel: (01) 283 0522

Rodney Mak has been expanding his restaurant empire recently, opening up Brooks restaurant just a door or so down from the Furama.

It is likely, however, that his greatest gift to the food culture of Dublin will remain the Furama, for here is a Chinese restaurant which makes the minimum of culinary compromises for its clientele, and which produces food that has terrific discipline and panache.

Professionalism and an air of grandeur and seriousness about their craft mean that the Furama is a good restaurant, a place which reads the needs of its customers and aims to satisfy them with precision. This care costs more, of course, but when the job is as well achieved as they manage here, then no one minds.

It is bourgeois Chinese cooking, in a bourgeois room with the company

of the Dublin 4 bourgeoisie all around you, and it works, somehow.

● **OPEN:** 12.30pm-2pm, 6pm-11.30pm Mon-Sat (Fri & Sat to midnight), 1.30pm-11pm Sun,
6pm-11pm bank holidays.
Last orders half-an-hour before closing time.
● **AVERAGE PRICE:** Lunch under £15. Dinner over £20.
Visa, Access/Master, Amex.
Opposite the rugby ground.

ROY FOX ⑤
Des Donnelly
49a Main Street
Donnybrook, Dublin 4
Tel: (01) 269 2892

The produce from Des Donnelly's shop positively tumbles out on to the little side street, just off the main strip of Donnybrook, and the be-decked trays of fruits and vegetables will guide you to a shop full of good things. Inside, there are all the excellent comestibles of the choice deli. Brilliant place, brilliant staff who love their work.

● **OPEN:** 9am-7pm Mon-Sun.

TERROIRS ⑤
Sean & Françoise Gilley
103 Morehampton Road
Donnybrook, Dublin 4
Tel: (01) 667 1311, Fax: 667 1312

What Terroirs enjoys, in the persons of Mr and Mrs Gilley, is a duet of decisively selective palates, and their shop is testament to their discrimination. Whether it's Burgundies or Bordeaux, magnificent artisan treats, or just fabulous sweeties for the baby, Terroirs has the best you will find.

Terroirs is, of course, a wine shop, and it is a very fine one at that, amongst the very best in the country.

But what makes Terroirs special is not just the wines. No, the special ingredient lies with everything else they sell. The Jelly Bellies. The teas by Benjamin & Barton. The Quernon's d'Ardoise from Angers. The confitures by Jean-Marc Chatelain. The olive oils from France and Italy. The flavoured vinegars by Consorzio. The stunning mustards from Champ's. No other shop, not to mention any other wine shop, has such a powerfully selective and stupendous range of complementary foods, and Terroirs is one of the best things to happen to Dublin in years.

● **OPEN:** 10.30am-8pm Mon-Sat.

DUNLAOGHAIRE

CAVISTON'S DELICATESSEN Ⓢ
The Caviston family
59 Glasthule Road
Sandycove, Dun Laoghaire
Tel: (01) 280 9120

The great ship Caviston sails ever onwards, its brilliant strengths as reverberant and resplendent as ever.

There is the fine cheese counter, there are great oils and savouries, excellent sarnies for lunch, in fact just about everything your heart could desire.

For special occasions – Xmas,

your big dinner party – they tune up a gear, finding great treats. It is a smashing shop, its fabric rich in personality and pleasure and a true sense of vocation in their work. There is now a small restaurant next door, which has already proven to be a great success.

● **OPEN:** 9am-7pm Mon-Sat.

KRISHNA INDIAN RESTAURANT Ⓡ
Paul Sahota
1st Floor, 47 George's Street Lwr
Dun Laoghaire
Tel: (01) 280 1855

The simplicity of the Krishna is welcome, making no attempt to ape the plushness which other Indian restaurants strive for, preferring to concentrate instead on temperate and particular use of organic ingredients and intelligent, well-focused food.

It is a small, upstairs room, dimly lit, and the take-away they operate adds to the air of community café. There is much to enjoy, with their breads, in particular, proving especially excellent.

Their work enjoys a particular air of authenticity – the cooking is in the succulent, buttery Northern Indian style – and everything works together to make this a special place.

● **OPEN:** 12.30pm-2.30pm Mon-Sat, 6pm-11.30pm Sun-Thurs, to 12.30am Fri & Sat.
● **AVERAGE PRICE:** Lunch under £10. Dinner over £15.
Visa, Access/Master, Amex, Diners.
A few doors up from Dunphy's pub, over the butcher's shop. Look for the sign.

MORELS BISTRO ®
Alan O'Reilly & John Dunne
18 Glasthule Rd, Dun Laoghaire
Tel: (01) 230 0210

Morels is probably the most successful restaurant to have opened in Dublin since the tearaway success stories that have been Roly's and the Elephant & Castle. Its concept is a clever one – affordable, creative food in a funky environment, but the key note in its success has been John Dunne's cooking, a splendidly evolved and astute style which is crushingly logical and delicious.

Mushroom risotto with tarragon; plum tomato soup with Parmesan; angel hair pasta with artichoke heart and home-dried tomatoes; goat's cheese crostini with rocket and balsamic dressing.

With cooking like this, you can't lose, and from the day it opened its doors, Morels has given the public what they want, and they have turned up in droves to get it.

● **OPEN:** 5.30pm-10.30pm Mon-Sun,
12.30pm-2.30pm Sun.
● **AVERAGE PRICE:** Lunch over £10.
Dinner – early bird under £15.
Dinner under £20.
Visa, Access/Master, Amex.
Over the Eagle Pub.

ODELL'S ®
John Waddell & Frank O'Connor
49 Sandycove Road, Dun Laoghaire
Tel: (01) 284 2188

Odell's is a friendly bistro, with understated, cosmopolitan food –

Cajun dishes, Mediterranean stylings, Chinese spicings – served in generous portions by kindly staff.

● **OPEN:** 6pm-10.30pm Mon-Sun.
● **AVERAGE PRICE:** Dinner under £20.
Visa, Access/Master, Amex, Diners.
Upstairs, opposite Fitzgerald's pub in Sandycove.

BISTRO NA MARA ®
Adrian Spellman
Dun Laoghaire, Tel: (01) 280 0509

Bistro Na Mara currently wears the smartest new livery in Dublin, a beautiful plain white coat with mega-mirrors which has radicalised this grand old institution. But the revision is not merely skin deep, for Adrian Spellman's cooking is more than a match for its bright new interior. He has shifted the focus onto modern, hybrid creations, and if the menu is now closer in concept to that of Na Mara's sister-ship, the Footplate Brasserie, in Heuston Station, in Dublin, it is much better executed.

Vegetarian choices are limited – salad of avocado, tomato and feta; a tian of vegetables with a herb flavoured couscous and a tomato coulis featured on an early menu, and one hopes Mr Spellman will extend this, for he is a talented cook, and the new bistro is a groovy space.

● **OPEN:**
1pm-2.30pm, 7pm-10.15pm Mon-Sat.
● **AVERAGE PRICE:** Lunch under £15.
Dinner over £20.
Visa, Access/Master, Amex, Diners.
Over the railway station.

FOXROCK

THOMAS' DELICATESSEN ⑤

Thomas Murphy
4 Brighton Road
Foxrock
Dublin 18
Tel: (01) 289 6579

Thomas Murphy has a very keen appreciation of his customers' demands, a fact which has firmly established the importance of Thomas's deli in the area. Lots of choice things, good wines, and friendly, helpful advice.

● **OPEN:** 7.30am-7.30pm Mon-Sat, 10am-2pm Sun.

MONKSTOWN

NAPOLEON OF MONKSTOWN ⑤

Michael & Noel Kelly
Monkstown Road
Monkstown
Tel: (01) 230 0387

The Kelly brothers have very cleverly brought together an eclectic range of foods for their little shop just across from the church.

Fine milk from the Kiltiernan dairy, breads from the Bretzel bakery in Rathmines, a small range of Irish dairy and farmhouse cheeses, good free-range eggs, excellent teas and coffees from Clive McCabe of Greystones, and an assortment of cooked foods prepared for them by the kitchens of John Howard's Le Coq Hardi in Ballsbridge. It's a sumptuous selection, abetted by

other choice comestibles, and a successful recipe.

● **OPEN:** 10am-7.30pm Mon-Sat.

SEARSON'S ⑤

Charles & Frank Searson
The Crescent, Monkstown
Tel: (01) 280 0405, Fax: 280 4771

Frank and Charles Searson may convey something of the image of claret and club tie chaps, but whilst they do specialise in fine wines, they also hunt down many cracking newcomers, and recent times have seen their gaze directed on French regional wines and the wines of eastern Europe.

But whatever they choose, it is selected with care and eagerness and – that vital ingredient – they are chaps who have good taste. It's always a pleasure to shop in Searson's.

● **OPEN:** 10.30am-7pm Mon-Sat.

VALPARAISO ®

Paul Foley & Con Galligan
99 Monkstown Road, Monkstown
Tel & Fax: (01) 280 1992

Spanish colourings of vivid blue and yellow are the template of the design, and Spanish accented food – tapas of tortilla and piparrada salad; vegetable stuffed aubergine; pisto stew of vegetables; vegetarian rice; – are the recipe of Valparaiso.

● **OPEN:** 6.30pm-11.30pm Mon-Sat, 5.30pm-10pm Sun.

● **AVERAGE PRICE:** Dinner under £20.
Visa, Access/Master, Amex, Diners.
Near the Church, over Goggin's Pub.

PORTOBELLO

BRETZEL KOSHER BAKERY ⑤
Morgan Hackett
1A Lennox Street, Portobello,
Dublin 8
Tel: (01) 475 2724

They set up the template of tastes in the Bretzel many years ago, and the gooey pizzas, the crumbly croissants, the chompish chocolates, the kiddy-cute gingerbread men, the onion bagels, are the same as they have always been, sweetly nostalgic, tried and trusted tastes.

● **OPEN:** 9.15am-5.30pm Mon-Sat,
9am-1.30pm Sun.

BU-ALI ®
Abi Abbasali
28 Lower Clanbrassil Street
Dublin 8
Tel: (01) 454 6505

In India and Pakistan, roadside eateries like the Bu-Ali are everywhere, and the great thing about the Bu-Ali is the authenticity of its simplicity. A counter, some chairs, garish lighting, a bleating telly, and scrumptious food are all they need. For the most part, it specialises as a take-away, and there is a delivery service in the locale. But be careful: such well-judged simple tastes may make you nostalgic for back-packing days, as you sit at

home with the delights of the sub continent all around you.

● **OPEN:** 5pm-2.30pm Mon-Sat,
5pm-midnight Sun.
● **AVERAGE PRICE:** Dinner under £10.
Visa, Access/Master, Amex, Diners.
Halfway up Clanbrassil St.

TEACH BAN ⑤
Ann Currie & Patrick Duggan
6 Parnell Road
Harold's Cross, Dublin 6
Tel: (01) 454 3943

Ann and Patrick not only run regular classes on wholefood cookery, but have also written and published "The Irish Macrobiotic Wholefood Cookbook". They also do personal dietary counselling, shiatsu treatment and alternative medicine. More details from the centre.

RANELAGH

PUNJAB BALTI HOUSE ®
Mohammed Latif
15 Ranelagh Village, Dublin 6
Tel: (01) 497 9420

Mohammed Latif's Balti House is a simple, comfortable room, basic in design, quietly lit, with the steamy activity of the kitchen a nice counterpoint to the calm of the dining room. Since opening, it has been a runaway success, its affordable food a God-send for locals.

There are vegetable samosas and kebabs, Balti vegetables, vegetable biryani and a good range of vegetarian dishes.

Service is excellent, and their bring-your-own-wine policy means that an evening in the Punjab Balti House can be extremely inexpensive, and extremely good crack. If you haven't a bottle or two with you, then Redmond's excellent off-licence just up the road will save the day.

● **OPEN:** 5pm-midnight Mon-Sun.
● **AVERAGE PRICE:** Dinner under £15.
Visa, Access/Master, Amex, Diners.
Centre of Ranelagh Village.

REDMOND'S ⑤
Jimmy & Aidan Redmond
25 Ranelagh Village
Ranelagh, Dublin 6
Tel: (01) 496 0552

They souped-up the style of Redmond's a while back, turning it into a garishly lit, modernist palace of grub and plonk. Some may miss the passing of the former fine old shop and wine merchant, with its agreeably archaic style, but what has not changed is that this remains one of the very best independent off-licences in Dublin.

Their range is imaginative and extensive, and good value, and there are frequently good bargains to be found in bin ends. They have cool bottles to take with you to nearby restaurants, lots of cool beers, and Redmond's is a vital part of Ranelagh.

● **OPEN:**
9am-10.30pm Mon-Sat,
12.30pm-2pm, 4pm-9pm Sun.

RATHMINES

FOTHERGILL'S ⑤
Terry & Breda Lilburn
141 Upper Rathmines Road
Rathmines
Dublin 6
Tel: (01) 496 2511

Fothergill's is one of the great Dublin delis, with a smashing range of handmade foods. The goodies range from the brilliant lunchtime sandwiches, the carefully composed salads, the plump cheeses, right through to the knockout cakes and desserts which local matrons – shame on you, girls! – often have the gall to pass off as their own. A terrific shop, where retaining self-control is almost impossible.

● **OPEN:** 9.30am-6pm Mon,
9am-6.30pm Tue-Fri, 9am-6pm Sat.

C. MORTON & SON ⑤
Alan Morton
15 Dunville Ave
Rathmines, Dublin 6
Tel: (01) 497 1254

Design fetishists adore the beautiful, 1960s style of Morton's shop front, whilst food lovers appreciate it as one of the most selective, personable, places to shop. Its gentle, almost distracted atmosphere, its human scale and helpful service, the obvious care which goes into selecting what they sell, all make it a refreshing, calming, quite inimitable shop.

● **OPEN:** 9am-6.30pm Mon-Sat.

NATURALLY NICE ⑤
Catriona Norton
Dunville Avenue, Rathmines
Dublin 6
Tel: (01) 497 3411

Good dried pastas, olive oils and their own salad dressings are just a few of the specialities in this busy little trove dedicated to Italian foods.

● **OPEN:** 9am-7.30pm Mon-Sat, 9am-2.30pm Sun.

ZEN CHINESE RESTAURANT ®
Dennis O'Connor
89 Upper Rathmines Rd, Dublin 6
Tel: (01) 497 9428

The Zen is actually housed in a converted religious meeting hall, which gives a style of missionary endeavour to the experience of eating here.

Actually, the room is a delightful contrast to the other laminate and lacquer Chinese restaurants in the city, and the generous acreage of space between the tables and a plenitude of light, is an important factor in allowing the service to be relaxed and affable.

If the architectural and design details are a happy accident, the food is a considered composition of ingredients. It runs along largely familiar lines, for sure – the black bean sauce combinations, the tofu, the noodles, the fried rice – but it can produce some excellent inventions.

● **OPEN:** 12.30pm-3pm, 6pm-11.30pm Mon-Sun

● **AVERAGE PRICE:** Lunch under £10. Dinner over £20.
Visa, Access/Master.
Take-away service available.
In Upper Rathmines, near the junction with Church Avenue.

RATHGAR

KIM CONDON'S DELICATESSEN ⑤
Kim Condon
99B Rathgar Road
Rathgar
Dublin 6
Tel: (01) 492 9148

A scion of the family who have powered Magill's delicatessen in the centre of the city for many years, Kim Condon's own shop has a panache and persuasiveness which is entirely the property of the lady herself.

She is a dynamic figure, always looking for good new things, open to suggestions from her customers, keen to establish the shop as a vital part of the little cluster of businesses which are Rathgar.

Like any good deli, you quickly build up a relationship with Ms. Condon, and you trust her discrimination, her taste. She knows the good things – the Olvi oils, the Torc chocolates, the farmhouse cheeses, the pastagusto sauces – and it is a treat to visit, and to be persuaded by Kim's vivacious character.

● **OPEN:** 10am-7pm Mon-Fri, 9am-6pm Sat, 10am-2pm Sun.
At the junction in Rathgar.

THE GOURMET SHOP ⓢ
Thomas Cronin
Rathgar
Dublin 6
Tel: (01) 497 0365

The Gourmet Shop is an old style deli, with an eclectic array of wines for sale, and part of its attraction is undoubtedly the sense of stepping back in time.

● **OPEN:**
9am-7pm Mon-Sat.
At the junction in Rathgar.

THE VINTRY ⓢ
Evelyn Jones
102 Rathgar Road
Rathgar
Dublin 6
Tel: (01) 490 5477

The Vintry is a confident little wine shop, with an eclectic, confident array of wines which ciucumnavigate the globe in their quest for rasping deliciousness and fruit-filled vivacity.

Evelyn Jones also organises the Vintry Wine club for her customers, holding monthly tastings and presenting visiting winemakers, a valuable process which helps to demystify – and to increase everyone's enjoyment – of the world of wine.

● **OPEN:**
10.30am-11pm Mon-Sat,
12.30pm-2pm, 4pm-10.30pm Sun.
At the junction in Rathgar.

CHINA-SICHUAN RESTAURANT Ⓡ
David Hui
4 Lower Kilmacud Road
Stillorgan, Co Dublin
Tel: (01) 288 4817

David Hui's restaurant is the most classical Chinese restaurant in the country, easily outpacing its many rivals when it comes to authenticity and the cooking of food with distinct, vital, exciting flavours.

They can do certain things in here which can achieve true greatness: fab hot and sour soup; wonderful braised hot and spicy bean curd; fried twin delight of bamboo shoots and Chinese mushrooms; golden fried bean curd in the home style.

Flavours are very true and crisply captured, and the array of dishes terrifically enjoyable.

In addition, the service is excellent – none of that standard brusque belligerence from the smiling Tim and his colleagues, and prices are fair.

This is real Chinese cooking and the China-Sichuan has long been one of the most valuable and memorable restaurants in the city.

● **OPEN:** 12.30pm-2.30pm, 6pm-11pm
Mon-Fri, 6pm-11pm Sat,
1pm-2.30pm, 6pm-11pm Sun.
● **AVERAGE PRICE:** Lunch under £10.
Dinner over £20.
Visa, Access/Master, Amex.
On the Kilmacud Road, just up from the Stillorgan Shopping Centre, and amidst a complex of shops, pubs and whatnot.

NORTH DUBLIN

BEAUMONT

OLVI OILS ●
Miriam Griffith
103, Elm Mount Avenue
Beaumont
Dublin 9
Tel: (01) 831 0244

The country is awash with prepared oils and sauces, but few of them are as good as the Olvi oils made by Miriam Griffith. Her range is wisely small – a smashing black olive paste; fruity tomato vinaigrette with fennel; excellent basil pesto; and juicy vinaigrettes flavoured with mango and basil respectively – and they have the precise, well-judged tastes which show that Ms Griffith is a fine cook.

● **OPEN:** Distributed nationally.

CASTLEKNOCK

BRANGAN & Co ●
Colm Brangan
15 Deerpark Ave
Castleknock
Dublin 15
Tel: (01) 821 4052

We have a phrase, whenever we come across a bottle of wine which is particularly exciting. What we say is: "It's bound to be a Brangan", for the French wines on Colm Brangan's list are unusually distinguished, irrespective of the price charged. No one else has such an idiosyncratic, distinctive, surprising list, and whilst Brangan is, of course, strong on both clarets and Burgundies, it is the little gems he unearths each year on his forays to France which are the most exciting. The wines are found on restaurant lists and in wine shops, and they never disappoint. So, the next time some inexpensive little gem knocks you sideways with pleasure, remember: "It's bound to be a Brangan".

● **OPEN:** Telephone for price list.

CLONTARF

VERLING'S ●
Jim & Julie Verling
360 Clontarf Road
Castleknock
Dublin 3
Tel: (01) 833 1653

They have a fine eye for a bargain in Verling's. Just about every time you go through the door of the shop, alongside the excellent range of fine wines there are likely to be a couple of new arrivals, snapped up by Jim or Julie, which offer knock-out value.

They also run wine appreciation courses, held upstairs, and it's the kind of shop where there is always an opened bottle, waiting to be sampled, a signal of their friendly, down-to-earth, unpretentious approach to the world of wine.

● **OPEN:**
10.30am-10pm Mon-Sat, 12.30pm-2pm, 4pm-10pm Sun.

ADRIAN'S ®

Catriona & Adrian Holden
8 Abbey Street
Howth
Tel & Fax: (01) 839 1696

Catriona Holden is a cook who loves the business of being creative in the kitchen, producing clever things such as a subtle three-pepper gateau; aubergine and polenta rarebit; garlic and honey lentil cakes. Lovely food, laid-back place.

● **OPEN:**
12.30pm-3pm Mon-Sat,
6pm-9.30pm Mon-Sun ('till 8pm Sun).
● **AVERAGE PRICE:**
Lunch under £15.
Dinner over £15.
Visa, Access/Master.

MALAHIDE

OLD STREET WINE BAR ®

Gail Sinclair
Old Street
Malahide
Tel: (01) 845 1882

A great, happening little room, where Gail Sinclair composes a happy, fun atmosphere and happy, fun food with lots of good choices: red cabbage pancake; curried parsnip soup; spinach and mushroom quiche; vegetable moussaka, and nice gooey desserts.

● **OPEN:**
Noon-3pm, 6pm-11pm Mon-Sun.

● **AVERAGE PRICE:** Lunch under £10.
Dinner over £10.
Visa, Access/Master.
Turn left before the traffic lights, and the wine bar is on the left.

STONEYBATTER

LITTLE ITALY ⓢ

Marise Rabitte
68 North King Street
Stoneybatter
Dublin 7
Tel: (01) 872 5208

A trove of all things Italian – arborio, big bottles of Bove, dried porcini, Lavazza coffee – in a quickly-smartening up part of town.

● **OPEN:**
9am-5pm Mon-Fri, 10am-1pm Sat.

TA SÉ MOHOGANI GASPIPES ®

Roy & Drina Kinsley
17 Manor Street,
Stoneybatter, Dublin 7
Tel: (01) 679 8138

Ta Sé is a pleasingly classless restaurant with eclectic, imaginative cooking that straddles the globe. There is music at the weekends.

● **OPEN:** 1pm-4pm Tue-Fri,
7pm-midnight Tue-Thur,
7pm-2am Fri-Sat.
● **AVERAGE PRICE:** Lunch under £10.
Dinner over £15.
Visa, Access/Master, Diners.
Near the pedestrian traffic lights at the top end of Manor Street (going North).

COUNTY KILDARE

TONLEGEE HOUSE Ⓐ Ⓡ
Mark & Marjorie Molloy
Athy
Tel & Fax: (0507) 31473

The Molloys are consummate restaurateurs, and Tonlegee is a model of what a couple who love their work can achieve. There is always a vegetarian starter on the menu, such as baked goat's cheese on a bed of salad leaves, and as Mark makes his own pasta, he can conjure up main course dishes such as a ragout of vegetables with homemade pasta and a cheese and herb sauce.

The rooms in the house are comfy, and it is a delightful, genuine place.

● **OPEN:** 7pm-9.30pm Mon-Sat
('till 10.30pm Fri & Sat). Residents only Sun.
● **AVERAGE PRICE:** Dinner over £20.
B&B over £30. Visa, Access/Master.
Take the Kilkenny road out of town, then look for their sign telling you to turn left.

CARBURY

DEIRDRE O'SULLIVAN & NORMAN KENNY Ⓕ
Deirdre O'Sullivan
& Norman Kenny
Nurney House, Carbury
Tel: (0405) 53337

Deirdre sells produce at the weekly Saturday food co-op on Dublin's Parse Street, her happy, bubbly manner every bit as captivating as the delicious organic vegetables which she and Norman produce.

● **OPEN:** The vegetables can also be found in Cindy and Larry Quinn's shop, Healthy Image, in Naas.

KILCOCK

MARY MORRIN Ⓕ
Mary Morrin
Kilcock
Tel: (01) 628 7244

Mary Morrin farms organically. She makes cheeses and country butter, and also pies.

● **OPEN:** You can buy the produce of Mary's farm at the Naas Country Market, Fri mornings, 10.45am-12.15pm.

MAYNOOTH

THE MILL WINE CELLAR Ⓢ
Michael & Effie Tennyson
Mill Street
Maynooth
Tel: (01) 628 9520

The Mill is an enthusiastic shop with a fine range from all over the world, and Michael and Effie also run a wine club for local enthusiasts.

● **OPEN:** 10.30am-10.30pm,
Sun 12.30pm-2pm, 4pm-9pm.

COUNTY KILKENNY

KELL'S WHOLEMEAL FLOUR ❻
Billy Mosse
Bennettsbridge
Tel: (056) 28310

Billy Mosse's stone ground flour is best known amongst professional chefs who buy it in 10kg bags.

Domestic cooks who want to enjoy its timeless, generous richness of flavour, should seek out the brown bread mix which is available in supermarkets.

● **OPEN:** The brown bread mix which can be found in shops and supermarkets.

NICHOLAS MOSSE POTTERY ❻
Nicky Mosse
Bennettsbridge
Tel: (056) 27126 (shop)
27105 (factory)

Nicky Mosse produces the most exquisite, adorable pottery. He has been a potter since the age of seven, and indeed there seems something charmingly childlike in his sponge-work, suffused as it is with a conscious element of naïveté in the figures of the animals and a sense of wonderment which perhaps owes something to the scale he works in.

● **OPEN:** Jul & Aug 10am-6pm Mon-Sat, 2pm-6pm Sun.

MOSSE'S MILL CAFÉ ®
Cynthia McClelland
Bennettsbridge
Tel: (056) 27664

Cynthia McClelland has come from New York to take over Nicholas and Susan Mosse's café, and with chef Michael Roberts they have created an imaginative, rather funky menu with some nice vegetarian inventions such as marinated roasted vegetables with melted fresh mozzarella as an intriguing sandwich filling, or a goat's cheese and roast pepper quiche served with a leaf salad, or hot artichoke and horseradish paté. "We are trying to create food which is as striking and cheerful as the pottery we serve it on" says Ms McClelland, an altogether noble ambition.

● **OPEN:** Lunch Wed-Sun, dinner Wed-Sat four miles south of Kilkenny, at the bridge.

STONEWARE JACKSON POTTERY ❻
Michael Jackson
Bennettsbridge, Tel: (056) 27175

Visitors to the pottery and show-room can see the pots being created, and then buy these hand-some artefacts in the shop.

● **OPEN:** 9am-5.30pm Mon-Fri, 9am-6pm Sat. Closed lunch 1pm-2pm.

THE WATERSIDE ® Ⓐ
Daniel Fitzpatrick
Graiguenamanagh
Tel: (0503) 24246

The Waterside is a rebuilt, converted grain mill, hard by the banks of the River Barrow. Its restaurant has been brought down to the ground floor since Daniel Fitzpatrick took over, for formerly it was in the top of the building with hostel accommodation underneath. This has now been reversed, and the accommodation has been restored to its rightful place.

It is a plain, unornamented space – polished quarry tiles on the floor, rough white walls, supporting beams – but the cooking is ambitious, and desserts are good – light grapefruit flan, good chocolate, pear and strawberry sorbet.

By the way, if you are taking a stroll in the main street of Graigue, do check out M. Doyle's splendid bar and shop, a perfectly preserved piece of the past.

● **OPEN:** 12.30pm-2.30pm, 7pm-10pm Mon-Sun. (Limited hours off season, closed 7 Jan-7 Feb).
● **AVERAGE PRICE:** Lunch under £15.
Dinner under £20.
Visa, Access/Master, Diners.
On the river front in Graigue.

THE MOTTE ®
Alan Walton
& Tom Reade-Duncan
Inistioge, Tel: (056) 58655

It is a fun place, The Motte, somewhere nobly dedicated to the noble pursuit of having a good time. Vegetarians need to give 24 hours notice, as the formal menu has little that is suitable, but the notice allows Tom to rustle up something that will be delicious, and undoubtedly fun.

● **OPEN:** 7pm-9.30pm Wed-Sun (open Tue from June-Sept).
● **AVERAGE PRICE:**
Dinner under £20.
Visa, Access/Master.
500 yards outside the village of Inistioge, overlooking the river.

KILKENNY

THE AUBERGINE Ⓢ
Mr Farrell
74 High Street
Kilkenny
Tel: (056) 63274

An excellent vegetable shop on the main shopping street of the city and a good source of locally grown organic vegetables.

● **OPEN:** 9am-6pm Mon-Sat ('till 7pm Fri).

CAFÉ SOL ®
Eavan Kenny & Gail Johnson
William Street
Kilkenny
Tel: (056) 64987

There is more than a touch of the charming naive style of the Silver Palate cookbooks not only in the design of the Café Sol menu, but in their alluring, attractive accessible style of cooking, and its smart embrace of simple foods and drinks and whatnots.

Vegetarian delights include nachos with chilli sauce; frittata with caramelised onions, potatoes, tomatoes and roasted red peppers; fresh pasta with tomato, chilli and basil.

"Two delicious dinners were as memorable as several of the comics" wrote a correspondent who discovered Café Sol during the Cat Laughs comedy festival in the city.

● **OPEN:** 10am-6pm Mon-Sat, noon-4pm Sun, 7pm-10pm Wed-Sat.
● **AVERAGE PRICE:** Lunch under £5. Dinner under £15.
Visa, Access/Master, Amex.
Off High Street, opposite The Tholsel.

KILKENNY DESIGN CENTRE Ⓢ Ⓡ
Kathleen Moran
Castle Yard, Tel: (056) 22118

The Kilkenny Design shops are always reliable places for flavoursome food, cooking which manages effortlessly the awkward act of picking you up just when you are dropping from the shopping. Sticky cakes and reviving bakes, good coffee and sweet things, and that hallmark of care and good taste which is a feature of the Kilkenny shops is evident throughout. There are also Kilkenny preserves to take away if you have any room in your shopping bag.

● **OPEN:** Café open 9am-5pm Mon-Sat, 10am-5pm Sun. Closed Sun off season.
● **AVERAGE PRICE:** Lunch under £10.
Visa, Access/Master, Amex.
Centre of Kilkenny, opposite the Cathedral.

LACKEN HOUSE Ⓡ Ⓐ
Eugene & Breda McSweeney
Dublin Road
Kilkenny
Tel: (056) 61085

It could almost be easy to take Eugene and Breda McSweeney's Lacken House for granted.

It is a handsome house, but unassuming, with little of the grandness of scale enjoyed by many of the country houses. Rather than being a centrepiece of the splendidly gorgeous, historical city of Kilkenny, it is just outside the pulsing metropolis.

And whilst both Mr and Mrs McSweeney are somewhat known in the media for their culinary and oenological successes – he for his skill with the skillet; she for her daunting skill as a sommelier – they have little truck with the fashion-fixated side of the business, preferring to just get on with their work.

But this deferential, modest method suits the McSweeneys, for when it comes to getting on with their work, they are a truly formidable team who have evolved a style that is refreshingly undidactic and appealing, something very much their own creation.

Eugene McSweeney's cooking manages to adapt everything he touches into his own métier, and his location between the city and the country has forged his style.

The food in Lacken House is some of the very best in the country, but it not only boasts culinary excellence, it is also terrifically enjoyable. This is spoon-lickin' cookin', and you may have to rack your brains for a very long time indeed to remember just when you last ate so well: summer vegetable soup with wild nettle pesto; vegetarian lasagne of crisp pastry with a tomato and lentil sauce; couscous with chick peas, ginger and tomatoes.

Where Eugene delivers the tastes on the plate, Breda delivers them in the glass. She has the knack of knowing not just what wine will suit the food you have ordered, but of knowing just exactly what wine you want to drink tonight.

● OPEN: 7pm-10.30pm Tue-Sat.
● AVERAGE PRICE:
Dinner under £25.
B&B over £35.
Visa, Access/Masters, Amex.
On the Dublin Road as you enter Kilkenny.

SHORTIS WONG ⓢ
Mary Shortis & Chris Wong
74 John Street
Kilkenny
Tel: (056) 61305

Chris and Mary's shop is one of the most enjoyable places to shop in the whole country. Mary's breads are splendiferous, the selection of wholefoods and oriental foods is second to none, and Chris's cooking, in particular his funky street food, such as vegetable samosas are fabulous. Go and eat them in the grounds of the Cathedral.

There's always something new to discover and enjoy and something to learn when shopping here. Your

cookery books come up with some previously unheard of exotica – go here and they will have it.

● OPEN: 9am-7pm Mon-Sat,
10.30am-2.30pm Sun.

THE WINE CENTRE ⓢ
Maureen & Eamonn O'Keeffe
15 John Street
Kilkenny
Tel: (056) 22034

A handsome shop with a good selection, and the prices are keen.

● OPEN: 9am-6pm Mon-Sat.
(Closed 1pm-2pm lunch).

LAVISTOWN FOODS Ⓕ
Olivia & Roger Goodwillie
Lavistown
Tel: (056) 65145

Olivia Goodwillie's Lavistown cheese is a pale, white, crumbly, lively Caerphilly type cheese which oozes well-trusted milkiness and assured expertise.

As if this weren't enough, Lavistown is also a study centre offering many outrageously interesting courses on subjects as diverse as wild flowers of the Burren and edible Christmas gifts. Amongst the very best however are the September mushroom hunts led by Roger, which are terrific fun.

● OPEN:
Lavistown cheese is distributed throughout Ireland.

WENDY & MICHAEL MIKLIS ⓕ
Wendy & Michael Miklis
Raheen, Piltown
Tel: (051) 643519

Wendy and Michael Miklis were amongst the first farmers to follow the creed of bio-dynamic farming in Ireland. Their produce – vegetables, herbs, fruit, cheese – is unfailingly excellent and richly diverse. It can be found in local outlets.

● **OPEN:** Outlets include The Rainbow Warehouse in Clonmel and farm gate sales.

MILEEVEN ⓕ
Joe & Eilis Gough
Owning Hill
Piltown
Tel: (051) 43368

Joe and Eilis's range has enlarged considerably in recent years and now includes a broad range of flavoured honeys including oil of star flower and evening primrose. Don't miss the honey and cider vinegar, which is in a class of its own. Perfect for a late autumn salad when the leaves are beginning to loose their sweetness.

● **OPEN:** The honeys and the cider vinegar are widely available in good shops.

JERPOINT GLASS STUDIO ⓕ
Keith & Kathleen Leadbetter
Stoneyford
Tel: (056) 24350, Fax: 24778

Distinctive hand-made glassware that will grace any dinner table. A team of eight glassmakers make and finish glass by hand. You can see for yourself at the studio.

● **OPEN:** 9am-6pm Mon-Fri, 11am-6pm Sat.

Kilkenny pubs

Two of Kilkenny's most famous pubs, Edward Langton's and Tynan's Bridge House reveal the ancient and modern of Irish pub culture. Langton's is a massive warren of rooms which extends far back from the original bar preserved at the front. It is well known for its professional, extensive menu of pub food.

Just over the bridge, meanwhile, we see a different aspect of the Irish pub. Tynan's Bridge House is a gorgeous old pub, with fine pints of porter and all the old fixtures, furnishings and fit things of yesteryear in perfect, pristine condition. No food, no music, no TV, just booze and chat.

EDWARD LANGTON ⓟ
69 John Street
Tel: (056) 65133

TYNAN'S BRIDGE HOUSE ⓟ
2 John's Bridge, Kilkenny
Tel: (056) 21291

● **OPEN:** Both open licensing hours. Langton's serves lunch and dinner.

COUNTY LAOIS

MORRISSEY'S ℗
PJ Mulhall
Abbeyleix
Tel: (0502) 31233

Is Morrissey's the finest pub in the country? And, if it is, then what does that say about those of us who love Morrissey's?

That we are suckers for nostalgia. That we are incurably romantic about the past? That our vision of the perfect pub is of a place which never changes?

Well, perhaps that is all true. But what is, perhaps, truest, is that we admire and love a place which shows the right sort of respect to the business of having a drink.

This calm space is an enclave of peace, of dignity, of sociability, and this almost Zen-like patience is what makes Morrissey's special, is what makes the business of having a drink in Morrissey's unlike the business of having a drink anywhere else.

● **OPEN:** Pub hours with sandwiches served all day.

ABBEY BLUE BRIE ℉
Pat & Joan Highland
Ballacolla, Abbeyleix
Tel: (0502) 38599

Pat and Joan Highland have worked hard ever since they began to make Abbey Blue Brie a few year's back,

and indeed they have worked wonders in terms of making this a high-profile cheese, seen almost everywhere, and a major factor in combating the dull blue cheeses which invade from Europe. Abbey Blue, though a cambozola-type cheese, has none of the plasticity and fakeness of those cheeses; this one speaks confidently of good milk and good care.

● **OPEN:** The cheese is widely distributed throughout Ireland.

PRESTON HOUSE CAFÉ ℞ Ⓐ
Alison & Michael Dowling
Abbeyleix
Tel: (0502) 31432/31662

Alison Dowling's cooking makes you feel good. Simple as that. And in the Preston House Café, the noble stone building in the centre of Abbeyleix village she has found the perfect place in which to make you feel good.

Mrs Dowling's cooking has always had this gift. For some years she ran Glebe House, a little hideaway where you could forget the rest of the world and immerse yourself in the sort of cooking that gave you an appetite the instant you saw it.

This is true country cooking, virtuous, flavour-filled, the sort of thing that creates happiness.

She keeps her cooking straight-forward, logical. The local Abbey

Blue brie, walnuts and croûtons in a salad; ratatouille crêpe with salad, tomato and basil soup; lemon ice cream or fruit charlotte pudding. Simple comfort food which, in Mrs Dowling's hands, screams out, Try Me!

There are six cosy rooms in Preston House, and it is the sort of place you look forward to finding yourself in. The fact that it is smack bang on the main road, and thus offers solace to car-addled folk who either need to grab something to eat or else want to call a halt to the driving and stop for dinner and a place to stay, makes it a treasure.

● **OPEN:** 10am-7pm Mon-Sun, dinner from 8pm Thur-Sat, Sun lunch 1pm-2.30pm.
● **AVERAGE PRICE:** Lunch under £10. Dinner over £20. Sun lunch over £10. Visa, Access/Master. In the centre of Abbeyleix, the southern end of the town, on the main N7 road.

MOUNTRATH

ROUNDWOOD HOUSE Ⓐ
Frank & Rosemary Kennan
Mountrath
Tel: (0502) 32120

What might be grandiose in another place, another province, tends to remain unassuming, unforced, in County Laois.

This modesty extends to Frank and Rosemary Kennan's Roundwood House, one of the most affectionately regarded places to stay in the entire country. Elsewhere, it would

become a staple of the glossy guidebooks. Here, it stays a secret, almost.

An air of lazy, pleasure-filled idyll pervades the house, creating a place so story-book super – with its commingling ducks and its horses, its wide rooms with tall windows, its slightly-knocked-about charm – that you might imagine yourself transported to some never-never land, a province straight from the pages of Janet and Allan Ahlberg.

Rosemary Kennan's cooking is expert, soulful, flavour-addled, full of intriguing twists which her hungry mind adds to the repertoire of country house fare. Breakfasts are scrumptious, and dinner a delight of modest, skilful food.

● **OPEN:** All year except Xmas, dinner available for non residents.
● **AVERAGE PRICE:** B&B over £30. Dinner over £20. Visa, Access/Mastercard, Amex, Diners. Roundwood is signposted from Mountrath, a few miles south of Portlaoise on the Limerick road. Follow signs for Slieve Bloom.

PORTLAOISE

CHEZ NOUS Ⓐ
Audrey Canavan
Kilminchy
Portlaoise
Tel: (0502) 21251

"A lovely, warm-hearted person" is the kind of thing people will tell you about Audrey Canavan, and you will hear no word of argument from anyone who has ever stayed at her cute bungalow, immediately adjacent to the main N7 Dublin-Cork road.

Mrs Canavan's ability to make a stop-over into an event is legendary. You might find yourself at Chez Nous, the first time, just because it is so convenient to the main road. But the second time you stay at Chez Nous will be because you want to stay there, because you want to indulge in the plenitude of Audrey's personality, and her fine food.

Breakfast is ordered at night, and may cause some sleepless anxiety as you dream of "Potato Cakes with Lashings of Pure Irish Butter and Sea salt". And how can you resist a dish which so sumptuously promises "Lashings" of butter? If only you had two stomachs. Nothing for it but to stay another day.

A correspondent described Audrey's breakfast table as "the most opulent looking table which we have ever seen in a B&B – flowers, home-made jams and marmalades, home-made bread, home-made scones, home-made biscuits, toast, tea, coffee...

"All this against the background of the garden and bathed in the soft light of an early autumn morning".

You can just see yourself sitting there, can't you? Heavens, you can taste that breakfast, feel those lashings of butter dribbling down your chin...

● **OPEN:** All year except Xmas.
● **AVERAGE PRICE:** B&B under £20.
No Credit Cards.
Chez Nous is signposted on the main N7 Dublin/Cork/Limerick road, a few miles north of Portlaoise.

JIM'S COUNTRY KITCHEN ®
James Tynan
Church Street
Portlaoise
Tel: (0502) 32616

James Tynan runs a good show in his Country Kitchen.

Step in off the street at lunchtime on a winter's day, and the welter of folk inside will astonish you. But, once you try the food, the presence of so many people will no longer be a surprise.

This Country Kitchen produces good country cooking, and Mr Tynan knows his customers, knows what they like, and knows just how to give it to them.

In wintertime, bright fires blaze away as you select just what you would like from the central table on which the salads and bakes are arranged. This is also the time of year when James holds his evening cookery classes, popular annual events that attract many locals.

And it is no surprise, for the food in Jim's is flavourful, fun, the sort of grub that hits the spot.

If you need a break from the torment of the N7, then the detour off the road into Portlaoise adds little extra time to the journey.

● **OPEN:** 9am-5pm Mon-Sat.
● **AVERAGE PRICE:**
Lunch under £5.
No credit cards.
In the centre of Portlaoise.

COUNTY LONGFORD

THE PIONEERING SPIRIT lives on in Longford. For a cheese maker such as Antoinette Trueman, who makes Glannagh cheese, or a chocolate confectioner like Ruth McGarry-Quinn, who makes Torc truffles, the fact that Longford doesn't enjoy the busy, creative food culture that one finds in other parts of the country is merely a call to arms.

The fact that there are no other artisans in the county to lead by example, to show the way, only acts to spur these indomitable women on. They are pioneers, creating something valuable and worthwhile in the midst of nothing,

They have a powerful vision of their own work, and an appreciation of just how important that work is. They have organised two festivals of Midland's food producers, to show that there is nascent growth, to show that there is an awareness of the need to create a food culture. Both have been terrific successes, demonstrating that the hunger for true artisan foods exists in the Midlands.

"Food in the Midlands region has a certain character and individuality", they wrote, and none more so than Ms Trueman's fine Glannagh cheese, made from the milk of her quartet of Jersey cows, or Ms McGarry-Quinn's splendiferous Torc truffles, some of the most delightful confections to be found in the entire country.

These are valuable foods, not merely because there is little other artisan production in Longford, but because they are excellent. And where they lead, then others, surely, will soon follow.

Isn't it high time, indeed, that you got to know this quiet part of the country somewhat better.

TORC TRUFFLES ℗
Ruth McGarry-Quinn
Convent Road, Longford
Tel: (043) 47353
Fax: (043) 41207

● **OPEN:** Available in good delicatessens nationwide as well as some in the locality.

GLANNAGH CHEESE ℗
Antoinette Trueman
Glannagh
Tel: (043) 71230

● **OPEN:** Sold in Woods of Longford, Tir na nOg in Sligo, Graham's of Mullingar and from the farm gate.

COUNTY LOUTH

McGEE'S BISTRO ®
Hugh Finnegan & Sheila Keiro
D'Arcy McGee Centre
Dundalk Street, Carlingford
Tel: (042) 73751

McGee's is a fizzy, fun place which has built a cultish reputation for Sheila Keiro's imaginative cooking, a culinary performance which the open kitchen allows one to spectate.

Her vegetarian choices are stylish and plentiful: sweet potato with spinach and dolcelatte; Middle Eastern aubergine slices, and Mexican aubergines; Magee's Cajun cakes, where chick peas are mixed with sautéed mushrooms, and leeks, then seasoned with Cajun spices before being coated with bread-crumbs and deep fried. In total, Ms Keiro works a marvellous series of improvisations around her favourite ingredients, and the care for vege-tarians which McGee's exhibits is fabulous.

● **OPEN:** Seasonally for dinner.
● **AVERAGE PRICE:** Dinner under £15.
Visa, Access/Master.
Beside the Heritage Centre.

THE HAZEL TREE RESTAURANT ®
Anna Breivik & Brendan Mulligan
Roden Place, Dundalk
Tel: (042) 32804

The Hazel Tree is a vegetarian rest-aurant and wholefood shop, and part of Dundalk's Iomlanu Centre. Most of the vegetables used in the kitchen come from the local organic growers at Philipstown Trust – these can also be bought in Maura Lenin's shop at the entrance to the Hazel Tree – and the restaurant space itself is a calm, simple little twin of rooms, likely as not with the collection from some local project used charmingly to decorate the walls.

The cooking has a pleasing savour. Smart dishes such as millet croquettes with a devil sauce come with some good crisp salads and the whole operation is family friendly.

● **OPEN:** 10am-6pm Mon-Sat.
● **AVERAGE PRICE:** Lunch under £5.
Visa, Access/Master.
Downstairs in the Lomlanu Centre.

FOOD SOLUTIONS Ⓕ
Richard Martin
Rath
Ardee Road, Dundalk
Tel: (042) 34862
Fax: (042) 39597

Richard Martin imports the wonderful Illy coffee from Italy and the wonderful Illy espresso machines, which means that he has had a significant impact on the quality of people's lives, all of it for the better.

● **OPEN:** Available throughout the country.

WHITE RIVER MILL Ⓕ
Gerard O'Connor
Dunleer
Tel: (041) 51141

The expression "restored to its former glory" is sorely over used but in the case of Gerard O'Connor's beautiful White River Mill, it is barely adequate.

This is a beautiful mill, the great stones powered entirely by the waters of the river Dee. To spend even a few minutes watching and listening as the stones turn is intensely therapeutic, calming, balming, a trip back in time, as far as the seventeenth century when a Quaker family built the original mill.

Mr O'Connor mills about 2 to 3 tons of flour every week, and plans to grow and mill his own organic wheat.

● **OPEN:** The excellent flour and bran is available locally.

KNOCKBRIDGE

CUCHULAIN DAIRY Ⓕ
Caroline Meegan
Dunbin
Knockbridge
Tel: (042) 35654

Caroline Meegan produces fine country butter with a mellow but distinctive taste, and both buttermilk and cream. They can be found for sale in Superquinn and Quinnsworth supermarkets in Dublin, under the Cuchulain Dairy label.

RAVENSDALE

PHILIPSTOWN TRUST FARM PROJECT Ⓕ
Colette Halpenny
Deerpark Organic Farm
Ravensdale, Tel: (042) 80048

The inspirational aim of the Philipstown Trust is to farm organically – they have an area of thirteen acres at Deer Park, in Ravensdale, north of Dundalk – and to produce food for customers which is delivered to them weekly.

Customers pay an annual sum, depending on how many people they wish to buy vegetables for, and this allows the Trust to get on with the business of growing and distributing, a practice which has become increasingly successful in southern England.

It allows the grower to budget for the year, it allows them to plant according to the volume of customers they must supply, and it means the cost is kept low.

But what it also means, of course, is that the lucky customers get just-picked vegetables delivered to their door, they have a genuine relationship with the person producing the food, and they get food in season: tomatoes, peppers, beans and so on in August, leeks, cabbages, carrots and kohl-rabi in mid winter.

Delightful.

● **OPEN:** Call for a brochure and price list.

COUNTY MEATH

SONAIRTE ⓕ
Mary Perry
The Ninch Farm, Laytown
Tel: (041) 27572

An experimental organic farm, interesting for its ancient varieties of apples and for other good produce. Useful for supplies if you are renting one of Liz Lyons' cottages down the road, tel: (042) 28104

● **OPEN:** Turn at Julianstown on the N1.

NAVAN

JANET'S COUNTRY FAYRE ⓕ
Janet Drew
The Steward's House
Ballinlough Castle
Clanmellon, Navan
Tel: (046) 33344

Janet Drew's relishes, jams and dressings are possibly the best in the country. The jars of goodies virtually jump off the shelves at you, decorated as they are by Janet's explosively marvellous calligraphy.

Get them home, open them up, and the jams and chutneys burst with flavour, but their expressiveness is never unbalanced. Ms Drew understands how to capture and then concentrate flavours.

The sweet pepper relish is some sort of a masterpiece, the sweetcorn relish irresistible, the jams are droolsome, the vinaigrettes are fab, the tomato relish a dream.

● **OPEN:** Janet Drew's produce is available in good delis.

HUDSON'S ⓡ
Richard & Tricia Hudson
Railway Street
Navan
Tel: (046) 29231

"All of our food is made from fresh ingredients" says Tricia Hudson.

And what lovely cooking: spicy Thai chickpeas simmered in coconut milk; pine kernel fettucine with a saffron cream; smart food which Richard Hudson understands.

"All of our desserts are made by Richard", says Tricia. And what lovely desserts: melt-in-the-mouth pecan pie; "funky" toffee pud; Zuccotto, filled with chocolate cream, nuts and candied fruit.

Each night, there is a "Richard's Special", as the chef visits his magic on whatever new ingredients have come to hand. "Our regular clientele eat these and love the surprise element", says Tricia. Can you think of a nicer surprise?

● **OPEN:** 6.30pm-11pm Tue-Sat, 6.30pm-10pm Sun.
● **AVERAGE PRICE:** Dinner under £20. Visa, Access/Master.
50 yards from the roundabout in Navan.

COUNTY WESTMEATH

LEFT BANK BISTRO ⓡ
M McCullough & A McNamara
Bastion Street
Athlone
Tel: (0902) 94446

It is a cracking place, the Left Bank. Casual and relaxed in a truly confident way, its food is perfectly understood, delightfully executed.

Annie McNamara is an Aussie by birth, and worked in various restaurants in Ireland before opening the Left Bank. Her food has a happy cosmopolitanism that unifies the Mediterranean with an Australian's affinity for the foods of the Far East.

So, the Left Bank offers crispy garlic foccacia; fried Halmoumi cheese with lime and caper vinaigrette, Mediterranean style tagliatelle with mushrooms, sun-dried tomatoes and olives, warm goat's cheese salad with roasted almonds, all of them dishes that are bright with flavour. Mary McCullough does front of house, and opens the bottles of New World wine. It is a lovely space, blessed with a vigorous, youthful buzz.

● **OPEN:** 10am-6pm Mon-Sat,
6pm-10pm Thur-Sat.
(Open six and seven days in high season).
● **AVERAGE PRICE:** Lunch under £10.
Dinner under £15. Visa, Access/Master.
In the old part of Athlone.

NANNIE MURPH'S ⓡ ⓟ
Thérèse Gilsennan
Grogan's Pub
Glasson Village
Tel: (0902) 85158

Thérèse Gilsennan was the original chef in Ray Byrne and Jane English's Wineport restaurant, before she moved up the road away from the water's edge, to set up her own venture, imaginative pub food in an olde worlde style pub in the centre of Glasson village.

Nannie Murph's serves classic pub grub, but Thérèse's skill is best seen in her clever, fun evening dinner menu: grilled goat's cheese and strawberry salad; tossed spinach salad with mushrooms, croûtons and Parmesan; chocolate truffle cake or home made meringues and home made ice cream.

It's really lovely cooking – generous, well-understood, very feminine and instinctive, in a great pub where they will – most likely - have to chuck you out sometime long after closing time.

● **OPEN:** Pub grub noon-9pm.
Dinner 5.30pm-9pm Mon-Sat,
4pm-8pm Sun.
● **AVERAGE PRICE:** Bar food under £5.
Restaurant under £20.
Visa, Access/Master.
In the centre of the village.

WINEPORT RESTAURANT ®
Ray Byrne & Jane English
Glasson Village
Athlone
Tel: (0902) 85466 85471

It seems that everybody loves The Wineport. Young and old, rich and otherwise, couples and families, golfers and sailors, those who hate golf and sailing.

They provide menus for just about everyone: Brunch for late Sunday, with dishes such as buckwheat and vegetable pies, menus for the kids, menus for golfers, and for those who pursue good food without the interruption of needless sporting behaviour, the menu is welcomingly balanced: baked goat's cheese and oven-dried tomatoes with a walnut and herb vinaigrette; ravioli filled with spinach and cheese with a tomato and basil sauce finished with shavings of Parmesan; fusilli with Mediterranean vegetables and mixed nuts; canneloni style aubergine stuffed with cottage cheese and basil with roast cherry tomatoes and black olives.

Inside, in one of the sweetest dining rooms in the country, with break-heart views across the water, it is a democratic ideal, an all-hands-on-deck place, and a winning success

● **OPEN:** 12.30pm-2.30pm Sun,
6pm-10pm Mon-Sun.
(Open noon-10pm high season).
● **AVERAGE PRICE:** Lunch under £10.
Dinner under £20.
Visa, Access/Master, Amex, Diners.
Three miles north of Athlone, leave the by-pass at exit 4, towards Glasson. Access by boat also.

MOATE

TEMPLE Ⓐ
Declan & Bernadette Fagan
Horseleap
Moate
Tel & Fax: (0506) 35118

Good food, good crack, good fun, is the trilogy of delights which the regulars of Temple appreciate. But we can make a quartet of this trilogy, for this is someplace special to relax, a feature which is pre-eminent for the Fagan family.

Declan and Bernadette give Temple an easy-going grace, which means it is very much the sort of place that, after one visit, you want to head back to, preferably with a clatter of your friends and your bevy of kids. You are likely to find, staying here, that many of the other guests have been here many, many times, and that these regulars adore the house party feel.

Mrs Fagan's cooking is a fine-tuned, well-understood cuisine paysanne: she takes pleasure in the preparation of food, and the generosity implicit in her culinary efforts is echoed in everything about the house. They welcome kids, are delighted to make something special for vegetarian guests, and you can even ask for aromatherapy or Ki-massage to be arranged, if you can cope with more blissfulness.

● **OPEN:** All year.
● **AVERAGE PRICE:** B&B under £25.
Visa, Access/Master.
Signposted from the N6 Kinnegad/Galway road. One mile west of Horseleap and four miles east of Moate.

CROOKEDWOOD HOUSE ®Ⓐ
Noel & Julie Kenny
Mullingar
Tel: (044) 72165

You must take the crooked road to find your way to Crookedwood, Noel and Julie Kenny's 200-year old Rectory, but when you arrive, at the summit of the crooked roads, uncertainty ends. Julie Kenny has that spontaneous hospitality which rushingly ushers you into the house, and Noel Kenny is a chef who loves decisive, earthy tastes, and who grows most of his own vegetables. Vegetarian choices are few, but something like baked stuffed aubergine with wild mushrooms show Mr Kenny's style: punchy, direct, satisfying.

● **OPEN:** 7pm-10pm Tue-Sat,
12.30pm-2pm Sun.
● **AVERAGE PRICE:** Dinner under £20.
Sun lunch under £15.
Visa, Access/Master, Amex, Diners.
From Crookedwood village, turn right at the Wood pub, then one and a half miles further along you will see the house.

WINES DIRECT Ⓕ
Siobhan & Paddy Keogh
Irishtown, Mullingar
Tel: (044) 40634
(freephone 1-800-579579)

Wines Direct is a smashing company, a saviour of the wine lover who lives away from the major cities in Ireland.

Give a freephone call to Paddy and Siobhan Keogh, select a brace of bottles from their choice list, and blow me but isn't that precious parcel with you the next day or the day after.

And what a parcel! The Keogh's travel extensively in France each year, sourcing new growers and producers, seeking and finding interesting bottles.

The Wines Direct list is relatively small, which means that new arrivals have great impact. A combination of choice and their efficient delivery service makes the Keoghs vital to the wine lover.

● **OPEN:** Telephone to obtain a Wines Direct list and to place your order.

LITTLE INDIA Ⓡ
Sunil & Meera Kumar
2 Dublin Bridge
Mullingar
Tel: (044) 40911

Little India is a much-loved restaurant, a great success since it opened in 1992, so much so that it has now spawned a big sister, for the Kumars have opened up Saagar, on Harcourt Street, in Dublin. As you would expect from a first-class Indian restaurant, vegetarian choices are excellent and imaginative.

● **OPEN:** 12.30pm-3pm Mon-Sat,
5.30pm-midnight Mon-Sat,
4.30pm-11pm Sun.
● **AVERAGE PRICE:** Lunch under £10.
Dinner under £20.
Visa, Access/Master.
On the main street in Mullingar.

COUNTY WEXFORD

CROGHAN CHEESE ⑤
Luc & Ann van Kampen
Ballynadrishogue
Blackwater
Tel: (053) 29331

Croghan is one of the truly great Irish cheeses.

A goat's milk cheese which owes something to the style of a Reblochon, it is yet another of those cheeses whose style has become unique, and uniquely Irish.

The crispness and cleanness of the flavour, the intensity and precision of the tastes, the harmony and completeness which a great Croghan can offer is stupendous. It manages that most difficult feat, of exhibiting the power of an aged, hard cheese – though it is neither aged nor hard – and exhibiting the dancing finesse of a soft cheese – though it inclines more towards a semi-soft cheese.

It is in achieving these resolutions that Luc and Ann prove their greatness as cheesemakers, for the challenge for anyone who sets out to make a cheese is not only to imbue it with personality, but to achieve a sinuous dialogue of tastes which speak with one voice. Croghan manages this, almost without effort.

● **OPEN:** Cheese can be bought from the farm, but telephone first.

INISGLASS TRUST ⑤
Anthony Kaye
The Deeps, Crossabeg
Tel: (053) 28226

County Wexford has a vigorous, dynamic group of bio-dynamic farmers, and Anthony Kaye is amongst the most philosophical of the bio-dyn producers.

Of course, the idea of a philosophical farmer sounds like the ultimate anachronism in an agricultural world predicated on chemicalised uniformity. But it is precisely because modern agriculture has abandoned thought, has abandoned intellectual discussion of its aims, that we have a developed society with so much bad food.

Mr Kaye, like the other bio-dyn and organic growers, produces foods which are complete, delicious, foods which are all they can be. His practices seek harmony and concord with the forces of nature, and his foods reveal the fruits of this dialogue. They are living foods, and eating them makes us feel truly alive.

● **OPEN:** Inisglass flour is widely available in wholefood shops throughout the country. There are farm gate sales of soft fruit, vegetables and fruit trees and some of their produce is sold in the Dublin Food Co-Op market.

P & E KOOMANS VAN DE DRIES O'REILLY ⓕ

Cnockfe
Ballyharran Upper
Crossabeg
Tel: (053) 28428

Bio-dynamic growers producing vegetables, herbs, wool.

● **OPEN:** Their outlets include Wexford Organic Grower organisations, the L&N supermarket, the Humble Food Shop, and Only Natural.

CARRIGBYRNE FARMHOUSE CHEESE ⓕ

Paddy Berridge
Adamstown
Enniscorthy
Tel: (054) 40560

Paddy Berridge's cheese is one of the most successful and well-known of the farmhouse cheeses, its distinctive, multi-sided box a familiar sight in supermarket chill cabinets and in good delis.

It is a mild cheese, much-favoured by chefs for cooking, but whilst this may be the element which most people know about Carrigbyrne, there is another side to the story.

In the British Cheese Awards, Carrigbyrne won the prize for "Best Soft White Rind Cheese" and, as the food writer Maureen Tatlow, one of the judges, pointed out, the award was for "a very mature specimen,

infinitely tastier than the babyish milky-bland versions which one almost always encounters here: I only wish the distributors and supermarkets would take note".

So, make friends with a good cheese seller, and ask them to age a Carrigbyrne for you. And, then, experience a slice of the other side of Carrigbyrne.

● **OPEN:** The cheese is widely distributed throughout Ireland.

SALVILLE HOUSE ⓐ

Jane & Gordon Parker
Enniscorthy
Tel: (054) 35252

Just like some folk have charisma, so some houses have character. Salville has character, and it is of a charismatic kind. There is something quite magical about it – its grandeur tempered by understatement, its formality underpinned by comfort, its distinctiveness acquired thanks to thought and care rather than cash. It really is a truly lovely place to stay, its nostalgic air an utter joy for the senses. The cooking is excellent, and Salville's charisma adds up to something addictive.

● **OPEN:** All year except Xmas.
Dinner for guests only.
● **AVERAGE PRICE:**
B&B under £20
(self catering also available).
Dinner under £20.
No credit cards.
Just off the N11 Dublin/Wexford road.

THE HONEY POT ⑤
Matt & Tina Kennedy
4 Main Street, Gorey
Tel: (055) 20111

A wholefood shop which also sells bread from Arklow's Stone Oven, good coffee and some crafts.

● **OPEN:** 9am-6pm Mon-Sat.

NICHOLAS REDMOND ⓕ
Nicholas Redmond
Gerry, Ballygarrett, Gorey

Bio-dynamic grower producing potatoes, vegetables, soft fruit.

● **OPEN:** For farm gate sales, and produce is available in the Ivory Stores and Pettits Supermarket locally.

KELLY'S RESORT HOTEL ⓐ
Bill Kelly
Rosslare
Tel: (053) 32114
Fax: 32222

For the scores of thousands of people who go to Kelly's each and every year, this is a place which can do no wrong and its secret lies in the name. Kelly's Resort Hotel. You come here to tune in and drop out, to vanish from normal workaday cares. It's a complete holiday package – food, wine, art, sport, chilling out – a veritable Barnum and Baileys of bliss.

● **OPEN:** Restaurant open to non residents 7.30pm-9pm Mon-Sun. Hotel closed early Dec-end Feb.
● **AVERAGE PRICE:** Dinner over £20. Visa, Access/Master, Amex, Diners. Signed from the Wexford/Rosslare road.

FURZIESTOWN HOUSE ⓐ
Yvonne Pim
Tacumshane, Tel: (053) 31376

Certain people encapsulate a trueness and an holistic maturity in their character and their work. Yvonne Pim is one of these people. Her intuitive style of vegetarian cooking, is complete and earnestly flavourful: strawberry soup; spinach and cream cheese roulade; chick peas in a lentil and coconut sauce; sesame tofu with stir-fried vegetables. Mrs Pim understands the country, orchestrates an idyllic farm with a tunnel which supplies much of what she needs for the table, and she is able, then, to offer the foods of the season in a storybook environment which completes a picture of almost hypnotic idyll. Some people are inspirational, in their quiet way. Mrs Pim, and her little farm, is quietly inspirational.

● **OPEN:** For dinner for residents only. Closed end Nov-Feb.
● **AVERAGE PRICE:** B&B under £20. Dinner under £20. No Credit Cards. Signposted from Tacumshane, but hard to find, so telephone for detailed directions.

FERRYCARRIG HOTEL ⒶA
Ferrycarrig
Wexford
Tel: (053) 20999

The place to wear your dinner jacket for Opera festival goers, the Ferrycarrig is an hotel which does try harder than most, with thoughtful food for vegetarians.

● **OPEN:** Bar open10am-11pm Mon-Sat, noon-11pm Sun.
Food served 12.30pm-2pm, 6.30pm-9pm.

GREENACRES Ⓢ
James G O'Connor
56 North Main Street, Wexford
Tel: (053) 22975

A good vegetable stall with an impressive selection.

● **OPEN:** 9am-6pm Mon-Sat.

NEWBAY HOUSE Ⓐ
Paul & Mientje Drumm
Newbay, Wexford
Tel: (053) 42779, Fax: 46318

Whilst the exterior of Newbay is quite forbidding, almost foreboding, the interior is bright, colourful, enlivened by great floods of light through the big windows and by Paul's stripped pine furniture.

Paul Drumm's cooking has a professional edge which sets the food in Newbay apart from many of the other country houses, with their amateurish styles. Dinners are communal, eaten at a great big,

ginormous table, and the crack can be mighty, and breakfasts are excellent.

● **OPEN:** All year, dinner for guests only.
● **AVERAGE PRICE:** B&B over £30.
Dinner over £20. Visa, Access/Master.
Signposted from the N25

HUMBLE NATURAL FOODS Ⓢ
Heike Weiehagen
Walker's Mall, Nth Main St,
Wexford
Tel: (053) 24624

Heike's is a good wholefood shop and a place in which to find many of the specialities of the county's growers.

● **OPEN:** 9.15am-6pm Mon-Sat.

McMENAMIN'S TOWNHOUSE Ⓐ
Seamus & Kay McMenamin
3 Auburn Terrace
Redmond Road, Wexford
Tel: (053) 46442

There are many words one can choose to describe the great breakfasts you can enjoy in many of the fine houses in Ireland, but the choice of words which an Aussie correspondent chose for the breakfasts in the McMenamin's fine house topped the lot.

The breakfasts, they said, were "phenomenal".

And they were right.

● **OPEN:** All year (except Xmas).
● **AVERAGE PRICE:** B&B under £20.
Visa, Access/Master.
Opposite the railway station.

COUNTY WICKLOW

THE STONE OVEN BAKERY ⑤
Egon Friedrich
65 Lower Main Street
Arklow
Tel: (0402) 39418

The Stone Oven is a tiny little bakery and shop, so everything produced here is mollycoddled from its humble beginnings as flour, water, yeast, sourdough and salt until the glorious breads finally emerge from Mr Friedrich's traditional ovens. There is goodness in every bite of the smashing nut-dusted party rings, the fine grey bread, the excellent rye breads, the kiddisome pretzels.

● **OPEN:** 9.30am-6pm Mon-Sat.
Closed half day Wed.

ARKLOW

THE TREE OF IDLENESS ®
Susan Courtellas
Sea Front, Bray
Tel: (01) 286 3498

Plonked inside the brace of rooms that is the Tree of Idleness, with a good bottle from their terrific wine list in front of you, the restaurant seems to have been imported direct from the hills of Cyprus.

With the intuitive work of Tom, the waiter, and Susan Courtellas completing the picture, the Tree is a cracking neighbourhood restaurant.

Greek-Cypriot food is simple, and its virtues of direct, delicious, expressive tastes are beautifully captured by Ismail Basharan's cooking in the Tree: terrific humous, great melitzanosalata, a mix of aubergine, feta, lemon and herbs, or the aubergine in the guise of Imam Bayildi, lovely vegetarian moussaka.

● **OPEN:** 7.30pm-11pm Tue-Sun ('till 10pm Sun).
● **AVERAGE PRICE:** Dinner over £20.
Visa, Access/Master.
Overlooking the seafront in Bray.

ESCAPE ®
Patrick O'Connor
1 Albert Walk
Bray
Tel: (01) 286 6755

Escape is one of the few strict vegetarian restaurants outside of the capital city, and Patrick O'Connor's place has carved a neat niche for itself and its generous cooking in Bray.

You can both shop and eat in the restaurant, taking time out from dinner to peruse the arts and crafts which adorn the walls and which they sell alongside their works of art on a plate.

It's a relaxed place, with good service that is friendly and well-informed, and which comes into its own as they explain the dishes.

The menu is described on blackboards, so it becomes the job of the staff to fill in the finer details of dishes such as cashew and tomato pâté, simple soups like leek and potato or spicy Italian pasta, batak chan or onion bhaji.

Main dishes such as spinach and mushroom lasagne, a fiery pasta pepperoni, Siciliana or mushroom and broccoli crêpes, Russian pie, are forthright in flavour, their generosity accented by side dishes of roast potatoes or potato gratin.

Escape is a clever mix of good times and good value, and the fact that you can bring your own booze has made it essential.

● **OPEN:** Noon-10.30pm Mon-Sat, noon-9pm Sun.
● **AVERAGE PRICE:** Meals under £10.
No Credit Cards.
On the seafront.

ENNISKERRY

ENNISCREE LODGE Ⓐ
Raymond & Josephine Power
Enniskerry, Tel: (01) 286 3542

Enniscree is a charming lodge, just the sort of base you want when walking through Wicklow. The views from its dining room are spectacular, and the good hospitality makes for a lovely hideaway.

● **OPEN:** 12.30pm-2.30pm, 3pm-5pm, 7.30pm-9.30pm Mon-Sun.
● **AVERAGE PRICE:** Lunch under £15.
Dinner under £30-£35.
Visa, Access/Master, Amex, Diners.
5 miles from Enniskerry on the Glencree Drive.

DONARD

CHRYSALIS RETREAT & WORKSHOP CENTRE Ⓕ
Ann Maria Dunne
Donoughmore
Tel: (045) 54713

Chrysalis run a splendid array of courses, and offer B&B accommodation with the cooking founded on the use of their own organically grown vegetables.

● **OPEN:** Telephone for details of courses.

GREYSTONES

CLIVE McCABE Ⓢ Ⓡ
Clive & Kathleen McCabe
Watson & Johnson Centre
Delgany Road
Greystones
Tel: (01) 287 4463

What a delightful shop Clive McCabe's is. The range of coffees is bigger and better than anyone else's – Monsoon Malabar; Sumatra Lingtung; Kenya AA; India Plantation; Mocha Djimmah – and there are many teas as well: excellent Earl Grey with a rich bergamot scent; good Kenyan for everyday drinking, fine Lapsang Souchong.

In their bright, neat bags, they make the business of tea and coffee a treat.

● **OPEN:** 10.15am-6pm Tue-Sat.
On the main street of Greystones.

THE HUNGRY MONK ®
Pat & Sylvia Keown
Greystones
Tel: (01) 287 5759

Pat and Sylvia's Hungry Monk is a sociable place, where Sunday lunches run from noon until eight o'clock in the evening. It's an unpretentious place, somewhere to enjoy spanokopitta and simple vegetarian dishes. Mr Keown is a wine lover, and the wine list is great.

● **OPEN:** 7pm-11pm Tue-Sat,
12.30pm-8pm Sun.
● **AVERAGE PRICE:**
Dinner under £20.
Visa, Access/Master.

NATURE'S GOLD ⓢ
Brod Kearon
Killincarrig Road
Greystones
Tel: (01) 2876301

This is a good wholefood shop, an excellent source of good foods as well as locally grown organic vegetables.

● **OPEN:** 9.30am-6pm Mon-Sat.

KILMACANOGUE
AVOCA HANDWEAVERS ⓢ®⊙
Joanna Hill
Kilmacanogue
Tel: (01) 286 7466
Fax: (01) 286 2367

"I never had designs on being a cook", says Leylie Hayes who, with head chef Joanna Hill is the mastermind behind the cooking in Avoca Handweavers.

Well, maybe not, but the team of Ms Hayes and Ms Hill is a demon double-whammy, a pair of cooks whose work is fun, and perfectly understood, women who seem to be able to cook out of pure instinct, and thus create food which is wonderfully pure. You look at the assembly of dishes at lunchtime, their sparkling integrity and appearance, and want to try everything.

"We have a very open policy", says Leylie Hayes, "and we have a great team of chefs. If one of them comes in at seven in the morning and wants to try something new, we will try it. If people like it and it sells, then we keep it. Plus we also often go out on the floor, and just ask people if everything is okay, if they are happy. We have a lot of regulars, so we have to dream up new things for them, and we have lots of people who always want to eat the same things, so we have to make sure it is always good."

And goodness but it is good: a bowl of roasted tomato and red pepper soup, which shows the fondness of this kitchen for sweet flavours.

Ms Hill's fantastic piperade tart, the slice topped with a ring of tomato, and the stew of peppers and onions bound up with goat's cheese, this accompanied by roasted fennel and red pepper salad, and grated carrot and sesame seed salad with a sesame dressing. Potato salad in a yogurt and mint dressing, and a lovely crunchy mixture of cauliflower, broccoli and peanut salad, with a mustard dressing.

Smashing food, food that draws in people from many miles around.

The synergy between the tastes – the goat's cheese in the tart with the vegetables, the heat of mustard with the broccoli and cauliflower, the clever splash of pesto in the soup – shows the very astute culinary thinking of Joanna Hill. And, on any given day, the place will be jumping, the buzz of people enjoying themselves, people who know they are on to a good thing.

The key to this discipline lies with constant enquiry. Ms Hayes travels widely, staff are allowed sabbaticals to travel and learn about new cuisines. The dread of dullness and repetition is thus kept at bay. And with this constant enquiry comes constant innovation. A new food hall, more seating, moving onwards.

"But we don't think we ever have it right", says Ms Hayes. "We are pumping money back into the business all the time, trying to make it better".

Of all the things to admire about Avoca perhaps this hunger to improve is the finest attribute of this fine venture.

● **OPEN:** 9.30am-5.30pm Mon-Fri, 10am-5.30pm Sat-Sun.
Food served all day, last food orders 4.45pm.

KILPEDDER

ORGANIC LIFE Ⓕ ✪
Marc Michel
Tinna Park House, Kilpedder
Tel: (01) 281 9726

Funky, stylish and trendy as all get out, Mr Michel has transformed the image of organic growers. Firstly, he has shown that not all organic producers are people who grow their own sturdy sandals and live lives of austere denial.

Secondly, he has shown that marketing organic foods wisely and slickly – he sells his produce under the Organic Life label – can work, and that one can persuade this food into the mainstream supermarkets with ease. This, indeed, is his great lesson for the organic movement, that there is no tension between idealism and commerce, and that one can prosper from the other. His produce, needless to say, is megatastic: just check out those tomatoes in summertime.

● **OPEN:** Organic Life produce is widely available in Supermarkets and Healthfood Shops in Dublin and Wicklow.

KILTEGAN

PENNY & UDO LANGE Ⓕ ✪
Penny & Udo Lange
Ballinroan House, Kiltegan
Tel: (0508) 73278

If you ever needed persuading that bio-dynamic farming is able to capture the essential flavours of food – that it can give you fennel with a pure anise strength, or carrots with an intense sweetness, or salad leaves with a concentrated greenness – then it is Mr and Mrs Lange's food which will convince you of the fact.

Their produce is peerless, and one finds that when you eat such unalloyed, pristine food, the sense of physical well-being it generates is almost as pleasurable as the perfect taste. You really do owe it to yourself to try this food, for the tastes are a true revelation.

● **OPEN:** The Langes' vegetables are sold by delivery, in the fortnightly Dublin Food Co-Op on Pearse Street and in certain branches of Superquinn and Quinnsworth.

RATHDRUM

THE OLD FARMHOUSE Ⓡ Ⓐ
Caroline & Tony Buck
Greenane, Rathdrum
Tel: (0404) 46676

Caroline and Tony's restaurant and B&B boasts the largest herb garden in Wicklow, which is quite a feat in the county known as the Garden of Ireland.

They source food from their own organic garden, and are thus easily able to cook for both vegetarians and vegans. Like another of the county's best-known cooks, Linda Saunders of The Old Rectory, Caroline makes a speciality of using edible flowers.

● **OPEN:** All year.
● **AVERAGE PRICE:** Lunch £5. Dinner £12-£18. B&B £14 pps. Telephone for directions.

WICKLOW

THE OLD RECTORY Ⓡ Ⓐ
Paul & Linda Saunders
Wicklow
Tel: (0404) 67048, Fax: 69181

You can praise the elegant rhythm of a dinner eaten in the tiny confines of The Old Rectory, the way in which one course will act as a prelude to another, the satisfying expansiveness in the middle of a meal, the happy way dessert will complete by reprising the confident notes of the food that has gone before.

You can also hymn the counterpoint between ingredients in Linda Saunders' cooking, and the true pitch they strike thanks to being local, organic foods.

There are many delicious things: spearmint tea sorbet; Andalucian pancake; viola flower crêpe filled with summer berries and cream with bilberry sauce; spicy red bean and parsnip soup; nasturtium flowers stuffed with cottage cheese and sage flowers; carrot and cucumber tart with a sauce provençale; dessert of chocolate pots with chocolate and Cointreau mousse served with candied oranges.

The celebrated floral dinners, all ten courses, are marvellous, and the rooms in the house are comfy, cosy.

● **OPEN:** 8pm Sun-Thur, 7.30pm-9pm Fri-Sat. Closed Nov-Mar.
● **AVERAGE PRICE:** Dinner under £30. B&B over £40. Visa, Access/Master, Amex. On the left hand side of the road as you drive into Wicklow town heading south.

shopping as warfare

They look normal. Perfectly normal in fact: cardys in cascade white or widow grey, wicker baskets. Sensible, efficient shoes. Toyota Starlets. Mini Metros.

They almost behave normally, too. Except you know that they are watching, waiting. Counting down. There is tension in the air. Kilternan. The Saturday Country Market. Shopping As Warfare.

An all-action contact sport. No holds barred. In Shopping As Warfare there is nothing but a cold logical chase. The rush for the last Battenburg. The dive for the final bunch of white turnips. The helter-skelter shove for the pot of gooseberry conserve.

Age doesn't matter either. Look at the matrons who, now that there are only ten minutes to go, are standing in front of the big red curtain that hides the hall. Silver haired. Committee ladies. Except there is a tension in their bodies, and you realise that they are behaving like teenyboppers, love-struck lassies waiting at the airport for The Beatles to touch down.

There are now only a few minutes to the off. Almost ten thirty. Inside the hall are the lucky folk, the chosen, those who hold the little cardboard cards with numbers on them from one to thirty or forty. We will be allowed in first, counted down into the hall. The tension is unbearable. People begin to stand up: three minutes. We crowd in front of the curtain with all the discipline and self-control of a

Sicilian bank queue. Granny-sharp elbows are readied. Shoulders pulled back. Slow, deep breaths.

Then, suddenly, after so long, it is all action. "Numbers 1 to 10", calls the man, and there is a flurry of speed. Bodies fall into the body of the hall, dispersing like shrapnel around the tables. Cakes are urgently requested. Pot plants are seized, bunches of flowers are called for. "One jam sandwich. And a battenburg", Eggs. Jade-dark lettuce. Tubs of blackcurrants.

And then on. Next stall. Next stall. In seven minutes, it is all over. A sign at the entrance to the car park states: Kilternan Country Market. Saturday 10.30-12. 00. It should read: Kilternan Country Market. Saturday 10.30-10.37.

Queueing up to pay, arms laden with goodies, there is a breathless exhilaration amongst us all. Veterans of the fight, survivors of the struggle.

KILTERNAN COUNTRY MARKET ⑤
Golden Ball, Kilternan
● OPEN: 10.30am-noon Sat.

NORTH WICKLOW COUNTRY MARKET ⑤
St Patrick's Hall
● OPEN: 10.30am-11.30am Sat.

ROUNDWOOD SUNDAY MARKET ⑤
Parish Hall
● OPEN: 3pm-5pm Sun.

MUNSTER

INCLUDING THE COUNTIES OF

CLARE

CORK

KERRY

LIMERICK

TIPPERARY

WATERFORD

COUNTY CLARE

AILWEE CAVE COMPANY ⓢ Ⓕ
The Johnson family
Ballyvaughan
Tel: (065) 77036

If the Johnson family did no more than orchestrate the thrilling complexion of caves which are the Ailwee complex, they would oversee one of the most extraordinary natural phenomena in the country. For a stroll through the warren, deep into underground, is an amazing experience.

But they are not people to simply take things easy. In addition to the caves, there is a smashing craft shop, a splendid tea rooms, and young Ben Johnson also makes richly flavoured Burren Gold cheeses.

● **OPEN:** 10am-5.30pm Mon-Sun.
● **AVERAGE PRICE:** Lunch under £5.
The Caves are signposted all over Clare.

AN FEAR GORTA Ⓡ
Catherine O'Donoghue
Pier Road
Ballyvaughan
Tel: (065) 77023
Fax: (065) 77127

Catherine O'Donoghue's tea rooms are a treasure. The cloistering, cottagey atmosphere inside the main cottage, their carefree, heat-straddled conservatory and gardens out at the back of the house, where Catherine has planted a carefully considered selection of plants – including cultivated varieties of plants which grow wild in the Burren, all make for the perfect environment in which to sup tea and scoff scones and home-cooked cakes.

● **OPEN:** 11am-5.30pm Mon-Sun.
Closed Oct-May.
● **AVERAGE PRICE:**
Lunch under £10.
No credit cards.
Overlooking the Quays.

HYLAND'S HOTEL Ⓡ Ⓐ
Marie Greene
Ballyvaughan
Tel: (065) 77037

Hyland's is an hospitable, fun place, which still retains much of the atmosphere of an old coaching inn.

The rooms upstairs are comfy and cosy, with the newer rooms at the rear the ones to really chase after.

● **OPEN:**
11am-5.30pm, 7pm-9pm Mon-Sun.
● **AVERAGE PRICE:** Lunch under £10.
Dinner under £20.
B&B over £20-over £30.
Visa, Access/Master, Amex.
In the town centre.

THE TEA JUNCTION CAFÉ ®
Marianne Krause
Ballyvaughan
Tel: (065) 77174

Situated right smack in the centre of the village – right at the t-junction, in fact – Marianne's café serves excellent vegetarian breakfasts, and there are also café specials such as Burren cheese salad.

● **OPEN:** From 8.30am.
(Closing times depend on the season).
● **AVERAGE PRICE:** Lunch under £10.

THE WHITETHORN ® ⑤
John McDonnell & Sarah Culligan
Ballyvaughan
Tel: (065) 77044

The location of the Whitethorn is jaw-droppingly gorgeous, and there is nothing quite like a quiet dinner eaten in here as the sun sets over the bay, a truly memorable experience.

John McDonnell brings to his work in the restaurant the same passion he brings to his work with wine. He is unabashedly enthusiastic and humorous, and this bonhomie and creativity lifts the Whitethorn into something special.

The wine list is, probably, the finest to be found on the west coast.

The craft shop is excellent, the cooking is bright with flavours in dishes such as vegetable and mixed nut stroganoff with herbed rice, and this is an unmissable stop in Clare.

● **OPEN:** For meals 10am-5pm, 6.30pm-9.30pm Mon-Sun.
(Check out of season).

● **AVERAGE PRICE:** Lunch under £10.
Dinner under £20.
Visa, Access/Master, Amex, Diners.
Just east of Ballyvaughan, signed before you enter the village.

BUNRATTY

MACCLOSKEY'S ®
Shaun & Eileen Smith-Roberts
Bunratty House Mews
Tel: (061) 364082

Shaun Smith-Roberts' cooking shows the involvement of someone who enjoys both a fine talent and a fine training.

He dedicated himself, whilst studying, to working with chefs who had particular specialities, with the result that his work is fluent through all the disciplines, and the elegant cellars of MacCloskey's is just the place for himself and Eileen to strut their confident, accomplished style of cooking and presentation.

MacCloskey's cheese parcels with a damson and apple jelly; iced melon rose with a watermelon sorbet; roasted goat's cheese in butter pastry, are a mere sampling of astute, personal cooking, where imagination coincides happily with skilfulness.

● **OPEN:** Tue-Sat from 6.30pm, Sun & Mon for groups on request.
● **AVERAGE PRICE:** Dinner £26.
Visa, Access/Master, Amex, Diners.
MacCloskey's is in the basement of Bunratty House, and the restaurant is signposted in Bunratty.

CAHERBOLANE FARMHOUSE ®Ⓐ
Brid & Patricia Cahill
Corofin
Tel: (065) 37638

A very pure streak of perfectionism runs through Patricia Cahill's work, and one senses a cook who wants to be in control at all times. In this ambition she is helped by the fact of cooking in Caherbolane, for it is intimately small. It is, in fact, the sitting room of the farmhouse, and in evening time is host to no more than five tables. Cooks like Patricia Cahill understand those flavours and savours which are best at cranking our pleasure dials to the max. She does this with stupendously simple things – a floury potato steamed to utter perfection; mashed turnips with a hint of cinnamon stirred in; crunchy, creamy cabbage – and the confident nature of her technique means that dinner becomes a solid sender of good tastes.

Alongside easy-going starters such as melon and avocado with a mint dressing, she may produce fine little ravioli stuffed with nuts and served with a pesto sauce, or perhaps a curried mushroom crêpe which is generous with comforting flavours. Desserts may be a thunderously good champagne parfait or a well-executed coffee crême caramel.

● **OPEN:** 7.30pm-9.30pm Mon-Sun.
● **AVERAGE PRICE:** Dinner under £20.
BYO.
No Credit Cards.
Three miles outside Corofin on Gort road.

CROIDE NA BOIRNE Ⓟ
Michelle Cassidy
Carron, Corofin
Tel: (065) 89109

The pub is a restored barracks, with wonderful views out cross the valleys, and the sarnies are ginormous, involved concoctions.

● **OPEN:** Noon-10pm Mon-Sun.
Closed Nov-Easter.
● **AVERAGE PRICE:** Under £10.
Visa, Access/Master.
Ask directions locally.

FERGUS VIEW Ⓐ
The Kelleher family
Kilnaboy, Corofin
Tel: (065) 37606
Fax: (065) 37192

Mary Kelleher's house is a landmark for hospitality and for fine food. Mrs Kelleher's interest and her expertise translates into delectable, delicious food which it is famously easy to enjoy. A perfect mushroom crêpe. A glorious potato gratin made with Kilnaboy cheese, and a purée of spinach, then pear frangipane and fine coffee. Vegetables and herbs have come from no further than the garden, so their vigour is bounteous.

The housekeeping in Fergus View is meticulous and the rooms extra comfortable: this is a homely house.

● **OPEN:** Easter-1 Oct, dinner for guests.
(Book by noon).
● **AVERAGE PRICE:** B&B under £20.
Dinner under £20.
No Credit Cards.
The house is two miles north of Corofin.

CRATLOE

CRATLOE HILLS SHEEP'S CHEESE Ⓕ
Sean & Deirdre Fitzgerald
Cratloe
Tel: (061) 87185

Cratloe is at its best in the mature form, recognisable from its dark mustard waxed coat, when the gentleness and spiciness is most clearly defined and most pleasing.

● **OPEN:** Cratloe cheese is widely available.

DOOLIN

BRUCH NA HAILLE Ⓡ
John & Helen Browne
Broadford
Doolin
Tel: (065) 74120

John and Helen Browne opened Bruch na hAille almost twenty years ago, when Doolin was a far cry from the rampant village it has since become. "We have tried to keep pace with the changes", they say, "and are always trying to maintain a very high standard of food".

They use many local foods – Kilshanny cheese will be deep fried, Inagh cheese will be baked with pimento, and the atmosphere has that breezy, carefree Clareness.

● **OPEN:** 6pm-9.30pm Mon-Sun.
● **AVERAGE PRICE:** Dinner under £20.
Visa, Access/Master.
Doolin centre, overlooking the bridge.

THE DOOLIN CAFÉ Ⓡ
Josephine & John Clinton
Doolin
Tel: (065) 74429

A trendy, slightly self-conscious, very vegetarian friendly café which many love, the Doolin is also good for coffees and a browse of the papers and assorted magazines.

● **OPEN:** 9.30am-2pm, 6pm-9pm May-Sept.
● **AVERAGE PRICE:** Under £5. No credit cards.

CRAFTS GALLERY & FLAGSHIP RESTAURANT Ⓡ
Matthew O'Connell & Mary Gray
Ballyvoe
Doolin
Tel: (065) 74309

This is principally a gallery devoted to Mr O'Connell's batik work and Ms Gray's jewellery, but there is also a café serving coffee, lunch and afternoon tea, seafood, scones and Guinness cake.

● **OPEN:** Shop opens 9am-8pm.
Restaurant opens from 10am Mon-Sun.
Limited hours off season.
● **AVERAGE PRICE:** Under £5.
Visa, Access/Master.
Beside the Cemetery and the Church.

THE FOOD EMPORIUM Ⓢ
TJ McGuinness & Brenda Dearing
Abbey Street
Ennis
Tel: (065) 20554

T J and Brenda's is a happy shop, the sort of place where you can find tons of good things, and they are experts in relieving you of the burden of party planning, and are delighted to remove the potential of celebration calamities.

● **OPEN:** 9am-6pm Mon-Sat.

THE CLOISTER Ⓟ Ⓡ
Jim Brindley
Abbey Street
Ennis
Tel: (065) 29521

A very professional pub which does enormous business at lunchtime, thanks to a well-established local trade who value the thoughtful, flavourful cooking. As an on-the-road stop, the Cloister is excellent, as it is close to the roundabouts which ring the town, and lunch is also served well into the afternoon. There is a restaurant also.

● **OPEN:** BAR – noon-11.30pm.
RESTAURANT – noon-3pm, 6pm-9.30pm
Mon-Sun.
(Closed Sun & Mon off season).
● **AVERAGE PRICE:**
Restaurant under £20.
Bar under £15.
Visa, Access/Master, Amex, Diners.

OPEN SESAME Ⓢ
Sally Smyth
29 Parnell Street, Ennis
Tel: (091) 31315 (home)

A conventional wholefood shop, but invaluable for local organic vegetables and other good things.

● **OPEN:** 10am-1.30pm, 2.30pm-6pm
Mon-Fri, 10am-6pm Sat.

UNGLERT'S BAKERY Ⓢ
Mr Unglert
Ennistymon
Tel: (065) 71217

Unglert's is a cute little bakery, wholly appropriate to the town. There are good breads, some of the best made using rye flour, and cakes, and a small coffee shop also.

● **OPEN:** 9am-7pm Tue-Sun.

INAGH FARMHOUSE CHEESES Ⓕ ✪
Meg & Derrick Gordon
Inagh, Tel: (065) 26633

From the storybook farm come the storybook cheeses. Meg and Derrick Gordon's Inagh cheese, made from the milk of their handsome herd of goats, are some of the finest made in Ireland.

Why? Well, care and affection are the secrets, most likely. All of the goats have names, the scale of the cheese production is small and so there is the most intricate care with every detail, with every detail of the Inagh cheeses stamped with the character of the Gordons.

The lush but delicate St. Tola soft cheese is often sold very young, and it is also worthwhile trying to find one with a little maturity. The hard Lough Caum is beautifully crisp and immediate in taste, and occasionally one can find the fresh cheeses.

● **OPEN:** The cheese is widely distributed, but do note that it is not available from the farm.

KILNABOY

BARTELINK **F**
Annaliese Bartelink
Poulcoin, Kilnaboy

Out of the rugged harshness of the Burren, Harry and Annaliese have carved a little vale of fertility and creativity. They farm according to the principles of bio-dynamics, and are leading lights in that organisation in the country. Whilst some of their produce can be found locally, it is actually for cheese-making rather than farming that they are best known.

Indeed, Annaliese Bartelink is one of the most senior cheesemakers in the country, and it shows. Her gouda style cheese – plain, some flavoured with cumin, others with nettle – are precise, perfect demonstrations of the cheesemakers art.

● **OPEN:** The cheese is available in shops, B&Bs and restaurants in the locality.

LAHINCH

BARRTRÁ SEAFOOD RESTAURANT **R**
Paul & Theresa O'Brien
Lahinch
Tel: (065) 81280

The Barrtra is such a sweet, good family operation, such a cloisteringly comfortable, logical little restaurant, that it is well nigh irresistible.

Paul does front of house, Theresa cooks, and at busy times the girls lend a hand and put together the desserts. The diners sit in what is, effectively, a room of the O'Brien's house, looking out at Liscannor Bay, a heartbreakingly beautiful vista. If there is a classic summertime restaurant, with all the holidaytime clichés – friendly food, good service, fine wines, the romance of looking out at the sea as the sun sets – then this is it.

The vegetables are grown organically, the wines are an interesting and diverting selection, and this is the sort of little restaurant you dream of stumbling across when on holiday.

● **OPEN:**
12.30pm-2.30pm Mon-Sun,
6pm-10pm Mon-Sat.
(Closed weekdays off season, closed mid Jan-Mar).
● **AVERAGE PRICE:**
Lunch under £10.
Sun lunch under £15.
Dinner under £20.
Visa, Access/Master, Amex, Diners.
Signposted from the Lahinch-Milltown Malbay Road.

KILSHANNY FARMHOUSE CHEESE ⒡
Peter & Aaron Nibbering
Derry House
Lahinch
Tel: (065) 71228

The fine Gouda style Kilshanny cheeses are some of County Clare's best-known foodstuffs, their distinctive mustard-yellow wax overcoats a familiar sight in the county, and they are much used by Clare restaurateurs, who appreciate the powerful flavours which the Nibberings are able to capture.

They flavour some cheeses with, respectively, pepper, cumin and garlic, as well as the plain milk, and all are interesting.

● **OPEN:** The Nibberings are delighted to sell from the house, which is well signposted ('Derry House') from Kilshanny village.

LISCANNOR

EGAN'S ⒫
Patrick Egan
Liscannor
Tel: (065) 81430

This is the most delightfully surprising pub in the west. Patrick Egan runs a fine bar – stylishly restored, full of good cheer, a sparky crowd – but his real passion is wine.

So, step in the door with your mind fixed on a pint, and you are suddenly confronted with the finest collection of fine clarets you could desire. Cheval-Blanc, Lynch-Bages, Latour, you name it, and Patrick

Egan has it. There are also some Burgundies and a smattering of good wine from elsewhere, but claret is the main focus, and whether or not you have a deep pocket, there is something here to suit. Wonderful.

● **OPEN:** Noon-9pm Mon-Sun.
No food Nov-Easter, Closed Jan-Feb.
● **AVERAGE PRICE:** Meals under £10.
Visa, Access/Master.
Centre of Liscannor.

SHEEDY'S SPA VIEW HOTEL ⒜⒭
Frank & Patsy Sheedy
Lisdoonvarna
Tel: (065) 74026, Fax: 74555

Sheedy's Spa View Hotel may look like just another member of that multitude of places to stay which one finds in Lisdoonvarna. But the surprise of Sheedy's comes, when you sit down to dinner. Sheedy's is different, because Frankie Sheedy cooks proper food, real food. The care which this kitchen shows, and the solecisms of the terrific staff, make dinner in Sheedy's a treat.

There is an excellent vegetarian menu: twice baked soufflé of St Tola cheese; chilled yogurt and mint soup; mushroom roulade with a fresh tomato coulis; symphony of vegetables in filo. Desserts are excellent, but don't miss the fine local Kilshanny cheese.

● **OPEN:** 6.30pm-9pm Mon-Sun.
Closed Nov-1 April (open New Year).
● **AVERAGE PRICE:** Dinner under £30.
Visa, Access/Master, Amex, Diners.
Lisdoonvarna town centre.

COUNTY CORK

Cork is divided as follows:

C O R K C I T Y

ARBUTUS LODGE ❶❷
Declan Ryan
Montenotte, Cork City
Tel: (021) 501237
Fax: (021) 502893

The grand old dame of Cork cooking sails serenely on, under the guidance of Declan Ryan. The essential mainstays of the Arbutus are as fine as ever – the wonderful collection of art, the staggering, award-winning wine list, the golly-gosh views out over the city from the hill of Montenotte, the calm and endearing service which has always been such a welcoming feature.

The informal food served in the bar is most enjoyable.

● **OPEN:** 1pm-2pm, 7pm-9.30pm Mon-Sat.
● **AVERAGE PRICE:** Lunch under £15.
Dinner over £20.
Visa, Access/Master, Amex, Diners.
Signposted from the Cork-Dublin road.

THE CRAWFORD GALLERY CAFÉ ❷
Chris O'Brien
Emmet Place, Cork City
Tel: (021) 274415

It would be absolutely impossible for the Crawford Gallery Café to change its menu – its devoted regulars simply wouldn't tolerate it.

"No spinach and mushroom pancake with hollandaise sauce – but it's Monday, I always have that on Monday."

"Now you know I always have Ballymaloe relish with my Mitchelstown Cheddar and soda bread".

Even if the new head chef of the café, Chris O'Brien, a man with a Ballymaloe school background, had a mind to change the splendid formula of cracking breads and cakes, the delectable open sandwiches, he would never be allowed. One of the Cork institutions.

● **OPEN:** 10.30am-5pm.
(Lunch served 12.30pm-2.30pm) Mon-Sat.
● **AVERAGE PRICE:** Lunch under £10.
Visa, Access/Master.
Ground floor of the Crawford Gallery.

GALVIN'S OFF LICENCES ❸
Barry Galvin
37 Bandon Road, Cork
Tel: (021) 316098
Watercourse Road, Cork
Tel: (021) 500818
22 Washington Street, Cork
Tel: (021) 276314

Barry Galvin's various wine shops are particularly strong on clarets, and the range of wines from the New world is always interesting. Do keep an eye out for the very regular sales and special offers they feature.

● **OPEN:** 10.30am-11pm Mon-Sat,
noon-2pm, 4pm-10pm Sun.

HAROLD'S ®
Harold Lynch
Douglas
Cork
Tel: (021) 361613

Harold Lynch has a Ballymaloe school background, and whilst elements of his cooking show that training, in classics such as a twice baked cheese soufflé, he also likes to bring a more modish complexion to some of his dishes, with tapas featuring occasionally on the menu.

● **OPEN:** 6pm-10pm Mon-Sat.
● **AVERAGE PRICE:** Dinner under £20.
Visa, Access/Master.
Douglas is just south of the City Centre.

ISAAC'S BRASSERIE ® Ⓐ AND HOSTEL
Canice Sharkey & Michael Ryan
MacCurtain Street, Cork
Tel: (021) 503805

Canice Sharkey is a classicist in the modern mould. His food effortlessly embraces the modern mania for multiculturalism – tagliatelle with asparagus as confidently delivered as Provençale bean stew or caramelised onion and blue cheese tart. The room is utterly delightful and service is friendly and excellent.

● **OPEN:** 12.30pm-2.30pm, 6.30pm-10.30pm Mon-Sat.
6.30pm-9pm Sun.
● **AVERAGE PRICE:** Lunch under £10.
Dinner under £20.
Visa, Access/Master.
Cork city centre, north of the river.

THE IVORY TOWER ® ✪ RESTAURANT
Seamus O'Connell
The Exchange Buildings
35 Princes Street
Cork
Tel: (021) 274665

Let us not mince our words: Seamus O'Connell is some sort of a genius.

When this man has a skillet in his hand, his consciousness enters a higher plane than that occupied by other mortal chefs. His inventiveness is extraordinary, his pursuit of excitement in food pursued at all costs.

There is no point in listing his dishes, for he cooks like that other great artist, Pierre Gagnaire, no sooner inventing something than he will be re-inventing it the next day.

Day in, day out, he sees what is available in the market, then goes to work. But his work is not like a standard restaurateur, someone who keeps an eye on price, and churns out staples which are popular. Every day, he writes the book anew.

He is as much of a performance artist as he is a chef, and he is scripting a culinary show that goes where no other Irish cook has ever gone before. His vegetarian cooking is not only enchanting, it is sublime.

● **OPEN:**
Noon-4pm Mon-Sat,
6.30pm-11pm Wed-Sun.
● **AVERAGE PRICE:**
Lunch under £10.
Dinner under £20.
Visa, Access/Master.
Princes Street leads off St Patrick's Street.

JACQUES ®

Jacqueline & Eithne Barry
9 Phoenix Street, Cork City
Tel: (021) 277387

They just can't stop, Eithne and Jacqueline. Their restlessness is seen in every aspect of Jacques, and after nearly 15 years the girls remain as enthusiastic and as determined as ever. The cooking, likewise, marches ever on: ribollita with extra virgin olive oil; ravioli with ricotta; cannelloni with spinach, almonds and cream; grilled polenta with tomato provençale, good flavours and savours in everything.

● **OPEN:** 11.30am-3pm Mon-Sat,
6pm-10.30pm Tue-Sat.
● **AVERAGE PRICE:** Lunch under £10.
Dinner under £20.
Visa, Access/Master, Amex, Diners.
Behind the main post office in Cork city.

LOVETT'S ®

Dermod & Margaret Lovett
Churchyard Lane, Well Road
Douglas
Tel: (021) 294909, Fax: (021) 508568

Lovett's have added a new brasserie area to the existing restaurant which has functioned so successfully for so many years. This continues the policy of Lovett's, which is to do their best to offer something for everyone. The wine list is splendid.

● **OPEN:** 12.30pm-2pm, 7pm-9.45pm
Mon-Sat.
● **AVERAGE PRICE:** Lunch under £20.
Dinner over £20.
Visa, Access/Master, Amex, Diners.
Signposted on the Well Road, off the R609.

NATURAL FOODS ⓢ

Wendy O'Byrne
26 Paul Street, Cork City
Tel: (021) 277244

It is a nifty little tuck-box of a shop, Natural Foods. Everything they have here is a delightful, special treat, with their own breads and cakes chief amongst them: the famous cherry buns; the soft pitta pouches; the apricot bakes; the fine sourdough loaves.

The shelves are lined with bags of good foods such as Macroom Oatmeal; Maldon salt; Puy lentils; the bunches of vegetables brought in by Joe Eats Organic.

This atmosphere of fun and this dedicated element of choice makes Wendy O'Byrne's shop one of the best wholefood shops in the country.

● **OPEN:** 9.30am-5.30pm Mon-Sat.
Behind Waterstones bookshop.

CAFÉ PARADISO ® ✪

Denis Cotter & Bridget Healy
16 Lancaster Quay
Western Road, Cork City
Tel: (021) 277939

Denis Cotter runs the best vegetarian restaurant in the country. Indeed, to describe it as a "vegetarian" restaurant does something of a disservice to Mr Cotter. He is, simply, a fine cook who doesn't use meat, and he doesn't need it either, for he has a limitless imagination, a fine team to help run this neat, youthful room, and the chutzpah to make Café Paradiso a very groovy, unique place. It is the sort of vegetarian restaurant where, at any given time, half the customers will probably be meat-eaters. They are here, like everyone else, because Denis Cotter can cook.

His genius lies in creating a vegetarian cooking which is rich, almost lavish, and yet which is perfectly poised. The purity of flavour found in some fresh braid beans with Parmesan shavings and olive oil is so simple, so perfect, that it knocks you sideways.

But he also loves funky flavours: a potato, aubergine and coriander stew with broccoli and blue cheese filo; pepperonata mozzarella; vine leaves stuffed with couscous. Daring, smashing cooking, served in a charming room. The service is fab.

● **OPEN:** 10.30am-10.30pm.
(Lunch 12.30pm-3pm, dinner 6.30pm-10.30pm) Tue-Sat.
● **AVERAGE PRICE:** Lunch under £10. Dinner under £20. Visa, Access/Master.
Opposite Jury's, on the Western Road.

PROBY'S BISTRO ®
Dervilla O'Flynn, Helen O'Leary
Proby's Quay, Cork City
Tel: (021) 316531

Dervilla O'Flynn cooks in a fervently modern fashion: savoury Tuscan sandwich; sun-dried tomato and pesto tart. Great fun.

● **OPEN:** 12.30pm-10pm Mon-Sun.
Lunch 12.30pm-2.30pm.
Dinner 6pm-10pm Mon-Sun.
(No lunch Sat, no dinner Sun).
● **AVERAGE PRICE:** Lunch under £10. Dinner under £15. Visa, Access/Master.
Near St Finbarr's Cathedral.

QUAY CO-OP ⓢ →
John Calnan, Anne-Marie Friend
24 Sullivan's Quay
Cork
Tel: (021) 317660

It is impossible to imagine Cork city without the Quay Co-Op. Like so many other restaurants in this blessed city, it has endured because it has developed and grown in a quiet, organic fashion. The vegetarian cookery has adapted to Pacific Rim themes – smoked tofu, spinach and tomato tart; lentil and coconut soup; a Caribbean casserole of blackeye beans with vegetables in a coconut and tomato sauce, this served with fried bananas. But the great stand-bys, so much loved by the very regular clientele of the Co-Op, are also still here – spanokopitta; nachos; broccoli roulade; lentil, cashew and aubergine timbale.

The shop downstairs is an invaluable source of organically grown vegetables and well-chosen wholefoods, with friendly, helpful staff.

● **OPEN:** SHOP – 9am-6pm Mon-Sat.
RESTAURANT – 9.30am-7pm self-service, 7pm-10.30pm table service.
● **AVERAGE PRICE:** Lunch under £5. Dinner under £15.
Visa, Access/Master.
Just south of the river in the city centre.

CHETWYND IRISH BLUE ⓕ

Jerry Beechinor
Castlewhite
Waterfall, Cork City
Tel: (021) 53502

Jerry Beechinor's mild blue cheese is made with pasteurised milk and has a quiet, tongue-teasing contrast between the spicy saltiness of the blue veining and the calm lactic canvas of the milk. It is vastly superior to any imported blue cheese, swapping their blandness for a considerate, gentle taste.

● **OPEN:** Widely distributed around Cork.

COLLINS' ICE CREAM ⓕ

Tom & Ann Collins
Castlewhite, Waterfall
Cork City
Tel: (021) 342050

Ireland has been invaded by salaciously scrummy ice creams from the United States in recent years, so it is wonderful that at last we have a serious competitor. Tom and Ann make scrummy ice creams in a variety of flavours, and their rum and raisin, for one, is truly a dessert to die for: packed with flavour, utterly seductive, wonderful.

● **OPEN:** Available around Cork in good shops.

the Cork sandwich

They respect the art of the sandwich in Cork. That sarnie may be of the traditional school, as found in a whacky pub like The Long Valley – chopped egg with salad, just the kind of ballast needed to provide the foundation for a clatter of pints.

Or it may be the groovy adaptations found in someplace like Barnaby Blacker's Gingerbread House – a French roll filled with cheese and relish, perfect food with a lunchtime coffee, or grub-to-go.

But the folk who have made the greatest strides in creating the sandwich for the new century are Sean Calder-Potts and his team in the Cork Market's wonderful Iago.

The lavishness, the deliciousness, the pell-mell piling on, make these the finest sarnies in the country.

Unapologetically magnificent, Iago's sarnies are everything a sandwich can be, should be, has to be.

THE GINGERBREAD HOUSE ⓡ

Barnaby Blacker
Paul Street, Cork City
Tel: (021) 276411
● **OPEN:** 9am-6.30pm Mon-Sat.

THE LONG VALLEY ⓟ

Winthrop Street, Cork City
Tel: (021) 272144
● **OPEN:** Sandwiches served all day.

IAGO ⓢ

Sean Calder-Potts
English Market, Cork City
Tel: (021) 277047 Fax: 277750
● **OPEN:** 8am-6pm Mon-Sat.

the English market

The wonder of the Cork Covered Market, or the English Market as it is popularly known, is not just that the people who work here manage to do so many things, but that they manage to do these things so well.

The Market has tapped into a vital source of energy in recent years, with the arrival of new blood who enjoy and appreciate its energy, its savvy.

This mix of the old and trusted and the new and exciting has created a Mecca for those whose job is to make and sell good food. The more it has become a Mecca, the more those who love good food come to pay their respects.

And so, there is new blood such as Toby Simmonds Real Olive Co., with its brilliant assortment of olives and oils, of salads and chillies, of breads and whatnots.

Around the corner we find the brilliant Iago, run by Sean and Josephine Calder-Potts. This dazzling cornucopia of good things really has to be seen to be believed. A fabulous cheese counter – second only to that maintained by Peter Ward in Nenagh, in Tipperary – is complemented by the best sandwich counter in the country, and there are also fabulous pastas, oils and condiments, in a palace of good things. Across the way is the ever-expanding stall of Mr Bell, with all the spices and seasonings you could ever require, all the Oriental specialities you need.

Just a little further along, Martin and Anne-Marie of Maucnaclea Cheeses will have their splendiferous range of soft, semi-soft and hard cheeses for sale and their fantastic salad leaves, herbs and vegetables.

Whilst all this is going on every day, upstairs in the Farm Gate Café, Kay Harte will be devising the day's menu for the Café entirely around foods bought in the market itself, a logical, and conscientious policy that makes for delicious food.

MR BELL'S ⓢ
Mr Bell
Tel: (021) 885333
● OPEN: 9am-5.30pm Mon-Sat.

THE FARM GATE CAFÉ ⓡ
Kay Harte
Tel: (021) 278134
● OPEN: 9am-5.30pm Mon-Sat.

IAGO ⓢ
Sean Calder-Potts
Tel: (021) 277047 Fax: 277750
● OPEN: 8am-6pm Mon-Sat.

MAUCNACLEA FARM CHEESES ⓢ
Martin Guillemot & Anne-Marie Jamand
Tel: (021) 270232
● OPEN: 9am-5.30pm Fri & Sat.

THE REAL OLIVE Co ⓢ
Toby Simmonds
Tel: (021) 270842
● OPEN: 9am-6pm Mon-Sat.

EAST CORK

LA BIGOUDENNE ®
Rodolphe & Noelle Semeria
28 McCurtain Street
Fermoy
Tel: (025) 32832

The food, the character, the nature and the ambience of La Bigoudenne all seem to have been imported direct from northern France, yet La Bigoudenne is not the slightest bit self-conscious or arch or, most vitally, patronising. In an area of the country which has few good eating houses, it has won a steady, devoted following, and you get a true sense from the regulars that they are grateful for the efforts of Rodolphe and Noelle, and so they should be.

The restaurant has two characters. During the day, it is a simple enough on-the-main-road eaterie, with good soups, good salads and, best of all, wonderful crêpes which are one of their specialities: egg and cheese, salad and blue cheese. Then, after closing for a couple of hours in the afternoon, La Bigoudenne is reborn, with napery and low lighting.

● **OPEN:** 12.30pm-10.30pm.
(The restaurant menu gets going around 7pm, but they are helpful and flexible).
● **AVERAGE PRICE:** Lunch under £10.
Dinner under £20.
Visa, Access/Master.

BALLYMAKEIGH HOUSE Ⓐ
Mrs Margaret Browne
Killeagh
Tel: (024) 95184

Margaret Browne is one of that select band of inimitable women who can manage to do just about everything, and manage to do it well. Confronted by her determination, her inquiry, her vision, you just gasp with admiration. How does she do it?

How does she rear a brood of kids, run a smashing B&B, get involved with local matters, oversee a farm, and do also the million and one little things that take the rest of us all week to accomplish?

There are probably two reasons. Firstly, she very obviously loves her work, loves the whole business of hospitality, of cooking, of making people happy. Secondly, she is a creative soul, who views everything as a challenge, and a challenge to be enjoyed. New dishes. New ideas. New plans. She seizes the day, does Mrs Browne, each and every day.

● **OPEN:** Dinner for guests only.
Book by 4.30pm.
● **AVERAGE PRICE:** Dinner under £20.
B&B. Under £20.
No Credit Cards.
Killeagh is between Midleton and Youghal.

THE FARM GATE ® ⑤
Maróg O'Brien
Coolbawn
Midleton
Tel: (021) 632771

Maróg's Midleton institution has been happily in business for more than a decade, serving food which is terrifically enjoyable.

The shop out front is a splendid repository of good things: farm-house cheeses, good breads, cakes and biscuits cooked by their own bakery. In the restaurant proper respect is shown to simple lunchtime dishes such as open sandwiches, fine pancakes, well-executed pastas, whilst at weekends Maróg cooks dinner in the restaurant with a philosophy that says buy the freshest – then leave it alone.

● **OPEN:** 9.30am-6pm Mon-Wed,
9.30am-5pm, 6.30pm-9.45pm Fri-Sat.
● **AVERAGE PRICE:** Lunch under £10.
Dinner under £20.
Visa, Access/Master.
Town centre.

JAMESON HERITAGE CENTRE ⓕ
Midleton
Tel: (021) 613594

Irish Distillers' principal plant for the production of whiskey is open to the public for guided tours which culminate in a tasting of the Distillers' brands of whiskeys.

● **OPEN:** 10am-4pm Mon-Sun.
Closed Nov-Mar except for bookings.

BALLYMALOE HOUSE ® ④
Ivan & Myrtle Allen
Shanagarry
Tel: (021) 652531
Fax: (021) 652021

Rory O'Connell has succeeded Myrtle Allen as the guiding light of the Ballymaloe kitchen, and has shown that he understands well the great Ballymaloe verities – superb soups, good salads, fine attention to detail – and can craft these staples as well as ever. He follows also in the the Ballymaloe tradition of offering a full vegetarian menu.

The rooms in the restaurant are as splendid and womb-welcoming as ever, the art collection gifted with an agelessness and vigour that makes it more luminescent with each visit.

● **OPEN:** Buffet Lunch 1pm. Dinner 7pm-
9pm Mon-Sun (buffet dinner Sun).
● **AVERAGE PRICE:** Lunch under £20.
Dinner over £30. B&B over £50.
Visa, Access/Master, Amex, Diners.
Signposted from the N25.

THE BALLYMALOE COOKERY SCHOOL ⓕ
Darina & Tim Allen
Kinoith House
Shanagarry
Tel: (021) 646785

The pre-eminent cookery school in the country moves ever on, and amongst their broad range of courses there are some short courses designed especially for vegetarians.

● **OPEN:** Contact for their brochure.

BALLYMALOE KITCHEN SHOP Ⓢ
Wendy Whelan
Ballymaloe House
Shanagarry
Tel: (021) 652032

Wendy Whelan's shop is the best kitchen shop in the country, the contents a tribute to her selectivity and her confidence. The shop treads a clever line between the professional – pricey Pentole pans, lethal-looking Victorinox knives – and the domestic – masses of glorious Nicky Mosse pottery, lots of furniture made by Mrs Whelan's son Sacha, a broad range of Stephen Pearce pottery, as well as glorious olive oils and many other foods.

● OPEN: 9am-6.30pm Mon-Sun.
In the grounds of Ballymaloe House.

BALLYMALOE RELISH Ⓕ
Yasmin Hyde
Caherlog
Glanmire
Tel: (021) 353358

The original Ballymaloe Country Relish is one of the essential staples of the larder, equalled almost by the cucumber relish, and the splendid Country Relish Sauce. Also sold under the Ballymaloe name is Myrtle Allen's soda bread mix, which is guaranteed to make failsafe nutty, wholesome soda bread using Donal Creedon's Macroom flour.

● OPEN: Widely available.

STEPHEN PEARCE POTTERY Ⓕ
Stephen Pearce
Shanagarry
Tel: (021) 646807

Stephen Pearce's work is lovingly distinctive, its earthy clay-coloured hues and soft white facings seem to be almost the unmediated result of the clay dug from near the river Blackwater, as if Mr Pearce has had to do little or nothing to it to create his pieces. Secondly, by placing function as the pre-eminent feature, his work is terrifically practical, always usable, and always pleasing. Things of beauty.

● OPEN: 8am-5pm Mon-Fri, 10am-5pm Sat, 2pm-5pm Sun.

ARDSALLAGH Ⓕ
Ina & Erwin Körner
Ardsallagh House
Youghal
Tel: (021) 92545

Ina Körner makes both soft and hard cheeses with the milk of her own purebred herd of goats.

There are flavoured varieties of cream cheese - garlic, horseradish - as well as an unsalted variety, whilst Ardsallagh itself is a semi-hard cheese with a soft centre. You can also find their goat's milk yogurt, both plain and in flavoured varieties, in shops throughout Cork.

● OPEN: Widely available.

NORTH CORK

the fabulous cheeses of North Cork

The farmhouse cheeses of North Cork are amongst the greatest cheeses of the country. What they share is a powerful strength of flavour, irrespective of the style in which the cheese is actually made. An eighteen-month old Coolea, made somewhat in the style of a Gouda, will have such an assault of fudgey, sweet flavours that the taste buds tumble into a dissolute delight.

A just-ripe Ardrahan, whose style is perhaps closest to an Havarti, can assemble such an array of pristine, perfectly realised flavours that it seems more like a confection of milk, than a farmhouse cheese.

Round Tower, matured to a respectable middle-age, has an intensity and persistence of taste which makes it behave like a fine wine – the taste goes on for ever.

The best-kept secret of the North Cork cheeses are the super Carraig goat's milk cheeses made by Aart Versloot. Sold only in the locality – and by the man himself at the Friday market in Bantry – the Carraig cheeses meld together painstaking technique with a richness and a subtlety of sweetness that makes them irresistible.

How do they do it? Perhaps the secret lies with the milk, and perhaps it lies with the pastures, but it is the personalities of the cheesemakers that transforms this milk into magnificent cheeses.

ARDRAHAN CHEESE ❶ ✪
Mary & Eugene Burns
Ardrahan House
Kanturk
Tel: (029) 78099

CARRAIG GOAT'S CHEESE ❶
Aart & Lieke Versloot
Ballingeary
Tel: (026) 47126

COOLEA CHEESE ❶
Dick & Helene Willems
Coolea
Tel: (026) 45204

ROUND TOWER CHEESE ❶
Nan O'Donovan
Enniskeane
Tel: (023) 47105

NORTH CORK CO-OPERATIVE ❶
Sean McAulis
Kanturk
Tel: (029) 50003

The lush pastures that go to make such superb cheeses also add a unique flavour to the local creamery milk. Look for both milk and cream sold under the label North Cork Dairies.

● **OPEN:** You can find the milk and cream in shops and supermarkets throughout north Cork.

BALLINEEN

MANCH ESTATE ● ✪
Iris Diebrook & Oliver Jungwirth
Ballineen
Tel: (023) 47507, Fax: (023) 47276

Everything which Iris and Oliver produce at Manch has the stamp of the farm, wears the character of the farm, enjoys the creativity and purity of purpose of the farm, and is definitively, decisively, their fruit of their own work.

Just think how rare a fact that is today, just think of how few places we can say that of. At Manch, the eggs have a Manch flavour; the vegetables have a Manch flavour; the flowers glimmer with the vibrancy of Manch; the sheep's milk cheese is resplendent with the flavours of Manch.

This is the total, complete, content farm. It is a model for every farmer, and an ideal to which the agricultural business should aspire.

How, then, with all this Manch flavour floating about the place, can one describe it? Simple.

The foods they produce taste of themselves. Iris and Oliver's techniques, practices and beliefs are unified to create a pristine environment in which everything – animal, vegetable, mineral – can thrive, can achieve its best. This is agriculture understood and practiced as an artistic calling, and it gladdens the heart to see it in action.

● **OPEN:** Manch produce is sold at the farm and at the Tuesday market in Macroom. The yogurt is available in good shops.

MACROOM

MACROOM OATMEAL ●
Donal Creedon
Walton's Mills, Macroom
Tel: (026) 41800

When you taste Donal Creedon's Macroom Oatmeal for the first time, the taste revelation is so profound that you have to ask: "If this is porridge, what is everyone else doing?!"

The answer, of course, is that commercial porridge production knocks much of the goodness out of the oats, where Mr Creedon is concerned only to capture and preserve it. It is so oaty, so toasty, so comfortingly perfect, that it stands as one of the great Irish foods. For breakfast, with oodles of cream and a splash of soft brown sugar, it is perfection itself.

● **OPEN:** Widely distributed around County Cork, and is available by post.

MALLOW

BLACKWATER VALLEY WINE ●
Billy Christopher
Mallow
Tel: (022) 21790

Billy Christopher makes a tiny production of white wine each year a good, dry white wine, which has a subtle suggestion of aniseed wrapped up in the clean, controlled crispness of its bouquet. It is sold in country houses and restaurants

● **OPEN:** Sold in restaurants locally.

the fabulous country houses of North Cork

Hazel Bourke and William O'Callaghan have a lot in common. Both are the second generation of their respective families to man the kitchens in their country houses, William succeeding his father Michael in Longueville, Hazel marrying young Joe Bourke and succeeding him in Assolas.

They work only a few miles apart, for Assolas is sited near to Kanturk, while Longueville is close to Mallow, in this quiet expanse of north Cork.

Both are young, and both are not only tenaciously talented, but are remarkable in being cooks who already have a mature style. This is the great gift they share: their tender years have not prevented them from discovering and refining styles of cooking which are truly signed with their own culinary signatures.

But, when it comes to analysing, and enjoying, these styles, that is where their common ground comes to an end. For they are so different in style as to make you believe they come from different planets. Their diverseness is a great thrill and joy and there are few greater pleasures in Irish food than to eat Mrs Bourke's food one evening, and Mr O'Callaghan's the next.

William O'Callaghan's style is meticulous, highly-wrought, and utterly intense. He works on a plate with the abandoned eagerness of a sculptor tearing the content from a piece of granite. His métier

is to rewrite the rule book. His cooking is indubitably impressive and confident.

Hazel Bourke likes simplicity in her food, so much so that her lack of convolution can seem almost more daring than Mr O'Callaghan's convolutions. The total lack of contrivance, the absence of any cheffy vanity, is breathtaking.

Mrs Bourke and Mr O'Callaghan are congratulated in their expertise by the expertise of their spouses at front of house. Joe Bourke and Aisling O'Callaghan are every bit as brilliant at their jobs as their partners, and this makes Assolas and Longueville truly accomplished.

ASSOLAS COUNTRY HOUSE Ⓐ
Joe & Hazel Bourke
Kanturk
Tel: (029) 50015, Fax: (029) 0795
● **OPEN:** 7pm-8.30pm.
(Non-residents booking essential).
● **AVERAGE PRICE:** Dinner over £30.
B&B over £60. Visa, Access/Master, Amex.
Signposted from the N 72.

LONGUEVILLE HOUSE Ⓐ Ⓡ
William & Aisling O'Callaghan
Mallow
Tel: (022) 47156, Fax: (022) 47459
● **OPEN:** To non residents for dinner, if pre-booked.
● **AVERAGE PRICE:** Dinner over £30.
B&B over £60.
Visa, Access/Master, Amex, Diners.
Signposted from the N 72.

SOUTH & WEST CORK

AHAKISTA

SHIRO JAPANESE DINNER HOUSE ®
Kei & Werner Pilz
Ahakista
Tel: (027) 67030

The mystical, magical Shiro has doubled in size, which is to say it now has four tables instead of two, with three of the tables in an elegant new room at the front of the house.

The menu revolves around constant themes, with an appetiser of various Japanese foods to begin – marinated tofu, pickled seaweed – followed by suimono, a clear soup, and then one chooses from an assortment of dishes, many of them vegetarian: a vegetarian tempura includes shiitake, bamboo sprouts and other vegetables dipped in Tenzuyu sauce, or vegetarian sukiyaki which includes vegetables with mock abalone and mock duck meat with Yum balls.

Kei does the cooking, Werner does front of house, and whilst the increase in size means the Shiro has become more like a standard restaurant, there is nowhere like it.

● **OPEN:** 7pm-9pm Mon-Sun.
● **AVERAGE PRICE:** Dinner over £30.
Visa, Access/Master, Amex, Diners.
(Credit card incurs a charge of 5%).
In the centre of Ahakista.

BANTRY

ESSENTIAL FOODS ⑤
Alan Dare
Main Street, Bantry
Tel: (027) 61171 (home)

Alan's is an invaluable shop, with organic vegetables for sale (Monday is delivery day), rare cheeses such as the local Ballingeary, Baby Organix and Hipp foods for the baby, and a great range of pulses, grains and staples alongside common-sense advice regarding herbal remedies.

● **OPEN:** 10.30am-5pm.
(Closed lunch 1pm-2pm) Mon-Sat.

5A CAFÉ ®
Cookie Susukie
Barrack Street
Bantry

A perennially popular little daytime place just off the main Bantry-Glengariff road, with flavoursome vegetarian food in the form of soulful soups, good bakes and breads, which can be bought to take away. The atmosphere is somewhere in between Beat meets Bohemia meets Bantry.

Quite an intoxicating mixture, when you think about it

● **OPEN:** 9.30am-5.30pm. Mon-Sat.

HAGAL HEALING FARM Ⓐ
Janny Wieler
Coomleigh, Bantry
Tel: (027) 66179

Fred and Janny Wieler practice the Reiki form of healing therapy at Hagal, and they can also offer B&B and vegetarian meals prepared with their own organic vegetables.

● **OPEN:** For details of courses and treatments, contact the farm.

GREEN LODGE Ⓐ
Chris Domegan
Trawnamadree
Ballylickey
Tel: (027) 66146

Individuals and families can stay at Green Lodge, where the rooms are in a single storey terrace in an enclosed courtyard. Organic vegetables are available, and the cooking is vegetarian. A well situated base for exploring the glories of the area.

● **OPEN:** All year.
● **AVERAGE PRICE:** Charged weekly.
8 Km from Bantry town going towards Glengarrif.

MANNING'S EMPORIUM Ⓢ
Val Manning
Ballylickey, nr Bantry
Tel: (027) 50456
For many people, Val Manning's Emporium is synonymous with the spirit that is West Cork.

Sociable, choice, creative, it is a shop where you can loiter for hours, chatting, discovering, selecting fine things such as Janet Drew relishes, Manch estate yogurt, Torc truffles, Yukon breads, all the great Irish farmhouse cheeses, and a choice array of good wines.

Mr Manning runs a fine shop, organises a great big food fair every year in June which celebrates the achievements of his suppliers – the cheesemakers, the growers, the wine importers – and Manning's is an integral part of the artisan food culture of the area.

● **OPEN:** 9am-9pm Mon-Sun.
Shorter hours in the winter, longer hours in the summer.
On the main N71 road.

RIVER LODGE Ⓐ
Gudrun Bernard
Pearson's Bridge
Ballylickey
Tel: (027) 66148

A handsome stone house, a few miles off the road from Ballylickey bridge, which operates principally as a B&B for vegetarians, with produce for meals coming direct from their own organic garden. Breakfasts, of course, are the speciality, with soft summer fruits a special treat in summer.

● **OPEN:**
Mar-Oct.
● **AVERAGE PRICE:**
B&B under £20.
No Credit Cards.

ANNIE'S ®
Annie Barry
Main Street, Ballydehob
Tel: (028) 37292

Annie's is a simple village restaurant, just a single room, and Dano's cooking complements this space, for everything is simply flavourful.

But Annie's is about an awful lot more than the food. There is a splendid ritual to the business of dinner here, with a drink or two in Levis's pub across the street, where you scan the menus before Annie comes to firstly take the order, and secondly to fetch you, and then there is the joy of the charming little room, the splendid service, the pop of wine corks, the mighty crack...

● **OPEN:** 6.30pm-10pm Tue-Sat.
Limited hours off-season.
● **AVERAGE PRICE:** Dinner over £20.
Visa, Access/Master.
Centre of Ballydehob. Annie also runs the café in the bookshop up the street.

HUDSON'S WHOLEFOODS ⑤
Gillian Hudson
Main Street, Ballydehob
Tel: (028) 37211

Gill Hudson is loved by her suppliers, and it's no wonder, for this is not a seasonal shop, taking advantage of the excellent West Cork foods in season to sell to bundles of tourists.

Ms Hudson is here all year long, selling the West Cork cheeses, the seaweeds, the necessary foods, and the best range of organic vegetables in the area. Her dedication energises Hudson's, and makes it a vital part of the local food culture.

● **OPEN:** 10am-6pm Mon-Sat, lunch 1-2pm.

ALLIHIES GLOBE ARTICHOKE CO-OPERATIVE ⑤
Tony Lowes
Reentrisk, Allihies
Tel: (027) 73025

Way down at the end of the country, Tony Lowes farms artichokes in an idyllic setting. Why artichokes? One suspects Mr Lowes likes a challenge. To farm artichokes on the wildness of the Beara is just about as unlikely a practice as one could imagine.

So, so much the better then that Mr Lowes has made a success of it, busily posting the crowns of the artichokes all over the country, eagerly proselytising on behalf of these wonderful vegetables, steadfastly becoming the celebrated face of the artichoke on television and elsewhere.

● **OPEN:** Follow the signs on the right hand side as you go from Allihies to Eyeries.

MILLEENS ⑤
Veronica & Norman Steele
Eyeries, Tel: (027) 74079

The very first of the Irish farmhouse cheeses is still the best known, thanks jointly to its distinctive, unassailable appeal, and to the tireless efforts of Veronica Steele to proudly trumpet the uniqueness of her cheese.

If Milleens was the first, it has also had a major importance in being the cheese that led the way. For what Mrs Steele did was to adopt a foreign template, a foreign style, but to then adapt that style, subtly, sensibly, organically, changing the influence to suit the milk of the herd, creating a cheese which spoke less of its influence and more of its place.

The result was one of the great Irish cheeses, and an artisan practice which was an example to the many others who have made cheeses on small farms since Milleens first appeared. Milleens began the revolution in Irish farmhouse cheeses.

● **OPEN:** The cheese is widely distributed.

B U T L E R S T O W N

DUNWORLEY COTTAGE RESTAURANT ®
Katherine Norén
Dunworley, Butlerstown
Tel: (023) 40314

Dealing in great tastes is the keynote of Katherine Norén's Dunworley Cottage Restaurant.

There have been many occasions when we have eaten in this modest, simple set of rooms, and been mesmerised by a tumult of flavours which no one else could even consider capturing, flavours no one

else seems to have access to.

As a restaurateur, Katherine Norén deals with the sublime. Her famous nettle soup is justly famous, but there are lots of choices here which show the pristine, pure flavours she can capture. If you have a glass of freezing cold aquavit to accompany the food, you will enjoy one of the greatest alliances of flavours in the food world.

● **OPEN:** Lunch 1pm-3pm, dinner from 6.30pm Wed-Sun.
Very limited hours off season, ring to check. Open for Xmas.
● **AVERAGE PRICE:** Lunch under £10. Dinner over £20.
Visa, Access/Master, Amex, Diners.
The restaurant is well signposted as you drive from Timoleague and from Clonakilty.

C A R R I G A L I N E

GREGORY'S ®
Greg Dawson
Main Street
Tel: (021) 371512

As one might expect of a chef with a Ballymaloe school background, Greg Dawson handles the essential staples of restaurant food with confident aplomb – excellent breads, a selection of local cheeses, fine coffee, well-judged classics – and his quiet confidence makes this elegant room a fine choice.

● **OPEN:** 12.30pm-2.30pm, 6.30pm-10pm Tue-Sat, 12.30pm-2.30pm Sun.
● **AVERAGE PRICE:** Lunch under £15. Dinner under £20.
Visa, Access/Master. Town centre.

CARRIGALINE COUNTRY MARKET ⓢ
The GAA Hall
Crosshaven Road
Tel: (021) 831340

Carrigaline enjoys one of the very greatest country markets. Calm, perfectly organised, the market has a true sense of by the community for the community and for the enjoyment of the community, and shopping here is a true pleasure

● **OPEN:** 9.30am-10.30am Fri.

JOE KARWIG WINES ⓕ
Joe & Betty Karwig
Kilnagleary
Carrigaline
Tel: (021) 372864

Joe Karwig stocks an excellent range of wines, and you can buy them direct from his warehouse. He has a penchant for wines which are florid and distinctively mineral, particularly his Italian and German wines, but everything – from quaffers to quality bottles – is choice, and well chosen.

● **OPEN:** Telephone to place an order.

CARRIGALINE FARMHOUSE CHEESE ⓖ
Pat O'Farrell
Marello, Leacht Cross,
Carrigaline
Tel: (021) 372856

Pat O'Farrell makes lovely, sinuous, subtle cheeses, using raw milk from his own Friesian herd.

The plain Carrigaline is partnered by a cheese flavoured with garlic and herbs, and they are both fine examples of the sheer goodness of West Cork milk and careful, patient cheesemaking.

Generally sold when rather young, they offer flavours which kids are especially comfortable with, but a little maturity adds some spice to the flavour, which is as soft and tender as Pat's own wonderfully whispery accent.

● **OPEN:** Widely distributed around Cork.

SEAN NA MBADS ⓡ ⓟ
Fiona McDonald
Ringabella
Carrigaline
Tel: (021) 887397

"This is a premises in which great care has been taken to preserve what is real", a writer who recently visited Sean na Mbads wrote afterwards, and indeed it is a handsomely restored bar and restaurant.

This care is evident also in the food, which is fun and great for hearty appetites established whilst trying to find the place, so telephone for directions.

● **OPEN:**
7pm-10.30pm Thur-Sun.
● **AVERAGE PRICE:**
Dinner under £20.
Visa, Access/Master.
Telephone for directions.

CLONAKILTY

FIONNUALA'S ®
Fionnuala
30 Ashe Street, Clonakilty
Tel: (023) 34355

The dining room of Fionnuala's, with its appropriately well-worn feel and its array of personal memorabilia, looks rather like the stage set of some amateur dramatic production, but there is nothing stagy about the friendliness and good heart of the cooking.

Fionnuala cleverly describes her raggle-taggle collection of tables, chairs, and candle-wax encrusted Chianti and Amarone bottles as a "Little Italian Restaurant", clever because this spells her culinary strengths. Pizzas and pastas are generous with spicy flavours, food that is comforting at lunchtime, and fun for the evening, with some thumping Italian wine.

● **OPEN:** 12.30pm-2.15pm, 6pm-9.30pm
Tue-Sun. Limited hours in winter.
● **AVERAGE PRICE:** Lunch under £10.
Dinner under £20.
Visa, Access/Master. Town centre.

O'DONOVAN'S HOTEL Ⓐ
Tom O'Donovan
44 Pearse Street
Clonakilty
Tel: (023) 33250/33883

The industrious O'Donovans run this hotel with vigour and enthusiasm. The bar, with its Guinness surfer roof mural, its old bottles and glasses, is a maze of family paraphernalia. There's a marvellous old polython in the café, and the corridors are lorded over by the five generations who have run the hotel since it opened.

● **OPEN:** Pub hours, with restaurant open all day and throughout the evening.
● **AVERAGE PRICE:**
Meals under £10.
B&B under £20.
Visa, Access/Master.
Clonakilty town centre.

COURTMACSHERRY

TRAVARA LODGE Ⓐ ®
Mandy Guy
Courtmacsherry
Tel: (023) 46493

Travara Lodge sits looking out on the sea in the beautiful, pastel-painted village of Courtmacsherry, and Mandy Guy works hard to make a success of both the little restaurant downstairs and the rooms upstairs. On Mondays vegetarian food is made a speciality in the restaurant, though vegetarians will find they are looked after throughout the week.

The rooms have pummelling showers and comfortable beds and those at the front of the house have super views across the calm inlet.

● **OPEN:** 7pm-9.30pm Mon-Sat
('till 9pm low season).
Closed Nov-Apr.
● **AVERAGE PRICE:** Dinner under £20.
B&B under £25.
Visa, Access/Master.
Just on the waterfront in Courtmacsherry.

DURRUS

DURRUS FARMHOUSE CHEESE ● ✪
Jeffa Gill
Coomkeen
Durrus
Tel: (027) 61100

Allowed to develop to its aristocratic maturity, Durrus is one of the best cheeses you can find in Ireland, and of all the West Cork cheeses, it is the one which most speaks of the area, reveals the flora and the rugged elemental nature of the place.

It has the precisely defined spice and nutmeg we find in a good tomme, and allies this controlled note with the full, milky bloom and effulgence that can only come from a semi-soft, raw milk cheese.

Its fullness is never overblown, for maturity gifts it only with more grace, with the tastes slowly assimilating to become more distinct, more poised. But there is also a vivacious lushness to be found and enjoyed in Durrus, a duality between politeness and lustiness that makes it seem as if it has been created by pure instinct.

● **OPEN:** The cheese is widely distributed, and sold from the farm. To find the farm take the Kilcrohane road out of Durrus, turn right after St James' Church and carry on up the hill for about 2 miles – it will seem longer – until you see the sign. Always telephone first to make sure someone is there to receive you.

GOLEEN

THE EWE ● Ⓐ
Sheena Wood & Kurt Lyndorf
Goleen
Tel: (028) 35492

The Ewe is an arts and crafts retreat which offers classes for both adults and children. Students can stay in the vegetarian B&B, or take self catering accommodation.

● **OPEN:** All year.
● **AVERAGE PRICE:** B&B under £20. Self-catering charged per week.

HERON'S COVE RESTAURANT Ⓡ
Sue Hill
Goleen Harbour, Goleen
Tel: (028) 35225

Heron's Cove has the most gorgeous location – right at the end of the country, overlooking the sea, it is truly a place apart.

The cooking has always been simple: pasta provençale; chilli beans with wild rice; vegetable stirfry, but if it is simple it is good hearted. Wines are selected from a collection which is on open display and there are also rooms.

● **OPEN:** Flexible opening times based around lunch between noon and 3pm. Dinner 6.30pm-9.45pm. Morning coffee and afternoon tea available. Reservations only during winter months.
● **AVERAGE PRICE:** Lunch under £10. Dinner under £20. B&B under £25. Visa, Access/Master, Amex, Diners. Signposted from Goleen.

KINSALE

THE BLUE HAVEN ⓟⒶⓈⓇ
Brian Cronin
Pearse Street
Kinsale
Tel: (021) 772209

Many people's favourite little hotel, the Blue Haven offers bar food, a wine shop, and a formal restaurant.

● **OPEN:** 12.30pm-11.30pm Mon-Sun.
● **AVERAGE PRICE:** Lunch under £10.
Dinner under £20.
Visa, Access/Master, Amex, Diners.

CHEZ JEAN MARC Ⓡ
Jean-Marc Tsai
Lr O'Connell Street
Kinsale
Tel: (021) 774625

Jean-Marc Tsai's restaurant has many admirers, and now includes an upstairs bistro – Time Out – with simpler food than that downstairs.

● **OPEN:** 7pm-10pm Mon-Sun.
Closed Mon off season.
● **AVERAGE PRICE:** Dinner under £20.
Visa, Access/Master, Diners.

THE OLD BANK HOUSE Ⓐ
Michael & Marie Reise
Pearse Street, Kinsale
Tel: (021) 772968/774075

Fine guesthouse with good cooking.

● **OPEN:** All year except Xmas.
● **AVERAGE PRICE:** B&B over £40.
Ask about evening meals.
Visa, Access/Master, Amex.

OYSTERHAVEN

THE OYSTERCATCHER Ⓡ RESTAURANT
Sylvia & Bill Patterson
Oysterhaven
Tel: (021) 770822

They may describe Kinsale as the culinary capital of Ireland, but it is the man outside the town, Bill Patterson, who is the boss when it comes to cooking. No one in the town can hold a candle to this brilliant, tumultuously inventive cook, and his cooking is amongst the very finest found in Ireland.

He is fortunate in having one of the sweetest little restaurants to work in, but if Bill and Sylvia cooked in a Nissen hut, you would still walk a country mile for his food.

His dinners are a pure bedazzlement, so much so that simply calling the names of the dishes cannot do justice to this brilliant cook: tortellini with fresh tomatoes and basil; Inagh goat's cheese salad; brioche filled with wild mushrooms on a port sauce. As the restaurant is small, a little notice can allow Bill time to pull something special out of the hat for vegetarians. Desserts are amazing, the wine list is excellent, and the Oystercatcher is one of the most unforgettable restaurants in Ireland.

● **OPEN:** 7pm-9.15pm Mon-Sun, May-Sept.
Private parties Nov-Apr, 24 hours notice.
● **AVERAGE PRICE:** Lunch under £20.
Dinner over £20. Visa, Access/Master.
Take signs for Oysterhaven.

SCHULL THE FOOD CAPITAL

The villages of the Mizen Head in West Cork have soft, reflexive names. There is the lovely elongation that is Ballydehob, the promise of good times that is Barleycove, the gentle Goleen, the smooth sound of Toormore.

And then there is the unambiguous, crunching certainty that is Schull. Skull, a bone-rattle sound, slightly threatening, disturbing and, amusingly, ironic. For with its dappled pastel colours, its snaky Main Street climbing between shops, houses and pubs, all these elements create one of the most enchanting villages to be found in Ireland.

What makes Schull different is the resonant fact that it produces, sells and serves some of the finest food to be found anywhere in Ireland. If any single place deserves to be called the food capital of Ireland, Schull is that capital.

Never mind that it is marked to the south by the famous Fastnet and to the north by Mount Gabriel. More significant, for the life and soul and stomach of the place, is the fact that it has two extraordinary cheesemakers at polar ends of the village. East of the village, Bill Hogan makes a trio of cheeses – Gabriel, Desmond and Mizen – cheeses which, in their ability to adapt and refine ideas and tastes are perfect exemplars of the modern movement in Irish cheesemaking.

At the other end of the town, on the road west down to Goleen, Giana Ferguson performs the same alchemy in order to make Gubbeen Farmhouse Cheese. The style, this time, is borrowed from the French Pont L'Evêque, and the cheese is creamy, smooth, with a dusty-pink natural rind. Mrs Ferguson also makes a smoked Gubbeen, full of lingering long flavours that intersperse with the cheese's fulsome creaminess.

But what is most impressive about these cheesemakers is not just the superb foods they make – eat some Gubbeen with a glass of good claret and you will likely not know when to stop; some Gabriel with a glass of good gewurzträminer is one of the most intoxicating combinations you can find – it is the comfort with which foreign styles and influences are adopted and then adapted by these people.

And this is something you find repeated throughout Schull. On Main Street in Adele Connor's brilliant bakery, café and restaurant, this catholicism of tastes lends itself smack bang with the Catholic talent for having a good time. Ms Connor's baking runs riot through buttery, crumbling croissants, petite sourdough loaves, carrot cakes that are altogether venal, hangover assuaging meat pasties, a lemon cake that is nowhere short of perfection. In the evening, when Simon Connor cooks, the embrace of this marvellous organisation comes full circle, his cooking confident, full of flavour and aplomb.

The welcoming and informal character of Adele's, its ageless energy and holiday-spirit bonhomie, suits this culinary internationalism, just as the sagacious characters of Denis and Finola Quinlan are the real secret of what makes The Courtyard, their pub-cum-shop-cum-restaurant-cum-tearooms so special.

The Courtyard is a true cornucopia of fine foods, and not just on the shelves of the shop, with their clutch and clutter of consumable delights, or in the cheese counter with its posse of handmade cheeses, or the breadbasket with its splash of still-warm, sweet-smelling loaves baked out back by Jackie Bennett.

All of this would be enough, but there are also the splendid ploughman's lunches, to be eaten outside in the courtyard itself if the weather is fine, with a pint of Beamish and your companion saying, happily, "It's always an excitement to go to Schull".

There might be a danger, elsewhere, that this culinary and cultural miscegenation would lead to a bland internationalism, but in Schull the rigorous sense of humour which the locals sport, the steady sang-froid of an agricultural community, tends to leaven and level-head everything.

What all these places and these people have in common is a vision that Schull is somewhere that can offer the enjoyment of the best of things, the best of times, in the best of places.

ADELE'S ®
Adele & Simon Connor
Main Street, Schull
Tel: (028) 28459

● **OPEN:** 9.30am-10.30pm Mon-Sun. (Check off season, closed Nov-Apr, open 3 weeks Xmas).
● **AVERAGE PRICE:**
CAFÉ – under £10.
RESTAURANT – under £20, B&B under £20.
No cards.

THE COURTYARD ⑤ ℗
Denis & Finola Quinlan
Main Street, Schull
Tel: (028) 28390

● **OPEN:** Shop open 9.30am-6pm, bar food available 10am-7pm Mon-Sat. (Food available until 4.45pm off season).

GUBBEEN ℉
Giana & Tom Ferguson
Gubbeen House, Schull
Tel: (028) 28231

● **OPEN:** Gubbeen and Smoked Gubbeen are widely distributed.

WEST CORK NATURAL CHEESE ℉ ✪
Bill Hogan & Sean Ferry
Ardmanagh, Schull
Tel: (028) 28593

● **OPEN:** Available in good shops throughout the country.

SKIBBEREEN

FIELD'S ●
John Field
26 Main Street, Skibbereen
Tel: (028) 21400

Field's is one of the finest supermarkets in Ireland and, square foot for square foot, it may be the very best. It allies cost keenness with an array of local foods from local folk, and with the breads and cakes of its own bakery, to put together a smashing shop.

If it is good, and it is produced in the locality, then it will inevitably, make its way to John Field's shop, simple as that.

● **OPEN:** 9am-6.30pm Mon-Sat (7pm Fri).

GABRIEL COTTAGE ●
Suzanne Dark & Dominic Lee
Smorane, Skibbereen
Tel: (028) 22521

A cutesy-pie little house, from where Suzanne and Dominic organise cycling holidays, and cook delicious vegetarian meals in the evening.

● **OPEN:** Call for a brochure. Signed on the N71 about 1 mile east of Skibbereen.

LISS ARD LAKE LODGE ● ● ●
Claudia Meister
Skibbereen
Tel: (028) 22365

The problem for many vegetarian cooks lies in the fact that their cooking often seeks to imitate, and compensate, for meat. This is a tired way of cooking and if you need proof that there is a better way, then just eat Claudia Meister's regular Saturday night vegetarian feasts.

She has evolved a style which is not merely culinarily confident, but intellectually confident. Dishes are concocted and flavours are revealed without any regard to meat whatsoever, a liberating leap which allows her food to become awesomely pure.

So, the feast might begin with parcels of Turk Head endive with a plum and ginger dip, before a ravishing bowl of miso and hijiki, and then a merry bowl of buckwheat noodles with roasted mushrooms.

A crystal-clear rosemary sorbet is followed by a delightful roulade of sun-warmed vegetables, strips of aubergine and pepper wrapped with pesto, and some couscous stuffing a courgette flower. Desserts are peachy prosecco sabayon with peach ice cream or perhaps brandy snap baskets with soft summer fruits.

This is dazzling, thrilling, soul-satisfying food which, in its intellectual rigour and accuracy of accomplishment, its minimal use of animal fats and dairy products, should set the template for Irish vegetarian cookery in the future.

● **OPEN:** 7pm-10pm Mon-Sun.
(Booking essential).
● **AVERAGE PRICE:**
Dinner over £20.
B&B over £50.
Visa, Access/Master, Amex, Diners.
Signposted on the Skibbereen/Traguma Road.

WEST CORK HERB FARM ● ➡

Rosarie O'Byrne
Church Cross, Skibbereen
Tel: (028) 22299

Rosarie O'Byrne's flavoured oils, vinegars and marinades reveal brilliantly pure flavours that are an essential component of the kitchen.

If that was all they made at the herb farm, it would be enough to ensure their fame. But get a taste of their terrific tarragon and green peppercorn mustard, or of the smashing concoction which is Clara's pesto sauce, and you realise that their confidence extends to every single thing they make.

● **OPEN:** 10am-6.30pm Mon-Sat, 12.30pm-6.30pm Sun. Winter noon-5.30pm. Signposted on the N71 road.

TIMOLEAGUE

DILLON'S ●

Isabelle Dillon
Timoleague
Tel: (023) 46390

Isabelle Dillon runs a pub in the continental style, with an easy atmosphere, big windows to let in the light, comfortable chairs in which to scan the groovy magazines.

The pub food is good, the menu including vegetable soup; pancakes stuffed with mushrooms and cheese and offered in a Port sauce; Greek salad with Feta Cheese, and pizzas.

● **OPEN:** Food served noon-9.30pm Mon-Sun. (Closed 2pm-4pm Sun.)
● **AVERAGE PRICE:** Meals under £10.

LETTERCOLLUM HOUSE ● ● ●

Con McLoughlin & Karen Austin
Timoleague
Tel: (023) 46251

Not only have they always made a great feature of vegetarian cookery at Lettercollum, they actually run vegetarian cookery classes in the autumn and winter, allowing one to attempt to replicate the true deliciousness which Con and Karen's cooking achieves.

Having a great deal of produce from their own organic walled garden helps, of course, but it is the sensitivity and the perceptiveness with which ingredients are treated here that makes their food special.

This means that they can take old favourites such as nut roast and make them truly delicious, truly modern, whilst also being able to deal a full hand of Cal-Ital specialities: stirfry vegetables and a ginger and coconut sauce will accompany corn, hazel-nut and rice croquettes; a red pepper sauce will team up with baked, stuffed aubergine; cannelloni will be stuffed with Gabriel cheese and spinach.

If you are five or fifty, rich or poor, frail or sound in limb and wind, Lettercollum promises delight for all. Rooms are simple, and they can play host to small conferences.

● **OPEN:** 7.30pm-9.30pm Tue-Sun, 1.30pm-3.30pm Sun. (Check times out of season).
● **AVERAGE PRICE:** Lunch over £10. Dinner under £20.
Visa, Access/Master, Diners.
Just outside Timoleague, and signposted.

COUNTY KERRY

THE KERRY PENINSULAS

CASTLEMAINE

PHOENIX CAFÉ & HOSTEL Ⓐ Ⓡ
Lorna & Billy Tycher
Shanahill East
Castlemaine
Tel: (066) 66284

A family-run hostel and café with interesting wholefood and orientally influenced cooking. The inspiration for much of the food comes simply from Lorna coping with whatever the sunshine has ripened. She contributed some imaginative recipes to Patrick Cotter's book "Irish Vegetarian Cookery" (Killeen 1996) including "Kofta baked in lemon, coconut and ginger sauce" and a fine chilled apricot crumble.

● **OPEN:** 9am-midnight Easter-Oct (booking only in winter).
● **AVERAGE PRICE:** B&B under £15, Lunch under £5.
Dinner under £10.
Three miles from Castlemaine and six miles from Inch.

DINGLE

BEGINISH RESTAURANT Ⓡ Ⓐ
John & Pat Moore
Green Street
Dingle
Tel: (066) 51588

There is a real sense of a hunger for progress and for perfection in Pat Moore's work, and these qualities have meant that the Beginish retains an energy and vitalism often lacking in other restaurants in Dingle. Vegetarian choices are limited, but Mrs Moore's keen work means that attention to detail in simple things like a vegetarian pot-pouri will always be paramount.

Do also note, there are some attractive, well appointed self-catering apartments just beside the restaurant available for weekly letting.

● **OPEN:** 12.30pm-2.15pm, 6pm-10pm Tue-Sun.
Closed mid Nov-mid Mar.
● **AVERAGE PRICE:**
Lunch under £15.
Dinner under £20.
Visa, Access/Master, Diners.
Near the Church.

DICK MACK'S ℗
Green Street
Dingle, Tel: (066) 51960

This is a beautiful bar of the classic mould, with high counters, and an assortment of leather goods.

● **OPEN:** Pub opening hours.

AN GRIANAN Ⓢ
Elaine Avery
Dykegate Street, Tel: (066) 51910

A great array of wholefoods and speciality items can be found here, but the shop is especially valuable for excellent breads. There are also fine cakes and bakes, and organic vegetables for sale.

● **OPEN:** 10am-6pm Mon-Sat.

THE OLD STONE HOUSE Ⓐ
Michael & Becky O'Connor
Cliddaun, Dingle
Tel: (066) 59882

A charming cottage, a few miles west of Dingle, and that short distance graces the house with a calmness that eludes the town. Michael and Becky know just about everything about the peninsula, so those who wish to explore the area in detail should first pick their brains and plunder their library.

● **OPEN:** All year, including Xmas.
Dinner for guests.
● **AVERAGE PRICE:** B&B under £20.
Visa, Access/Master.
Just outside Dingle on the Ventry road.

THE RIVER GOD Ⓡ
Patric Juillet
The Roundabout, Dingle
Tel: c/o the fish shop (066) 51825

A funky, snappy place, the River God offers a modern menu and aims to have you in and out quickly, and for under a tenner – both food and wine are keenly priced. Patric Juillet comes from France and owned a restaurant in Australia – and this mix of Med meets Pacific suits the style of Dingle well.

● **OPEN:** Noon-9pm Mon-Sun.
(Closed Wed).
● **AVERAGE PRICE:** Meals under £10.
No credit cards.

THE WOOD Ⓡ
Noreen Fanning
Dingle, Tel: (066) 51465

Close to the town and full of atmosphere, this vegetarian restaurant has been in business since 1992, preparing all the food on the premises, including good Vegan cooking. You can also bring your own wine.

● **OPEN:** 6pm-10pm Jun-Sep.
● **AVERAGE PRICE:** Dinner under £15.

THE WATERSIDE Ⓡ
Dingle, Tel: (066) 51458

Seasonal restaurant which can produce some exciting food.

● **OPEN:** Lunch and dinner in season.
● **AVERAGE PRICE:** Lunch under £15.
Dinner under £20. Visa, Access/Master.
Near the seafront.

LIOS DÁNA ®Ⓐ❶

Anne Hyland
Inch
Annascaul
Tel: (066) 58189

Lios Dána is an holistic centre which specialises in natural health and creative activities. Good wholefood cookery and some relaxation therapy in this most beautiful part of the peninsula sounds just like the sort of thing you need. Ring for details of their introductory bank holiday weekends and for the various courses.

● **OPEN:** Lunch & Dinner Mar-Oct
● **AVERAGE PRICE:** Lunch under £10.
Dinner under £15.
B&B under £15.

RING OF KERRY

CAPPAROE GOAT'S CHEESE ❶

The Hensel Family
Greenane, Blackwater

The fashion for immersing cheeses in olive oil has spread like a bushfire in Ireland in recent years, so it is worth remembering that the Hensel family's goat's cheeses in olive oil were amongst the first to appear.

The cheese manages to be both lush and yet austere, partly because they use olive oil in the jars. It remains a local curiosity, and one worth hunting down.

● **OPEN:** You can often buy the cheese in The Pantry in Kenmare.

THE OLD SCHOOLHOUSE ®

Ann O'Kane
Knockeens
Cahirciveen
Tel: (0667) 2426

Simple cooking and a warm welcome are the principal ingredients of Ann O'Kane's restaurant. Indeed, her willingness to accommodate the wishes of vegetarians, of groups, of families, of anyone who wants something done slightly different, explains the success of the Schoolhouse.

● **OPEN:** 11am-9pm Mon-Sun.
Closed Nov-Mar.
● **AVERAGE PRICE:**
Lunch under £10.
Dinner under £20.
Visa, Access/Master, Diners.
On the Ring of Kerry.

KENMARE

AN LEITH PHINGIN ®

Con Guerin
35 Main Street
Kenmare
Tel: (064) 41559

Con Guerin's restaurant has been working happily for over a decade now, specialising in northern Italian cooking – ravioli filled with aubergine and courgette, or ravioli filled with ricotta and parmesan served with a sauce of rosemary scented potato purée; bruschetta with Mileens cheese, tomatoes and basil oil.

The wine list has interesting

Italian wines alongside France and the New World.

● **OPEN:** Lunch and dinner during the season. (Dinner only off season).
● **AVERAGE PRICE:** Meals under £15.
Visa, Access/Master.
Kenmare town centre.

THE LIME TREE ®
Tony & Alex Daly
Shelbourne Street, Kenmare
Tel: (064) 41225

Tony and Alex Daly's restaurant occupies one of the most handsome buildings in Kenmare, and inside it is equally splendid, with gallery space upstairs and a buzzy atmosphere.

Michael Casey cooks, and the menu is very democratic: potato and cabbage soup, penne with black olives, goat's cheese potato cake.

● **OPEN:** 6.30pm-9.30pm Mon-Sun.
Weekends only off season.
● **AVERAGE PRICE:** Dinner under £25.
Visa, Access/Master. Beside the Park hotel.

D'ARCY'S ®
Matthew d'Arcy
Main Street, Kenmare
Tel & Fax: (064) 41589

Since moving to Main Street Matt d'Arcy's cooking has just got better and better. He has always been a great technician, but now his food has a drop-dead gorgeousness which is invigorating. And as Mr d'Arcy has developed into a more confident cook, his staff have grown in confidence also

If you have the opportunity, vegetarians should consider giving a little notice, as this allows the kitchen time to do something special.

● **OPEN:** 6pm-11pm Mon-Sun.
(Closed Sun off season).
● **AVERAGE PRICE:** Dinner under £25.
Visa, Access/Master.
At the top end of Main Street.

THE PANTRY ®
30 Henry Street
Kenmare
Tel: (064) 41320

A fine wholefood shop, where you can buy locally grown organic vegetables, local cheese and many other interesting things which separate it from the run-of-the-mill wholefood store.

● **OPEN:** 10am-5pm Mon-Sat.

PACKIE'S ®
Maura Foley
Henry Street, Kenmare
Tel: (064) 41508

Maura Foley is one of the finest cooks in Ireland. For thirty years she has cooked wonderful food with the skill and love of the patient, modest woman she is.

Her devotion to her standards, has made her the grand-mère of Irish cooking. She has defined a style which is without artifice – potato gnocchi with tomato and basil; tagliatelle with chanterelles and cream; potato cakes with garlic butter. The dignity in her work and her cooking conjoin to make Packie's one of the best restaurants in Ireland.

● **OPEN:** 5.30pm-10pm Mon-Sat.
Closed end Dec-end Feb.
● **AVERAGE PRICE:** Dinner under £20.
Visa, Access/Master.
In the centre of Kenmare.

THE PARK HOTEL Ⓐ Ⓡ
Francis Brennan
Kenmare
Tel: (064) 41200

If they wished to crown a king in the kingdom of Kerry, they could only choose one man. Francis Brennan, the hotelier's hotelier. No one does it better in Ireland, and we would happily take bets that no one does it better anywhere. He is consummate, in a class of his own.

True, he has some of the finest staff imaginable working with him – Jim McCarthy and Tony Daly, to name but two, but The Park is, all told, all about Mr Brennan.

Bruno Schmidt directs the kitchen, and his cooking perfectly understands and answers the hotel's need for disciplined sumptuousness. The wine list is fabulous, service is immaculate, and The Park Hotel is an unforgettable experience.

● **OPEN:** 1pm-2pm, 7pm-8.45pm Mon-Sun. Closed mid Nov-Xmas.
(Open for Xmas period) early Jan-Easter.
● **AVERAGE PRICE:**
Lunch under £20.
Dinner over £30.
Visa, Access/Master, Diners, Amex.
At the top of the town.

PURPLE HEATHER BISTRO Ⓡ
The Foley family
Henry St, Kenmare
Tel: (064) 41016

The Foley family simply understand the business of making people happy, making them feel comfortable, knowing how to show them a good time. In The Purple Heather, they bring all their skills to bear in a cosy, friendly bar, where cosy, friendly, simple food usually proves to be just exactly what you feel like eating.

There are good soups, good breads, good sandwiches, good omelettes, good drinks. Everything is good, and it's been like this for over twenty years.

● **OPEN:** Noon-6.30pm Mon-Sat.
● **AVERAGE PRICE:** Lunch under £10.
Visa, Access/Master. Centre of town.

KILLARNEY

GABY'S RESTAURANT Ⓡ
Geert & Marie Maes
17 High Street, Killarney
Tel: (064) 32519

Geert Maes has spent two decades making locals and holidaymakers happy in Killarney. The move to new premises a few years back has allowed them slightly more space, but the formula of good food and service is unchanged. The wine list is excellent.

● **OPEN:** 12.30pm-2.30pm Tue-Sat, 6pm-10pm Mon-Sat. Closed mid Dec-mid Mar.
● **AVERAGE PRICE:** Lunch under £10.
Dinner under £20.
Visa, Access/Master, Amex, Diners.

THE STRAWBERRY TREE ⓡⓟ
Evan Doyle
24 Plunkett Street
Killarney
Tel: (064) 32688

Evan Doyle is a very astute and conscientious proprietor. Based in the absurdly touristic town of Killarney, he could simply cash in on the waves of folk who visit here during the year. But not only does he not conform to the norm, he decided a few years back to source all of his produce for The Strawberry Tree from organic and free-range suppliers.

Admirable and forward-thinking, of course, and happily he has the culinary skills to make it work.

Downstairs, on the street, there is Yer Man's Pub, with bar snacks to marry with that pint of Guinness.

● **OPEN:** 6.30pm-10pm Tue-Sat.
(Open Mon & Sun in Jul and Aug).
Always check off season.
● **AVERAGE PRICE:** Dinner under £25.
Visa, Access/Master, Amex, Diners.
Killarney town centre.

AN TAELANN ⓡ
Deirdre Donohue
7 Bridewell Lane
Tel: (064) 33083

An intimate little vegetarian restaurant tucked in a narrow lane is the setting for Deirdre Donohue's cooking. Her style is poly-cultural: courgette fritters with tzatziki, for example, or a tofu and ginger stir-fry. Nice breads and desserts are one of their specialities, and organic foods are used whenever possible.

● **OPEN:** 12.30pm-4pm, 6.30pm-10.30pm Tues-Sun.
● **AVERAGE PRICE:** Lunch under £5.
Dinner under £10.
Opposite Dunnes Stores.

LISTOWEL

ALLO'S BAR & BISTRO ⓡ
A Whyte & H Mullane
41 Church Street, Listowel
Tel: (068) 22880

Those marvellous restaurateurs, Helen Mullane and Armel Whyte, have recently been in charge of Allo's, transforming its cuisine and turning it into a roaring success.

As you would expect from this pair, the food is fun: deepfried spicy potato wedges, crostini of grilled goat's cheese with an Italian salad, vegetable stir-fry with rice pilaff

● **OPEN:** 10.30am-7pm Tue-Sat.
● **AVERAGE PRICE:** Lunch under £10,
Dinner under £15.
Visa, Access/Master.

TRALEE

BRATS ⓡ
Bríd Brosnan & Pat Galvin
18 Milk Market Lane

A decade in business is proof of the endurance and the success of the Brats formula of simple, accessible vegetarian cooking.

● **OPEN:** 12.30pm-3pm Mon-Sat.

KERRY FARMHOUSE CHEESE ⓕ
Sheila Broderick
Coolnaleen, Tralee
Tel: (068) 40245

Using the unpasteurised milk of
their own herd, Sheila makes the
fine territorial style Kerry cheese,
with four flavoured varieties.

● **OPEN:** Cheese is sold from the house,
or you can buy it in O'Connor's
delicatessen.

ROOTS RESTAURANT ⓡ
Ruth O'Quigley
76 Boherbue, Tralee
Tel: (066) 22665

A timeless little vegetarian restaurant, where Ruth cooks in open
view and brews up happy stuff for
the many regular customers: celery
and apple bake; good salads;
mushroom and tomato quiche.

● **OPEN:** 10.30am-5.30pm Mon-Sat.

TUOSIST

OLD ARDAGH ⓕ
Lisette & Peter Kal
The White House
Tuosist
Tel: (064) 84500

Home-made bread, cheeses, chocolates, everything for the picnic.

● **OPEN:** You can order direct from the
house, and the Kal's produce is available
locally.

KILLORGLIN

THE BIANCONI ⓡ ⓟ
Richard & Raymond Sheedy
Annadale Road, Killorglin
Tel: (066) 61146, Fax: (066) 61950

Good pub food is served all day in
the friendly Bianconi, but the true
imaginativeness and quality is best
seen in the evening.

● **OPEN:** Bar food 10am-9.30pm,
restaurant 6.30pm-9.30pm Mon-Sun.
● **AVERAGE PRICE:** Bar food under
£10. Dinner under £20.
Visa, Access/Master, Amex, Diners.

NICK'S RESTAURANT ⓡ ⓟ
Nicholas Foley
Lower Bridge Street, Killorglin
Tel: (066) 61219

It takes about two minutes spent in
this snappy, happy bar and restaurant to understand why it is an
institution. A good time, good food,
good fun.

● **OPEN:** 12.30pm-3pm, 6.30pm-10pm
Mon-Sun.
● **AVERAGE PRICE:** Lunch under £10.
Dinner under £25.
Visa, Access/Master, Amex, Diners.

WILMA'S KILLORGLIN FARMHOUSE CHEESE ⓕ
Wilma O'Connor
Ardmoniel, Killorglin
Tel: (066) 61402

Fine gouda-style cheeses. There are
also three flavoured varieties –
garlic, cumin and clove.

● **OPEN:** Distributed in the locality.

COUNTY LIMERICK

THE INN BETWEEN ®
Catriona O'Mahony
Adare
Tel: (061) 396633

This popular, relaxed bistro in the gorgeous village of Adare is owned by the nearby Dunraven Arms Hotel, and has cleverly found a space in between the formality of Adare Manor and the Wild Geese, and the resolutely relaxed ambience of its parent hotel. The food is simple – soups, some pastas and good breads at lunchtime, with a more extensive evening menu.

● **OPEN:** 12.30pm-2.30pm, 6.30pm-9.30pm Wed-Sun. Closed Nov-Easter.
● **AVERAGE PRICE:** Lunch under £10. Dinner under £20.
Visa, Access/Master, Amex, Diners.
In the centre of the Village.

THE WILD GEESE ®
Lorcan Roche & Serge Coustrain
Adare
Tel: (061) 396451

Mr Roche and M. Coustrain bring a considerable depth of experience with them to the Wild Geese.

Mr Roche is a Dubliner, M. Coustrain from Toulon, and they shared spells working together in both Dromoland Castle and the Castletroy Park Hotel, before deciding to set up shop and move down the road to Adare.

"Every guest is important to us and we will do our utmost to ensure that your meal with us is a memorable one", they write, a statement which should be the intent of every restaurant in the country, but often isn't.

● **OPEN:** 6.30pm-10.30pm Tue-Sat, noon-3pm, Sun.
● **AVERAGE PRICE:** Dinner under £30.
Visa, Access/Master.
In the centre of the Village.

THE MUSTARD SEED AT ECHO LODGE ® Ⓐ
Dan Mullane
Ballingarry
Tel: (069) 68508

"It looks like it's been here forever", Dan Mullane says of echo Lodge, and indeed it does. But Mr Mullane has made changes: he has, quite simply, made it gorgeous.

A romantic soul, who loves the meeting and greeting, the sharing and caring of the hospitality business, his grasp of the necessary skills of the restaurateur is absolute.

With chef David Norris, the cooking in the new Mustard Seed promises a style of cooking that plays games with the disciplines of the classics.

● **OPEN:** For non residents 7pm-.9.30pm Mon-Sat. House Dinner Party 8pm Sun. (Residents only).
● **AVERAGE PRICE:** Dinner under £30. B&B over £60.
Visa, Access/Master, Amex.

● **OPEN:** For non residents 7pm-.9.30pm Mon-Sat. House Dinner Party 8pm Sun. (Residents only).
● **AVERAGE PRICE:** Dinner under £30. B&B over £60.
Visa, Access/Master, Amex.

KILMALLOCK

CUSSENS COTTAGE Ⓐ
Ita West
Ballygrennan, Bulgadden,
Kilmallock
Tel: (063) 98926

All the food prepared in Cussens Cottage is vegetarian, for both breakfast and dinner, and dinner can include chilli nonecarne, vegan shepherd's pie, mushroom and tomato Italian, vegetarian cheese macaroni, leek and garlic pie with spring greens, with the produce coming from their own organic garden. All the rooms have their own entrance so one can come and go as you please, and it is a smashing base for exploring this gorgeous area.

● **OPEN:** All year
● **AVERAGE PRICE:** B&B under £15, Lunch under £5. Dinner under £10.

LIMERICK

GREEN ONION CAFFÉ Ⓡ
David Corbett
3 Ellen Street, Limerick
Tel: (061) 400710

The Green Onion features a standard "daily specials"-plus-veg-or-salad formula, which they do simply and carefully, with things getting slightly more expansive in the

evening. Prices are keen, so Green Onions represents fine value for money.

● **OPEN:** Lunch noon-3pm, snack menu 3pm-6pm, dinner 6pm-10pm Mon-Sat.
● **AVERAGE PRICE:** Lunch under £5. Dinner under £15.
Visa, Access/Master.

EATS OF EDEN Ⓢ
Nancy Flexman & Rita O'Mahony
Spaight's Centre, Limerick
Tel: (061) 419400

Eats of Eden is a helpful, well-run wholefood shop – indeed one of the best in the country – with local vegetables, breads and farmhouse cheeses for sale alongside the complete panoply of wholefoodery.

● **OPEN:** 9am-6pm Mon-Fri, 9am-6.30pm Sat.

FINE WINES Ⓢ
Ralph Parkes
48 Roches' Street,
Limerick
Tel: (061) 417784, Fax: 417276
(also at Castletroy and
Dooradoyle)

There is indeed a fine range of wines to be found in Fine Wines, and their trio of shops always have a good buzz, with friendly, knowledgeable staff on hand to help. The range is strong throughout the vinous world, and there are some good bargains.

● **OPEN:** 10.30am-11pm Mon-Sat, noon-2pm, 4pm-11pm Sun.

Limerick Saturday Market

"I don't know any shop that looks like mine" says Marie Murphy of Greenacres Delicatessen, one of the new shops that string around the inner walls of the quadrangle that houses the Limerick Saturday market. The market has been renovated by the Civic Trust, and its new pedestrian link to the town centre is one of the many reasons why this area of town is buzzing.

Aside from Greenacres, the new shops in the market mix trendy vintage clothes, fabrics and lace, down-to-earth chips, and the fast expanding Yukon Bread Company, selling its sourdoughs and sweet bagels and other breads.

Greenacres itself mixes the oriental with the Mediterranean with the local. There are bundles of beans and barrels of grains. There's fresh Turkish delight and, Marie's current joy – a wonderful range of cheeses from Ireland, France and, unusually, England. Marie sells the great Territorials: sweet Lancashire, Devonshire and Shropshire cheeses and the very best of Stiltons.

And then there are olives, sun-dried tomatoes, Illy coffee and Italian biscuits to go with it and some of the gorgeous preserves made by Sally Walshe.

Sally sells her marvellous chutneys, jams and pickles in the market on Saturday as well as in Greenacres – "I can ask anything I want for her marmalade" says Marie. "They're so good, once somebody's tried them they come back and back".

Indeed Sally's stall sags with a breathtaking array of preserves. She makes between fifty and eighty types of jam, seventeen types of marmalade. All are different. Sally Walshe is unusual in striding two sections of the market, the shops and the stalls. Otherwise stallholders pitch up either inside the market walls, where there is a nominal charge for a stand, or outside, where the site is free.

So there's the Kilshanny Cheese stall, Toby from the Real Olive Company, better known from the Cork Market, there's home-pressed apple juice from Co Wexford, there's the genteel family who sell their own vegetables in season – parsnips, spuds, swedes and apples for cooking. There are free range eggs, brown breads, country butters.

These are just the regular stallholders. In the summer students pitch up to sell handpainted terracotta pots, you might find home made sweets and toys, and, typical of Irish markets, there's also plenty of things that aren't edible – second hand clothes, friendship bracelets and even, on occasion, cuddly puppies.

● **OPEN:** The Limerick Market is open every Saturday 7.30am-1.30pm. Shops are open during the week.

GREENACRES DELICATESSEN ⓢ
Marie Murphy
Limerick Market
Tel: (061) 400334
● **OPEN:** 10.30am-5.30pm Tue-Sat.

COUNTY TIPPERARY

KILLALOE

WATERMAN'S LODGE ©
Brid & Anne Ryan
Ballina, Killaloe
Tel & Fax: (061) 376333

Waterman's is a simply lovely house, distinguished by a meticulous degree of selection in both the furnishings and the food. It is a house which has no more than it needs, and yet has everything it needs, an effect which makes it marvellously comfortable.

Anne Ryan's cooking is maternal, soulful: perfect roasted peppers, gorgeous sweet onion soup. A perfect onion and shallot tart with a little concasse of tomato. It is food which, like the house, is perfectly judged, as   perfectly rendered as breakfast. In total, Waterman's is a tactile delight, a house whose sense of restraint contributes, ultimately, to a splendid sensuality.

● **OPEN:** All year.
● **AVERAGE PRICE:** Dinner under £30, B&B £30. Weekly and weekend rates.
The house is signposted from the road in Ballina, on the Lough Derg road.

BALLINDERRY

LAKESHORE FOODS ©
Hilary Henry
Coolbawn, Ballinderry
Tel: (067) 22094

"I always liked mustard", says Hilary Henry, a simple explanation for the creation of the dynamic business that is Lakeshore Foods. But Irish mustard lovers are lucky that Mrs Henry's love of the spicy seed should be so well served by her considerable business acumen, for she is a prototype of just what a talented individual can achieve.

The small factory which produces Lakeshore mustards and dressings is located in a gorgeously sympathetic building in Ballinderry which adds charm to this sweet little village. There is also a tea rooms, Lakeshore Cottage, to allow you to grab a bite as you explore Tipperary lakeland.

● **OPEN:** Lakeshore mustards and dressings are widely available.
Lakeshore Cottage is open for teas, coffees and lunches.

BIRDHILL

MATT THE THRESHER ℗
Ted Moynihan
Birdhill
Tel: (061) 379152

One of the staples of Irish on-the-road- eating, Matt the Thresher's is a pristine operation, hard on the road at the border of Tipp and Limerick.

● **OPEN:**
11am-11.30pm Mon-Sun.
● **AVERAGE PRICE:**
Lunch under £10.
Dinner under £15.
Visa, Access/Master, Amex, Diners.

BALLYCORMAC HOUSE Ⓐ
Herb & Christine Quigley
Aglish
Borrisokane
Tel: (067) 21129, Fax: 21200

M.F.K. Fisher. Carol Field. Richard Olney. The titans of the world of food writing decorate the walls of the Quigleys' kitchen, and were these great cooks and writers able to sample the cooking of Herb and Chris they would be delighted at their influence, delighted that their strictures are so well understood by this couple.

For the Quigleys' are fabulous cooks, people in thrall to the magic that talent can conjure and create in a kitchen. We cannot compare their work to that of any other amateur/domestic country houses in the country, for no one else can match their fluency: terrific breads baked by Herb, including an extraordinary cherry and chocolate soda bread; remarkable vegetable purée bakes such as their legendary potato, goat's cheese and scallion gratin, incredible soups, great vegetarian inventions like canneloni stuffed with chard with a walnut sauce.

It is perfectly thrilling food, and the Quigleys make just the right sort of ceremony of it. Do note that Herb runs weekend bread baking classes.

● **OPEN:** All year. Dinner for guests only.
● **AVERAGE PRICE:** B&B under £25.
Dinner under £25.
Visa, Access/Master.
Telephone for directions.

BALLYBRADO HOUSE Ⓕ
Joseph Finke
Cahir
Tel: (052) 66206

A smart government, with a progressive and sensible policy towards agriculture, would take a simple step when it came to developing a workable, sustainable agriculture to take us seamlessly into the next century.

The Minister for Agriculture would get into his black Mercedes, and head down to Ballybrado House, to enlist the services of Joseph Finke. For Mister Finke is a strategist and thinker on organic agricultural matters like no other. His expertise is in marketing, but aside from his clever ideas in this field, he understands the need to make organic agriculture the method of the future, for the sake of the nation's health, for the sake of the nation's land, for the sake of the nation.

He sees no tension between organic food being slickly, cleverly marketed and he understands that the slow progress of the organic message will soon speed up, as the depredations of conventional agriculture become ever more apparent. Until then, he remains a figure well known in organic circles, thanks principally to his fine Ballybrado flour, but the sheer intelligence and strategic thinking of this man actually belongs in the mainstream.

● **OPEN:** Distributed nationally.

CASHEL PALACE Ⓡ Ⓐ

Michael Bolster
Cashel
Tel: (062) 61411, Fax: 61521

Recently taken over and extensively renovated, the Cashel Palace now has the dynamic talent of Michael Bolster in the kitchens, which should see this fine old hotel cutting some sort of stylish culinary shapes in the near future.

During the day he serves an all day grill menu in the Bishop's Brasserie and The Three Sisters Restaurant will open in the evening where Michael intends to cook "modern food" fusing Irish ingredients with the more exclusive European specialities.

● **OPEN:** BUTTERY – 10am-10pm.
RESTAURANT – 6.30pm-9.30pm Mon- Sun.
● **AVERAGE PRICE:**
Buttery under £15.
Dinner under £30.
Visa, Access/Master, Amex, Diners.
Centre of Cashel.

CHEZ HANS Ⓡ

Hans Peter & Jason Matthias
Cashel
Tel: (062) 61177

Hans Peter Matthias is heading towards thirty years in the business of producing fine food for the folk of Tipperary, but you would never guess that this distinguished restaurant is so long in the tooth.

On the right night, it positively hums and fizzes with energy, a space where the controlled panic of a bistro meets the calm of a church, which is precisely what the building in which the restaurant is housed used to be.

Jason Matthias loves sumptuous food, and generous portions, which makes for special occasion food, and the happy folk who have been coming to Chez Hans for years make a special occasion of dinner here, all of them hell-bent on enjoying the treat that this restaurant always manages to be.

● **OPEN:** 6.30pm-9.30pm Tue-Sat.
● **AVERAGE PRICE:** Dinner over £20.
Visa, Access/Master.
Just beside the Rock of Cashel, and clearly signposted from the Dublin-Cork road.

THE SPEARMAN Ⓡ

The Spearman family
Main Street
Cashel
Tel: (062) 61143

They prepare enjoyable, approachable food in the Spearman, and since the day they opened, standards have steadily improved as the Spearman family have gained more confidence.

Lunch is casual and enjoyable with its great multi-layered toasted sandwiches, the soups deep big pools of flavour, and dinner is considerate and quietly accomplished.

● **OPEN:** 12.30pm-3pm, 6.30pm-9.30pm.
● **AVERAGE PRICE:**
Lunch under £10.
Dinner under £20.
Visa, Access.
Town Centre.

CLOGHEEN

BAYLOUGH CHEESE ⓕ
Dick & Anne Keating
Mount Anglesby
Clogheen
Tel: (052) 65275

Dick and Anne Keating's cheese is one of the friendliest, most agreeable cheeses you can find in Ireland. The Keatings produced a brochure some years back which actually had a drawing of Baylough on it, with the cheese saying "Hello", like an animated character from a Nick Park movie.

Well, Baylough does, in its own way, speak to you, and it speaks of timeless tastes which are yielding, gentle, beautifully captured in the cheesemaking. It speaks softly when it is young – whispers of good milk – but with a few months ageing – preferably by Peter Ward of Country Choice, in Nenagh – it becomes thunderously vocal, a true Callas of the cheeseworld, dramatically rich, with strong bass notes of fudgy complexity like Count John McCormack. At this stage, it is a cheese which you cannot stop eating, simple as that, the perfect everyday cheese, the perfect cheese to accompany a glass of Tipperary cider.

● **OPEN:** All year.
Much of the cheese is sold in Peter Ward's shop in Nenagh.
Ring for accurate directions.

CLONMEL

ANGELA'S WHOLEFOOD & THE HONEY POT ⓢⓡ
Pam O'Driscoll & Angela Ryan
14 Abbey Street
Tel: (052) 26899 (Restaurant), 21457 (shop)

The Honeypot shop has always been a centre for wholefoods and organics in Clonmel, and indeed the local organic growers pitch up every Friday and Saturday to sell their wonderful vegetables.

Meanwhile, under the same roof, but run as a separate business is Angela's Wholefood restaurant, where New Zealander Angela Ryan produces wholesome cooking on weekdays.

● **OPEN:** REST – 9am-5pm Mon-Fri.
SHOP – 9am-5pm Mon-Sat.
Organic growers sell 9.30am-1pm Fri & Sat.
● **AVERAGE PRICE:**
RESTAURANT – under £10.
No Credit Cards. Clonmel town centre.

RAHEEN HOUSE ⓐ
Elizabeth Day
Clonmel, Tel: (052) 22140

That fine cook Michael Quinn has charge of the kitchen in Elizabeth Day's handsome house, and has already made his stamp with fine concoctions such as chargrilled polenta with wild mushrooms and basil oil, mushroom bruschetta, grilled goat's cheese salad with roast beetroot, walnuts and a sun-dried tomato vinaigrette.

● **OPEN:** All year.
● **AVERAGE PRICE:** Bar Food under £10. Dinner under £20.

CASHEL BLUE Ⓕ
Jane & Louis Grubb
Beechmount
Fethard
Tel: (052) 31151

Cashel Blue is so well established on the cheese map of the world that one might expect Jane and Louis Grubb to simply sit back, do what they do, and not worry about anything else.

Of course, they aren't like that, the cheesemakers of Ireland. Give them half a chance, and there they go fiddling around with a plain cheese – Cashel White – or experimenting with sheep's milk for a cheese, always trying something new.

Of course, it is the gold-wrapped Cashel Blue which has made the Grubb's reputation, and these days most of the production is made with pasteurised milk. However, some production is still made with raw milk, and these are the cheeses to hunt down if you get the chance.

The raw milk affords a richer tableau against which the blue veining can work, and the eventual meld into greatness which happens when a Cashel Blue is about three and a half months old, when the blue has set to a slight tint of green, is still best achieved by the raw milk cheeses. Get one at this stage, and you get one of the finest tastes any Irish food can offer.

● **OPEN:** Widely distributed throughout the country.

BROCKA-ON-THE-WATER Ⓡ
Nancy & Anne Gernon
Kilgarvan Quay
Ballinderry, Nenagh
Tel: (067) 22038

"They just fuss over you so much" is how one correspondent described his experiences in Brocka-on-the-Water. And indeed how about this for fussing: "I have one customer, and I know her favourite colour is yellow, so whenever she comes I always make sure she has a yellow table cloth and yellow china on the table" says Anne Gernon, who cooks in the restaurant with her mother Nancy.

Each table is always dressed differently in long-loved pieces of china, with silver and different linen tablecloths. "It's a place with a lot of fabrics" says our correspondent.

The food in the restaurant is seasonal – Anne shops before she creates her menus, which might include: Cooleeney cheese croquets with home-made chutney.

● **OPEN:** Mon-Sat 7pm-9.30pm.
● **AVERAGE PRICE:** Under £25.
No credit cards.
On the Lough Derg lake drive, between Puckane and Ballinderry.

COUNTRY CHOICE Ⓢ
Peter Ward
25 Kenyon Street, Nenagh
Tel: (067) 32596

Was a shop ever so well named? Peter and Mary Ward's Country

Choice has all the choicest things from all over the country, but chief amongst these are actually the foods they make themselves.

Mrs Ward's jams are knockout, a tribute to her skill in extracting flavour from fruit, a tribute to her personality in that they, like her, are sunny and sweet.

Mr Ward cooks and bakes, with a strong leaning to the traditional things, but everything is informed by someone with a fine appreciation of flavour. Everything in this shop is the best it can be, from the dried fruits at Xmas to the bakes every day in the restaurant in the back, from the olive oils to the salad leaves. It is an inspiring place, a shop without a careless gesture or action.

■ **OPEN:** 9.30am-6.30pm Mon-Sat.

NENAGH COUNTRY MARKET ⑤
The New Institute
Nenagh

As you would expect in Nenagh, this is a buzzy, zappy market, running every Friday from 11am. As you would expect, the market is a good place to buy home-made and home-grown produce.

● **OPEN:** 11am-1pm Fri.

ABBEY STONEGROUND WHOLEMEAL FLOUR ⓕ
The Brothers
Mount Saint Joseph Abbey,
Roscrea
Tel: (0505) 21711

A celebrated flour, with excellent earthiness that gives great zest to soda bread but also adds depth to yeast breads.

● **OPEN:** The flour is available in shops throughout the country.

COOLEENEY CHEESE ⓕ
Breda Maher
Cooleeney House
Moyne
Thurles
Tel: (0504) 45112

Breda Maher's is one of the most sensitive of the Irish cheeses, needing fine handling to bring this delicate concoction to its very best.

When that happens, if you buy one from the farm, or from a good cheese shop, then you find a cheese that can speak glowingly of its place and the people who made it. The very intensity of the milkiness of Cooleeney speaks of the boggy pastures on which the cattle graze, the richly ripened bloom of the texture speaks of Mrs Maher's care and concentration.

● **OPEN:** Cooleeney House is about three miles off the main N7 road.

COUNTY WATERFORD

BLACKWATER VALLEY

Wine, cheese, bread, pure fruit juices, good cooking, it has a little of all the good things, the Blackwater valley. Flowing south of Cappoquin and Lismore, down past Clashmore and into Youghal, in County Cork, the river orchestrates the countryside, providing a focus for the producers who work here.

Barron's Bakery has been operating since 1887, and the bread is still baked in traditional brick ovens. It looks somewhat like commercial bread, but Esther Barron's bread bears no relation to the fraudulent mass-produced gunk of today. This is real baking, and not just "water standing up", the expression good bakers use to describe mass-produced bread. Do note that they also produce that interesting rarity which is the Waterford blas, a soft white roll only found in the county.

Others have arrived more recently. Wolfgang and Agnes Schliebitz came to Waterford six years ago to make Knockalara, a Balkan-style cheese.

It is the only sheep's milk feta made in Ireland, the produce of the milk of a herd of Friesian dairy sheep who are milked by hand, and they also produce excellent cheese in olive oil.

Eamon Lonergan another cheese-maker, producing the range of Knockanore cheeses, including a smoked cheese. Look out especially for his mature Ballyneety cheese.

Julia Keane makes the wonderful Crinnaghtaun apple juice, a brew which is splendidly golden and cloudy in colour, as a real juice should be. She uses Bramleys and Cox's Orange Pippins from her own orchards, and the juice flows naturally from the press into the bottle. Like a good wine, Crinnaghtaun has bouquet, structure, and is full of goodness.

What could be finer, on a fine day, than to collect the foods of the producers and to picnic somewhere peaceful in this gracious place. You might call to Ina and Erwin Körner's farm, Ardsallagh House near Youghal, and buy some soft goat's cheese, maybe some yogurt, maybe some ice-cream, all made from goat's milk. Or just pop into a local shop to pick up some of Mary McGrath's homemade jam, made at the foot of the Kockmealdown Mountains.

A good base to use for exploring the area is Richmond House, where Paul and Claire Deevy have recently joined Paul's mum, Jean, in the family business. The house was built in the eighteenth century and has been restored to accommodate ten comfortable bedrooms. The restaurant is open to non residents where Paul Deevy's cooking shows fine imagination.

ARDSALLAGH GOAT'S PRODUCE ●
Ardsallagh, Youghal, Co Cork
Tel: (024) 92545
● OPEN: Distributed throughout the area.

BARRON'S BAKERY ●
Esther Barron
Cappoquin
Tel: (058) 54045, Fax: 52012
● OPEN: 8.30am-6pm Mon-Sat and the bread is distributed within a 15 mile radius.

CRINNAGHTAUN APPLE JUICE ●
Julia Keane
Cappoquin
Tel: (058) 54258
● OPEN: Widely distributed.

KNOCKALARA SHEEP'S CHEESE ●
Wolfgang & Agnes Schliebitz
Cappoquin
Tel: (024) 96326
● OPEN: Available in good delicatessens.

KNOCKANORE ●
Eamonn Lonergan
Ballyneety, Knockanore
Tel: (024) 97275
● OPEN: Widely distributed.

MCGRATH'S HOMEMADE JAM ●
Mary McGrath
Tel: (058) 54087
● OPEN: Sold in the locality.

RICHMOND HOUSE ●
Paul & Claire Deevy
Cappoquin
Tel: (058) 544278, Fax: 54988
● OPEN: For dinner for non residents 7pm-9pm Tue-Sat (7 days for residents).
● AVERAGE PRICE: B&B over £25.
Dinner over £20.
Visa, Access/Master.

WEST WATERFORD VINEYARDS ●
David & Patricia McGrath
Cappoquin
Tel: (058) 54283

David McGrath was a heating engineer and Patricia McGrath worked for BT, but, happily stating that "We started with negative money", this dynamic duo came to west Waterford to set up a vineyard and make wine.

Using primarily the Schönburger grape, they make a dry, mildly spicy, white wine – available as a house wine, this blended with the three other grapes they have planted (Madelaine Angevine, Seyval Blanc and Siegrebbe). If you see it, snap up the fine Reserve. The wine is extremely keenly priced, at £4 a bottle and £10 for the reserve. All the wine is sold from the vineyard, at which they have a shop.

● OPEN: 10.30am-8pm Mon-Sun.

McALPIN'S SUIR INN ●
Mary & Dunstan McAlpin
Cheekpoint
Tel: (051) 82182/82220

Years ago, we were eating in McAlpin's one evening when a youngish couple came in to the bar. They had that look which said that they had parked the kids with granny for a couple of hours, and were stealing some quality time on their own. They ordered swiftly, were served swiftly, ate leisurely, paid the bill and left, happy.

That's the kind of place McAlpin's is. Essentially a seafood bar with limited vegetarian choices, it is full of cheer and buzz.

● **OPEN:** 6.45pm-9.30pm Tue-Sat, pub open from 6pm.
● **AVERAGE PRICE:** Dinner under £15.
Visa, Access/Master.
At the harbour in Cheekpoint.

HANORA'S COTTAGE Ⓐ Ⓡ
Seamus & Mary Wall
Nire Valley
Clonmel
Tel: (052) 36134
Fax: 25145

Snuggled within the silent embrace of one of the Comeragh Mountain valleys, Hanora's Cottage overlooks the river Nire and is overlooked itself by the Nire church, set slightly higher at the foot of the mountains. Many folk come here to partake in hill-walking, but another attraction is the fact that Seamus and Mary's son Eoin – a Ballymaloe trained chef – carefully sources good foods for the breakfasts and dinners that add the final touch of quietude to this quiet place.

● **OPEN:** For dinner for non-residents, from 7.30pm.
● **AVERAGE PRICE:** Dinner under £20.
B&B over £20.
Visa, Access/Mastercard, Amex, Diners.
Turn off the Clonmel/Dungarven road at Ballymacarbry. The house is four miles down this road, beside the Nire church.

RING FARMHOUSE CHEESE Ⓕ
Eileen & Tom Harty
Gortnadiha House
Ring
Dungarvan
Tel: (058) 46142

The Harty's is a lovely lusty, trusty cheese, ever-so piquant, especially when it reaches an age of about 8 months, when it develops a glorious Parmesan sweetness.

"It's not a gouda, not a cheddar, it's just Ring", says Eileen Harty, and indeed it is: Ring and nothing but Ring. Do note that it is wonderful to cook with: in the Farmgate Café in Cork, Kay Harte teams Ring with mushrooms in the most wonderful tart.

● **OPEN:** Mature cheeses can be ordered from the farm.
Otherwise widely distributed.

BUGGY'S GLENCAIRN INN Ⓟ Ⓡ
Ken & Cathleen Buggy
Glencairn
Tel: (058) 56232

"Everybody in Ireland is busy exporting the idea of the Irish bar throughout the world", says Ken Buggy. "So, I decided to open an English inn in Ireland".

The bar does look somewhat like an old inn, but it looks like an old inn designed by Ken Buggy. That pell-mell perfection, that air of abandoned contrivance, makes Buggy's Glencairn Inn a testament to some people's ability to place the right thing in the right place.

It achieves just the right effect; you want to sit down in front of the fire and drink a brace of pints and a tray full of whiskeys, chat away for the whole evening. If you hate the way modern pubs are so streamlined and self-conscious, then Buggy's is for you. And the best news is that there are now two bedrooms if you want to stay in this quite charming corner of Ireland.

● **OPEN:**
12.30pm-3pm, 7.30pm-9pm Mon-Sun.
● **AVERAGE PRICE:**
Meals under £10.
No credit cards.
Take the Tallow road from Lismore, turn right at the garage from where Glencairn is signposted. Buggy's is in the centre of the village.

LISMORE

KILMORNA FARM HOSTEL Ⓐ
Sibylle Knobel
Kilmorna
Lismore
Tel: (058) 54315

Sibylle Knobel runs a farm hostel. Simple, super and people love it.

● **OPEN:** All year.
Breakfast offered.
● **AVERAGE PRICE:**
B&B under £10 for both dormitory, double and family accommodation.
No credit cards.

WATERFORD

CHAPMAN'S DELICATESSEN & THE PANTRY Ⓡ Ⓢ
Mr Prendergast (Chapman's)
Gabriele Kneisel (The Pantry)
61 The Quay, Waterford
Tel: (051) 74938/76200
(Chapman's)
Tel: (051) 71142 (The Pantry)

A fine deli, with many of the best foods from the county, Chapman's is an elegant, spacious shop with more than a touch of class. The Pantry, at the rear of Chapman's, offers a simple and successful tea rooms, that is extremely popular with locals.

● **OPEN:** 9am-6pm Mon-Thur, 9am-9pm Fri, 9am-6pm Sat.
Pantry open from 8am-6pm Mon-Sat.

FULL OF BEANS Ⓢ
Ian & Sonia McLellan
9 George's Court, Waterford

Cute wholefood shop, which sells Ian and Sonia's own home-grown vegetables, amongst many other good things.

● **OPEN:** 9am-5pm Mon-Sat.

HARICOTS WHOLEFOOD RESTAURANT Ⓡ
11 O'Connell Street, Waterford
Breda & Elaine Ryan

Despite its name, Haricots is not a strict vegetarian restaurant, and does cater for non-vegetarians. It's a well-established place by now, set into a comfortable groove of good food and amiable, simple surroundings which suit the atmosphere perfectly.

● **OPEN:** 9am-9pm Mon-Fri,
9am-5.45pm Sat.

McCLUSKEY'S ®
Paul McCluskey
High Street, Waterford
Tel: (051) 57766

Paul McCluskey cooked with considerable distinction in Waterford Castle when he had tenure of the kitchen. He has now moved into town to a much leaner, simpler and more modern space, but, in truth, the move is a good one, for his food has always been modern and expertly achieved, a very personal style which has always featured good vegetarian cookery.

Prices are very, very keen, for it is Mr McCluskey's determination to make his restaurant not only approachable but affordable.

● **OPEN:** Noon-2.30pm, 6pm-10pm Mon-Sat. (Open all afternoon in the summer).
● **AVERAGE PRICE:** Lunch under £10.
Dinner under £20. Visa, Access/Master.
Town centre.

PRENDIVILLE'S RESTAURANT & GUESTHOUSE ® Ⓐ
Paula Prendiville
Cork Road, Waterford
Tel: (051) 78851

Prendiville's is a good place, whether you are staying in Waterford, maybe passing through having just gotten off the ferry, and want a good on-the-road stop if you are heading out of the city, as it sits immediately adjacent to the main road. The rooms in the guesthouse are basic, principally an adjunct to the real business which is Mrs Prendiville's work in the restaurant.

● **OPEN:** 12.30pm-2.15pm, 6.30pm 9.30pm Mon-Fri, 6.30pm-9.30pm Sat.
● **AVERAGE PRICE:** Dinner under £20.
Visa, Access/Master, Amex.
On the way out of Waterford on the N25 heading in the direction of Cork.

THE WINE VAULT ®
David Dennison
High Street, Waterford
Tel & Fax: (051) 53444

"Our main idea with our food is to keep it simple", says David Dennison. "Less sauces, more olive oil, contrasting flavours with different wines. One dish we tried was a simple vegetarian nut cake matched with an Alsace Riesling".

This is the key to the Wine Vault. David Dennison's passion for wine spills over into his food, for he conceives and creates dishes and styles which will match all the better with the fine range of wines he sells.

The food, thus, should be considered in direct relationship with the wines, and the wisest advice of all is to take the boss's advice.

● **OPEN:** Noon-2.30pm, 6pm-10pm Mon-Sat. (Open all afternoon in the summer).
● **AVERAGE PRICE:** Lunch under £10.
Dinner under £20. Visa, Access/Master.
In the centre of town.

U L S T E R

INCLUDING THE COUNTIES OF

CAVAN

DONEGAL

MONAGHAN

COUNTY CAVAN

BALLINAGH

BAVARIA HOUSE ⓐ
Rolf & Ilse Kleiber
Garrymore, Ballinagh
Tel: (049) 37452

"We love cooking", says Ilse, and the Kleibers' 19th century Georgian house plays host to carefully considered vegetarian dinners, made using carefully sourced foods – they buy cheese from Silke Cropp, and grow their own vegetables, fruits and herbs organically.

● **OPEN:** Apr-Oct.
● **AVERAGE PRICE:** B&B under £15.
Dinner under £15.
No credit Cards.
Telephone for directions to the house.

BELTURBET

CORLEGGY FARMHOUSE CHEESE ⓕ
Silke Cropp
Corleggy, Belturbet
Tel: (049) 22930

Silke Cropp began to make cheese eight years ago, experimenting constantly to try to hit on the style she wanted. "The first cheeses I made were too strong", she says, "so I invented a milder recipe by washing the curd".

She feels a natural rind is vital for a cheese to mature properly and watching her at work one sees a cheesemaker with a powerfully tactile sense, someone who conveys not just an awareness, but also a motherly concern over the well being of all her charges.

She has added a cow's milk cheese – Drumlin – to her assortment, flavouring some of the cheeses with peppercorns, some with cumin and some with garlic. In addition there is the splendidly fresh Quivvy cheeses, fresh unsalted goat's cheeses preserved in olive oil which has been flavoured with garlic and rosemary and decorated with nasturtium flowers.

● **OPEN:** Corleggy cheeses are available in delicatessens in Dublin, Sligo and Cork.

BLACKLION

MacNEAN BISTRO ⓡ ⓐ
Neven Maguire
Blacklion
Tel: (072) 53022

Neven Maguire is a brilliant chef. Audaciously talented, modest as all get out, his food is a treat for the senses, with his skills utilised throughout dinner to delight the diner.

Amongst his various menus, he offers a special vegetarian menu: garlic mushrooms on a puff pastry pillow, a thrilling salad of eden organic leaves with a blue cheese vinaigrette, a smashing leek and potato soup, avocado and ratatouille in a filo parcel with a tomato coulis, gratinated broccoli and cashewnut platter; garlic pasta with a brunoise of vegetables. All his food has a freshness and spiritedness which is captivating. His desserts, meantime, have to be seen to be believed, and are likely the finest in the entire country.

Neven's mother, Vera, offers some counterbalance to this youthful brilliance, and the Bistro menus continue to offer relatively simple dishes alongside this young man's flights of fancy. There are also comfy rooms in the house, and a great time to be had.

● **OPEN:** 5.30pm-9pm Tue-Sat, 12.30pm-9pm Sun.
● **AVERAGE PRICE:** Lunch under £15. Dinner over £20. Visa, Access/Master. On the main street in Blacklion.

CAVAN

LIFEFORCE MILL ●
The Mill Rock
Cavan
Tel: (049) 62722

This beautifully restored old mill still stonegrinds flour using stones powered by an original 1850s water turbine. There is a coffee shop where the food has that just-baked freshness. Best of all, if doing a tour, you bake a loaf at the beginning and collect the finished bread at the end.

● **OPEN:** For lunch with tours Tue-Sun at 11am, noon, 3pm and 4pm.

VIRGINIA

BOILIE CHEESE ●
Anne & John Brodie
Ryefield House
Virginia
Tel: (049) 47416

The enormous success of Anne and John Brodie's Boilie cheese – a soft cow's milk cheese preserved in oil and sold in small jars – has offered proof, if proof were needed, that a fine artisan product can cross-over into the commercial food marketplace with no loss of integrity. Originated and orchestrated from the Brodie's farm, Boilie has also shown that one can have a commercial success with a food without the dubious benefit of "marketing", that you can retain your original vision, and that small can be both beautiful, and successful.

But, in truth, Boilie was a success waiting to happen, for this interaction between truly produced food, originating on a small farm and rich in the textures and details which that gives, and an engagement with the food business has long been a feature of the Brodie's work. They were a vital staple of the Mother Redcap's market in Dublin for years, and have always allowed the requests and concerns of customers to influence their work.

This direct dealing means that the cheeses are friendly and pleasing, packed full of the character of Anne and John and their family.

● **OPEN:** Distributed throughout Ireland.

COUNTY DONEGAL

DUNKINEELY

CASTLEMURRAY HOUSE Ⓐ Ⓡ
Thierry Delcros
Dunkineely, Tel: (073) 37022

Thierry Delcros is such a good cook
that you could run the risk of taking
his expertise for granted. His style is
so subtle and skilful that he can
produce food which seems to speak
of pure culinary logic, and it is so
deliciously persuasive that, as you
eat it, you can't imagine that anyone
would ever do things differently.

He is a true Donegal cook, for a
Frenchman, in that his style owes
nothing to fashion and is embedded
in the true flavours and tastes of the
countryside, creating cooking that
emerges from cuisine paysanne and
cuisine bourgeois to take on its own
mantle. Vegetarian choices are
limited, but dishes such as vegetarian
gateau reveal his skill.

For many regulars, the trip is
completed by staying overnight in
the affordable, cosy bedrooms. But
don't imagine that you are going to
an hotel: this is a restaurant with
rooms, so you carry your own bags
and there is no room service.

But that actually suits the
straightforward, very honest nature
of the house and the kitchen.

● **OPEN:** 7pm-9.30pm Mon-Sun ('till
10pm Sat and Sun).
(Closed Mon-Wed off season).
● **AVERAGE PRICE:** Dinner over £20.
Visa, Access/Master. Signposted after
Dunkineely, heading west out of Donegal.

BURTONPORT

THE LOBSTER POT Ⓟ
Gerard O'Donnell
Burtonport
Tel: (075) 42012

This is a simple pub, down near the
waterfront in Burtonport, but it
enjoys a surprisingly expansive
menu and flavoursome cooking.

● **OPEN:** For pub food from noon,
dinner 6pm-9.30pm Mon-Sun.
● **AVERAGE PRICE:** Lunch under £10.
Dinner over £20.
Visa, Access/Master.
The pub is down near the port.

DONEGAL TOWN

SIMPLE SIMON Ⓢ
Andrew Cape
Anderson's Yard
The Diamond, Donegal Town
Tel: (073) 22687

Andrew Cape has long been a
pioneer of good food in Donegal, a
county which can boast disappoin-
tingly few artisan producers.

What good things there are tend
to make their way here, so Simple
Simon is valuable for good breads,
fresh organic vegetables, farmhouse
cheeses and other local exotica,
alongside the paraphernalia of a
thoughtful wholefood shop.

● **OPEN:** 9.30am-6pm Mon-Sat.
Signposted in The Diamond.

STELLA'S SALAD BAR ℗
Stella McGroarty's Pub
The Diamond
Tel: (073) 21049

Stella can make a mighty sandwich, a hearty bowl of soup, a spot-on stir-fry of vegetables, and cracking salads. Don't think of this merely as pub food or workaday catering. Stella may cook in a pub, but this is clever, concerned, and mightily regenerative, cooking.

● **OPEN:** For pub food from noon.

FAHAN

RESTAURANT ST JOHN'S ®
Reggie Ryan
Fahan
Tel: (077) 60289

Reggie Ryan's Restaurant St. John is a solid, enduring establishment, innately customer-conscious, a place which works charmingly to its own imprimatur.

● **OPEN:** 6pm-10pm Tue-Sun.
● **AVERAGE PRICE:**
Dinner over £20.
Visa, Access/Master, Amex, Diners.
Clearly signposted in Fahan village.

GLENTIES

THOMAS BECHT ℉
Thomas & Lucy Becht
Dorrian
Glenties
Tel: (075) 51286

Thomas Becht is a model farmer who works a model farm, according to bio-dynamic principles. Alongside these principles, he exhibits a wisdom which is surely as important to the quality of his produce as the theories of Rudolf Steiner.

One day, visiting the farm, we saw a calf being born without the need for any assistance. Because the mother had been covered by a small bull, the process was simple. Of course, this means that the calf would be smaller, but it also gifts the mother with a trouble-free birth and a longer life.

That is not a fashionable practice amongst conventional farmers, always looking to extract the maximum yield from every conceivable animal and product, but Mr Becht's farming is concerned with a more significant, and profound totality, than just making a fast buck. He works with nature, not against it, and this sense of harmony is evident in his produce. It is startlingly fine, true-tasting, food as good as it can possibly be.

● **OPEN:**
For farm gate sales.
You can also buy the produce from local health food shops, country markets, and from a market stall in Letterkenny every Friday morning.

BIO-DYNAMICS

The principles of bio-dynamic farming were established by Rudolf Steiner, in a series of eight lectures, given to a group of farmers in Silesia, in 1924. Notoriously complex and baffling, the lectures nevertheless enjoy moments of simple truth.

In Lecture One, for example, Steiner asks: "Why, for instance, is it no longer possible to find potatoes as good as the ones I ate when I was a boy?". How many of us, in the intervening years, have asked that same question, time and again?

Put as simply as possible, Steiner figured that the solution lay in viewing each farm as an individuality, an entity where mixed farming meant that the farm produced its own manure.

And it is with the basic business of compost that we find one of the planks of his theory. For what Steiner advocated was that you feed the land, not just the plants. Bio-dynamics goes one step further than organic farming, for not only must the soil not be further polluted by chemicals, it actually must be rescued from its depleted state.

This is done by a series of preparations which should be both added to manure and sprayed on the land. In addition to this, it advocates ideal times for planting and spraying, based on the interaction of the lunar cycle. The leading proponent of this system, Maria Thun, would maintain that it is nothing new, merely a systematic analysis of traditional farming customs. Thomas Becht, who

farms bio-dynamically in Glenties in County Donegal confirms this wisdom: "Every farmer planted like this. Maybe they couldn't explain it, but experience taught them to plant by the half moon, or the full moon".

What bio-dynamic agriculture offers, then, is the simple, essential fact of uniqueness, a uniqueness in food which speaks of the place from which it comes. When you taste bio-dynamically produced food, you encounter pure characteristics: a carrot tastes like a carrot, profoundly, purely.

There is an intense directness of flavour in the food which comes, initially, as a shock. Bio-dyn food is, simply, the best, and bio-dyn will slowly, surely, march forward, because it is not only superior produce, it is produced humanely, soundly, sympathetically.

With many organic growers latching onto the discipline of bio-dyn, the produce is becoming more available. It is still small beer, but only ten years ago the term organic meant little to most folk. All that has changed, and creeds and codes heretofore marginalised have come into the mainstream. The qualities which instigate people into buying organic produce – regionality, lack of pollution, the local economy, distinctiveness – are multiplied in the case of bio-dyn. And, just as the practices of organic farming have become mainstream, we believe the theories of bio-dyn will become increasingly influential.

CO CLARE

HARRIE & ANNALIESE BARTELINK ⓕ
Poulcoin, Kilnaboy
- **PRODUCE:** Cheese.
- **OUTLETS:** Farm gate sales, Local shops, B&Bs and restaurants.

DERRICK & MEG GORDON ⓕ
Inagh
Tel: (065) 26633
- **PRODUCE:** Cheese.
- **OUTLETS:** Inagh cheese is sold countrywide in good shops and supermarkets.

CO CORK

IAN PAUL & KIM LANGEN ⓕ
Holyhill, Ballineen
Tel: (023) 47667
- **PRODUCE:** Vegetables, Butter & Cheese.
- **OUTLETS:** Telephone for details.

GERD NEUBECK ⓕ
Incharoe, Kealkill, Bantry
Tel: (027) 66263
- **PRODUCE:** Vegetables, Livestock.
- **OUTLETS:** Telephone for details.

CO KILDARE

MARY MORRIN ⓕ
Belgard, Kilcock
Tel: (01) 628 7244
- **PRODUCE:** Vegetables.
- **OUTLETS:** Naas Country Market, Fri 10.45am-noon.

DEIRDRE O'SULLIVAN ⓕ
Nurney House, Carbury
Tel: (0405) 53337
- **PRODUCE:** Vegetables.
- **OUTLETS:** Dublin Supermarkets, Dublin Food Co-Op, farm gate sales.

CO WEXFORD

EVE & ANTHONY KAYE ⓕ
Inisglas Trust Ltd, Crossabeg
Tel: (053) 28226
- **PRODUCE:** Trees, vegetables, soft fruit.
- **OUTLETS:** Farm gate sales.

PAULA & ELMER KOOMANS VAN DE DRIES O'REILLY ⓕ
Cnockfe
Ballyharran Upper
Crossabeg
Tel (053) 28428
- **PRODUCE:** Vegetables, herbs.
- **OUTLETS:** Wexford Organic Growers, L&N supermarket, Humble Food Shop, Only Natural.

NICHOLAS REDMOND ⓕ
Gerry, Ballygarrett, Gorey
- **PRODUCE:** Potatoes, vegetables, soft fruit.
- **OUTLETS:** Farmgate sales, Ivory Stores and Pettits Supermarket.

CO KILKENNY

WENDY & MICHAEL MIKLIS ⓕ
Raheen, Piltown
Tel: (051) 643519
- **PRODUCE:** Vegetables, herbs, fruit, cheese.
- **OUTLETS:** Clonmel Organic Growers, The Rainbow Warehouse, Clonmel and farm gate sales.

CO WICKLOW

PENNY & UDO LANGE ⓕ
Ballinroan, Kiltegan
Tel: (0508) 73278
- **PRODUCE:** Vegetables, herbs.
- **OUTLETS:** Dublin supermarkets, Dublin Food Co-Op and farm gate sales by arrangement. Ring for details of home delivery service.

COUNTY MONAGHAN

HILTON PARK Ⓐ Ⓡ
Johnny & Lucy Madden
Scotshouse
Tel: (047) 56007
Fax: (047) 56033

It is an indicator of the intellectual resonance which Lucy Madden brings to her work that the food book on which she has been slowly working for several years now is neither a conventional cookbook, nor one of those profuse books about "country house cuisine" – whatever that may be.

Instead, Mrs Madden's labours have been tuned to an exhaustive study of the potato, and recipes for using the humble spud. This autodidactic approach is typical of her work, and gives a clue to the charm, and strength, of Hilton Park.

For Hilton is perhaps the most experimental of the country houses, a template of what the country house could be, can be, should be. Where other houses appear to have simply fallen together to act as a warehouse for old furniture and old ideas, one gets the impression in Hilton that everything is considered – composed, even.

This is a house where the owners seem clearly to have considered the very idea of the country house existing at the end of the twentieth century, have reassessed the idea of country house cooking, have thought about the idea of country house hospitality.

Indeed, this analysis of what country house cooking can be is vital. Mrs Madden's imprimatur is to avoid the dewy-eyed, Beetonesque brouhaha which some think appropriate to the country house. Instead, the basis of her cooking lies in the very relationship between farming and eating. The gardens are farmed organically, and, then, their produce is put at the service of Mrs Madden's intricate, considered cooking, where the vibrant energy of these foods is assessed and then simply released. Once again, the backbone of the food here is the careful consideration and analysis it enjoys, and the result is food which is expressive and truly delicious.

But don't imagine that this experiment is arid or unfeeling, that Hilton Park is some sort of Bauhaus Country House. It is not, and the cleverality of the Maddens means that unlike other places, Hilton doesn't wallow in the embrace of its considerable history. It is not a nostalgic house, where you are invited to trip out for a few days into some moribund idea of "gracious living". It is gracious, certainly, but the consideration of each aspect of the house, and the wit of Johnny and Lucy, make it a very real space.

● **OPEN:** Apr-Sept.
● **AVERAGE PRICE:**
B&B over £50.
Dinner for residents over £20.
Visa, Access/Master.

NORTHERN IRELAND

INCLUDING THE COUNTIES OF

ANTRIM

DOWN

B E L F A S T

Belfast is a city of Culinary Tribes. There is, first and foremost, the COOL SCHOOL, clustered around Roscoff and its offspring and its imitators, a lean-dream California-cool ethos of food and style

There is the CHINESE TRIBE, longer and more securely established here than anywhere else, and with a splendid cuisine and excellent shops.

The noisiest bunch are, of course, the PUB TRIBE, larger than life, and game-ball for anything.

The ITALIAN TRIBE are a mixed bunch, running the gamut from speedy takeaway to bustling trattoria to overblown temple, the loyalty of their customers matched point-for-point by the BISTRO TRIBE.

Clustered around a handful of city centre places whose authenticity is not something you might wish to dwell on, the Bistro crowd are diverse, democratic, and, frankly, rather fond of a drink.

Differences of style and background may divide them, but what unifies the Tribes is that unique Belfast savvy, built around a raucous fondness for a good time.

THE COOL SCHOOL

NICK'S WAREHOUSE ®
Nick & Kathy Price
35/39 Hill Street, Belfast BT1
Tel: (01232) 439690

If restaurants are built in the image of their owners – and they most definitely are – then we can say that the Warehouse is unpretentious, enjoys a joke, likes a drink, and has an appreciation of how to conjure up the pleasures of food and wine which is simply instinctive. Just like Nick and Kathy.

But what underpins the found-ation of the Warehouse is a streetwise, sassy style of cooking, combined with a streetwise, sassy style of service. Like many modern cooks, Mr Price is a magpie, filching, foraging and finding ideas and influences from books and cooks, from cultures and countries: braised lentils with chestnuts and pasta; cabbage leaves with ricotta and spinach; bulgur wheat pilaf

The wine list is smashing.

● **OPEN:** 11.30am-11pm Mon-Sat.
(Closed Mon evening).
Lunch served noon-3pm, dinner 6pm-9pm.
● **AVERAGE PRICE:**
Wine Bar under £10.
Restaurant over £20.
Visa, Access/Master.
Hill Street is near the University of Ulster in the centre of Belfast.

CARGOES ⑤
Rhada, Mary & Daphne
613 Lisburn Road
Belfast BT9
Tel: (01232) 665451

Cargoes is one of the most judiciously selective shops in the country. Little notes pinned to the shelves alert you to the fine provenance of the goods, and everything they sell is good: the buttery shortbread with its sedate sweetness; the gorgeous Colli d'Abruzzo oils and others bought from Charles Carey; the carnaroli risotto rice and the Castiglioni pasta; the Maya Gold organic chocolate; the Tamisee flour; the lentils from Puy; the Illy coffee; the Tracklements condiments; the Maldon salt and Wynad peppercorns; the crisp salads and scrumptiously yearning cakes; the blackboard announcing the cheeses they sell.

There is also a further board with the day's lunchtime specials written on it, for Cargoes has become as much of a lunchtime restaurant as a splendid deli with food-to-go.

When you taste the food, you realise just why Cargoes has become a success. The lunchtime cooking in Cargoes is blissfully flavoured and light as a sybarite's conscience, perfectly seen-to dishes such as panzanella, or simple pastas. Like everything else in Cargoes, from the style of the shop to the service, from the discrimination to the discernment, the cooking is the best it can be, and the best they can possibly make it.

● **OPEN:** 9.30am-6pm Mon-Sat.

EQUINOX CAFÉ ⓡ ⑤
Kay Gilbert
32 Howard Street
Belfast BT1
Tel: (01232) 230089

The establishment of a café at the rear of Equinox, Kay Gilbert's modish temple of good taste, was a logical and laudable step, but what is most impressive about it – apart from the thunderingly fine coffee and the calm, understated cooking – is the fact that the theory of the shop has been so successfully transferred across the glass partition into the little seating area.

So, the music is dreamily correct, the staff are crisply collected, the crockery and the cutlery bear the fine breeding found in the shop itself, the furnishings are mighty and the food orchestrates that ziggurat of northern Italian peasant – bean soups; bruschetta; easy pastas – found in all the most bourgeois eating places in the West.

Yet the food only plays a small part in the success of Equinox, for what they have really succeeded in creating is an oasis of refinement, the sort of place where you slip in for a blast of caffeine and slip out feeling refreshed by the balm of beauty. It is a very successful space, with each element of the café and the shop playing its part.

● **OPEN:**
SHOP - 9.30am-5.30pm Mon-Sat ('till 9pm Thur).
CAFÉ - 9.30am-5pm Mon-Sat ('till 8pm Thur).
● **AVERAGE PRICE:**
Lunch under £10.

ROSCOFF ®

Paul & Jeanne Rankin
7 Lesley House
Shaftesbury Square
Belfast BT2
Tel: (01232) 331532

Apart from a glorious period in the early days of Roscoff, when a quartet of Paul Rankin, Robbie Millar, Eugene Callaghan and Noel McMeel were actually sweating behind these stoves together, Roscoff has perhaps never produced better food than it is doing right now, the stupendous quality of the cooking perhaps explained by the fact that the Rankins have continued to allow their cooking to evolve intellectually.

The style of menu now – no set dinner, no à la carte, just a panoply of starters, main courses and desserts at a fixed price – allows Mr Rankin to pursue his idea of integral, essentially flavoured cooking.

A little notice allows them to swing into action, and the vegetarian cookery is wonderfully sympathetic, perhaps explained by the fact that Mrs Rankin herself is vegetarian. But they just love a challenge, so set them to it: ragout of summer vegetables with a lemon and tarragon beurre blanc; oriental pasta with soya, ginger and stir-fried vegetables; sun-dried tomato and artichoke pastry turnovers. Wonderful.

● **OPEN:** 12.15pm-2.15pm Mon-Fri, 6.30pm-10.30pm Mon-Sat.
● **AVERAGE PRICE:** Lunch under £20. Dinner under £30.
Visa, Access/Master, Amex.
Belfast City centre.

ROSCOFF CAFÉ ®

Gillian Hayes & Jeanne Rankin
27 Fountain Street, Belfast BT1
Tel: (01232) 315090
Fax: (01232) 328340

Gillian Hayes' Roscoff Café is subtle and stylish, and somewhat the sort of space where you would expect to find Belfast's cool tribe sippin' cappuchino's and munchin' muffins. Yet it also manages to be homey, in a home-from-homey sort of way. Whilst it is vivid and smart, any trace of selfconsciousness is absent.

This is a bakery and café as they make them in San Francisco or Vienna, in Basle or Bilbao. The orientation of the Café compares to the best, quite deliberately, for Gillian Hayes did her research in London and on California's west coast, examining how you show the proper respect to the business of coffee and cakes, sandwiches and cookies, bread and pastries.

What underpins this venture is a simple truism of Ms Hayes which is implicit in everything you find here: "It's simple, but it's difficult".

What is perhaps most impressive is the confident flavours of the fine breads they bake. From ciabatta to foccaccia, from wholewheat to wheaten, from the chilli and garlic to the soda farls, tastes and textures are very true, and in eating the breads we realise that when these simple but difficult things are done right, the pleasure they give is profound.

● **OPEN:** 7.30am-5.30pm Mon-Sat, 'till 8.30pm Thur, 8pm Fri.
● **AVERAGE PRICE:** Under £10.
Belfast city centre, behind Boots' chemist.

THE BISTRO TRIBE

What all these Belfast eating houses share is a concentration on speedy eating, simple food and keen prices. Hence, they are bistros by design, or default.

Depending on what you want, you make your choice: a modern faux style of French food in La Boheme or the Belle Epoque or Chez Delbart, where the style of cooking can seem interchangeable but where the crack can be mighty.

The perennial Strand, on the Stranmillis Road, with its domesticated, comfort food, or its near-neighbour, Bonnie Turkington's lofty, light-filled Museum Café.

Saints and Scholars and Aubergines and Bluejeans offer that grab-bag of grub which can be described as eclectic and cosmopolitan, though if this is the style you crave then around the corner on the Malone Road, Maloney's does a similar thing with considerably more finesse.

The newest interloper, however, is one of the best things to have happened to the bistro tribe. Mizuna, a lean collection of rooms on Botanic Avenue, has the populist, democratic spirit of the other bistros, enjoys extra-friendly staff, a good mix of ambience and attitude, but the cooking is more accomplished and enjoyable.

MIZUNA ®
99 Botanic Avenue, Belfast BT7
Tel: (01232) 230063
● **OPEN:** Noon-2.30pm, 6pm-10pm Tue-Sat.
● **AVERAGE PRICE:** Lunch under £15. Dinner under £20. Visa, Access/Master.

LA BELLE EPOQUE ®
61-63 Dublin Road, Belfast BT2
Tel: (01232) 323244
● **OPEN:** Noon-3pm, 6pm-11.30pm Mon-Fri, 6pm-11.30pm Sat.
● **AVERAGE PRICE:** Lunch under £15. Dinner under £20.
Visa, Access/Master, Amex, Diners.

LA BOHEME ®
103 Gt Victoria St, Belfast BT2
Tel: (01232) 240666
● **OPEN:** Noon-3pm, 6pm-11.30pm Mon-Fri, 6pm-11.30pm Sat.
● **AVERAGE PRICE:** Lunch under £15. Dinner under £20.
Visa, Access/Master, Amex, Diners.

CHEZ DELBART/FROGITIES ®
10 Bradbury Place, Belfast BT7
Tel: (01232) 238020
● **OPEN:** 5.30pm-midnight Mon-Sat, 5pm-9.30pm Sun.
● **AVERAGE PRICE:** Dinner under £25.
Visa, Access/Master, Amex, Diners.

BONNIE'S MUSEUM CAFÉ ®
11a Stranmillis Rd, Belfast BT7
Tel: (01232) 664914
● **OPEN:** 11am-11pm Mon-Sun.
● **AVERAGE PRICE:** Lunch under £5. Dinner under £10. No Cards.

MOLONEY'S ®
33-35 Malone Road, Belfast BT7
Tel: (01232) 682929
● **OPEN:** Noon-11pm Mon-Fri, noon-11.30pm Fri-Sat, noon-10pm Sun.
● **AVERAGE PRICE:** Lunch under £10. Dinner over £10.
Visa, Access/Master, Amex.

STRAND ®

12 Stranmillis Road, Belfast BT9
Tel: (01232) 682266
● **OPEN:** Noon-11pm Mon-Sat,
'till 10pm Sun.
● **AVERAGE PRICE:** Over £10.
Visa, Access/Master.

SAINTS & SCHOLARS, ABJ'S ®

1-3 University Street, Belfast
Tel: (S&S) (01232) 325137
Tel: (ABJ'S) (01232) 233700
● **OPEN:** (S&S) Noon-11pm Mon-Sat,
noon-10pm Sun (no lunch Sat); (ABJ's)
noon-11pm Mon-Sat, 12.30pm-10pm Sun.
● **AVERAGE PRICE:** (S&S) Under £15.
(ABJ's) Under £10. Visa, Access/Master.

THE CHINESE TRIBE

Think of every cliché you know
about Chinese restaurants:
indifferent food, tacky style,
brusque service and, at the end of it
all, the sort of bill which causes
severe bruising to the credit card.

Now, take yourself and the family
along to the Sun Kee, a little dining
room on Donegal Pass, just off
Shaftesbury Square in the heart of
the city, and across the street from
another Chinese restaurant, The
Manor House.

Push through the pair of doors,
and there, in all its modest glory, is
a little four-square, mirror-walled
room. There are a couple of doors
at the bottom end, there is a little
counter over on your left, and in
between is a collection of tables,
with a television set over against
the wall oozing some mindless sport
or whatnot. Perfect.

The Sun Kee is the real thing, a
reminder that Chinese restaurants
do not need to look like they have
been kitted out from a car boot sale
of lacquer panels.

Unadorned, uncompromised, this
is the friendliest Chinese restaurant
in the country, and its simple, true
food is awesome.

It is also cheap, a thrill which is
further helped by the fact that they
allow you to bring your own booze.
Your dining companions, for the
most part, will be members of
Belfast's Chinese community
enjoying some time out, having just
as good a time as you are.

If you want to meet your fellow
diners at work, then head down to
the Ormeau Road end of the Pass,
turn right up the hill, and you will
hit upon the Asia Supermarket after
half a mile or so. It is easy to spot,
because it is particularly ugly. Don't
let that put you off.

People who live in Belfast don't
know how lucky they are to have
this trove of culinary treasure in
town, for this is the best ethnic
shop in the country, and one of the
most exciting, inspiring places to
shop.

It is a great big barn of a place,
with entirely appropriate minimalist
décor – they have shelves, fridges,
freezers, a counter, and that's it –
and it is priceless.

The staff are delightful, the
accoutrements are seductive – woks
and steamers, shoes and cleavers –
and if you get out without having
spent twice what you intended, you
are made of stern stuff.

But don't blow all your money,

for just across the street from the Asia Supermarket is a little cabin called The Forever Chinese Home Bakery & Grocery.

The FCHB&G makes and sells some of the most ring-a-ding-ding dim sum savouries you can buy, just the thing to nibble on when the thought of what you are going to make for dinner has left you famished. This is real Chinese canteen cooking and kids adore these sticky, sweet, savoury masterpieces, so don't forget to indulge the inner child in yourself.

To get to the final member of the quartet of quality in this Chinese puzzle, we head back to Donegal Pass, to the Manor House. It is a more conventional style of Chinese restaurant – an unchanging menu, that ubiquitous décor and service – except that the cooking here is more than well above average, and the care which they take with vital details is evident in, for example, the fact of a decent wine list, sourced from Jim Nicholson of Crossgar.

In truth, the food doesn't put a foot wrong in the Manor House, and they are expert at preparing vegetarian feasts, given a little notice.

SUN KEE ®
38 Donegal Pass
Edmond Lau, Belfast BT7
Tel: (01232) 312016

● **OPEN:** 5pm-1am Sun-Thur, 5pm-11.30pm Sat. (Closed Fri).
● **AVERAGE PRICE:** Under £15.
No Cards.
Donegal Pass runs off Shaftesbury Square.

ASIA SUPERMARKET ⑤
Mrs Pau
189 Ormeau Road,
Belfast BT1
Tel: (01232) 326396

● **OPEN:** 10am-7pm Mon-Sun.

FOREVER CHINESE HOME BAKERY & GROCERY ⑤
Derek Lui
1 Agincourt Avenue
Belfast BT7
Tel: (01232) 235429

● **OPEN:** 11am-5pm Mon-Thur, Sat (closed Fri).

MANOR HOUSE ®
Tony Wong
47 Donegal Pass, Belfast BT7
Tel: (02232) 238755

● **OPEN:** Noon-midnight.
● **AVERAGE PRICE:**
Lunch under £15.
Dinner over £20.
Visa, Access/Master.
Donegal Pass runs off Shaftesbury Square.

WELCOME CHINESE RESTAURANT ®
22 Stranmillis Road, Belfast BT9
Tel: (01232) 681359

● **OPEN:** Noon-2pm, 5pm-11.30pm Mon-Fri, 5pm-midnight Sat, 5pm-11.30pm Sun.
● **AVERAGE PRICE:** Lunch under £15.
Dinner over £20.
Visa, Access/Master.
In the University area of Belfast.

THE ITALIAN TRIBE

While a lot of the ethnic cooking found in Belfast sells a style which seems to date from 25 years ago – the fishtank in the Chinese restaurant; the red-velvet banquette in the Indian restaurant; the cane-chair and Toulouse Lautrec posters in the bistros – no one has done a better job of selling an outdated and adorable image of an ethnic cuisine than the Italian tribe.

The image of Italian cooking which the brotherly restaurants Antica Roma, Villa Italia and Speranza conjure and sell is so clichéd that it is the culinary equivalent to John Ford's cod-Oirish movie "The Quiet Man". And, just like that daft piece of cinematic whimsy, the success of these places is testament to the power of nostalgia.
For this is an idea of Italy, and an idea of Italian cooking, as dreamt up by advertisers trying to sell mass-market pizzas and ice cream: Mamas and Mario Lanzas, fiascos and Alfa Romeos, a soundtrack of Pavarotti singing Puccini.

The food, therefore, is that curious polyglot Italian style only found far away from Italy, a style which will serve pasta alongside pizza, lather most things in a tomato sauce, dish up some cassata with a glass of sambucca and set fire to that slithery, syrupy drink and, then, give you a modest enough bill at the end of it all.

The brothers are well-suited: Speranza is elderly and modest, Villa Italia is functional and frenetic, and Antica Roma is slick and over-the-top, a film set which has wandered away from Cinécitta and somehow found itself on Botanic Avenue.

Their styles of cooking match their temperaments and it is highly likely, finding yourself in any one of them as the small hours approach, and that splash of Lambrusco nestles confidingly on your tie beside the stain from the tomato sauce, both of them awaiting the final splash from that slurp of sambucca, that you will be having a great night out.

ANTICA ROMA ℝ
Garrid Trainor
67 Botanic Avenue, Belfast BT7
Tel: (01232) 311121
● OPEN: 6pm-10.45pm Mon-Sat.
Closed Xmas week, 12 Jul.
● AVERAGE PRICE: Dinner over £20.
Visa, Access/Amex.
Just up from Shaftesbury Sq.

VILLA ITALIA ℝ
Gillian McCullough
39 University Road, Belfast BT7
Tel: (01232) 328356
● OPEN: Noon-2.30pm, 5pm-11.30pm Mon-Fri, 4pm-11.30pm Sat, 4pm-10.30pm Sun.
● AVERAGE PRICE: Lunch under £10. Dinner over £20.
Visa, Access/Master, Amex.

SPERANZA PIZZERIA ℝ
Bob Kerry
Shaftesbury Square, Belfast BT2
Tel: (01232) 230213
● OPEN: 5pm-11.30pm Mon-Sat.
● AVERAGE PRICE: Dinner under £15.
Visa, Access/Master. City Centre.

BELFAST SHOPS

ARCADIA ⑤
Willie Brown
378 Lisburn Road, Belfast BT9
Tel: (01232) 666779

Arcadia is one of the essential staples of the mecca of good food which rests at the top of the Lisburn road. Crammed from floor to ceiling with food, which further gives it the air of an old curiosity shop, it is a vital place which can usually manage to house whatever it is you want. Excellent, helpful staff who are as droll as the notices they write about the foods.

● **OPEN:** 7.30am-6pm Mon-Sat.

EATWELL ⑤
Jim Hunter
413 Lisburn Road, Belfast BT9
Tel: (0323) 664362

Jim Hunter's shop is one of the most discriminating wholefood shops, and is especially valuable as one of few places in the north where you can buy organic vegetables, produced for Eatwell by John Hoey. But there are lots of other sweet surprises to be found in store.

● **OPEN:** 8.30am-6pm Mon-Sat.

JUNE'S CAKE SHOP ⑤
June Henning
376 Lisburn Road, Belfast BT9
Tel: (01232) 668886

June Henning's shop is one of the great staples of the top of the Lisburn road, packed to the rafters at lunchtime with office workers buying soups and sarnies, and at other times it is otherwise crammed with matrons aiming to pass off not only the well-behaved baking, but also the smart savoury cooking, as their own.

● **OPEN:** 7.30am-5.30pm Mon-Sat.

MULHOLLAND'S ⑤
Jack Whiteman
382 Lisburn Road
Belfast BT9
Tel: (01232) 381920

Mulholland's always manage to have not only a good range of fruit 'n' veg, but also to have it in excellent condition. Along with June's and Coffey's, we might describe this little trio of quality as the Lisburn Road Triple Whammy.

● **OPEN:** 9am-6pm Mon-Sat.

SAWERS ⑤
Mr Graham
Fountain Centre
Belfast BT1
Tel: (01232) 322021

Sawers is a shop where they try to get things in season, endeavour to get things at their best, and then complete the process by making it enjoyable to shop here, thanks to amiable, confident staff.

A smart cook will find lots of inspiration in a tiny space which is, nevertheless, almost a one-stop shop.

● **OPEN:** 9am-5.30pm Mon-Sat.

DIRECT WINE SHIPMENTS Ⓢ
Kevin McAlindon
Corporation Square
Belfast BT1
Tel: (01232) 238700
Fax: (01232) 240202

"We had to make ourselves different", is how Jeremy Hinds of Direct Wines explains their success.

To this end, Jeremy Hinds and his youthful colleagues Peter and Neal McAlindon, have begun to travel the world of wine, taking in producers in the Rhone and the Midi, with Peter McAlindon working the 1995 vintage with the family firm of Brown Brothers in Australia.

"Your education becomes the customer's education", explains Mr Hinds. "Meeting the winemakers means that you are able to discuss and explain more about the wines. I feel this is important because the love of wine is in a large part being able to share it and being able to talk about it".

What DWS has created is its own style, its own milieu, by virtue of selling well-chosen wines from good estates.

The principle upon which they have hinged their future, combining education, exhibition and the enjoyment of wine, is a sound trinity of good sense, and a policy which will allow Direct Wines to improve organically and effortlessly. DWS have made themselves different, by making themselves better.

● OPEN: 9.15am-6.30pm Mon-Fri ('till 8pm Thurs), 10am-5pm Sat. Follow signs for the Seacat terminal.

THE PUB TRIBE

Belfast's pubs are not like the reflective, abstract, type of boozer you find in Dublin. Where Dublin pubs can be hedged about with flim-flam and caught up with social consciousness and touristic self-consciousness, Belfast's pubs are places you go to in order to drink.

Booze is what they are about, first, foremost, and finally. The serving and the drinking of it are their modus operandi, their raison d'être. Their orientation demonstrates an efficiency and practicality about drinking which Dubs just don't understand. Dublin has temples for boozing, Belfast has factories. These are some of the best boozers in Belfast.

CROWN LIQUOR SALOON
46 Great Victoria Street, Belfast

THE CUTTER'S WHARF
Lockview Road, Stranmillis, Belfast

THE DUKE OF YORK
11 Commercial Court, Belfast

KELLY'S CELLARS
30 Bank Street, Belfast

THE KITCHEN BAR
16 Victoria Square, Belfast

LAVERY'S BAR
14 Bradbury Place, Belfast

THE MORNING STAR
17 Pottinger's Entry, Belfast

MORRISON'S SPIRIT GROCERS
21 Bedford Street, Belfast

ROBINSON'S
38 Great Victoria Street, Belfast

THE ROTTERDAM BAR
Pilot Street, Belfast

It's not easy being green

When John Hoey talks about his work as a grower of organic vegetables and herbs, he will use terms such as "the wholeness" to describe the content, character and taste of a food.

When his friend and fellow grower John McCormick talks about the little stall he operates in Holywood, he will call it, half-jokingly, half-seriously, his "consulting rooms".

For here are two growers who not only share an holistic approach to their work, but also share penetrating intellects. They are not a couple of chaps well known to people in the North, but their influence on the restaurant culture has been profound.

Indeed, without Hoey and McCormick, it would be fair to say that the renaissance of restaurant cookery which has taken the North by storm would have happened much, much slower.

They have been a vital part of the equation, their restless, inquiring minds moving their work onwards, their ability to conceptualise their toil a further factor in influencing a sceptical public of the merit of what they do.

For there is a curious paradox at play when we consider the availability of organic foods in the North. If you eat in the best restaurants in Northern Ireland – the restaurants described in this book – you will eat foods grown by the two Johns. That glorious spinach with its life-giving vibrancy? That's Hoey's. Those mega-tastic Arran Victory potatoes with their purpled, tender skin and waxy-floury texture? McCormick grew those in Holywood, or down in Helen's Bay

Yet, if you try to buy these foods for yourself, in retail outlets, you will have a hard time finding them.

They have shaped the restaurant culture, but the retail culture remains fossilised, time-locked. There are only a few exceptions to this dismal picture, but one can be certain that this will begin to change soon.

For what will cause the public to turn on and tune in to organic food will be the increasing consciousness that we are what we eat and, so, if we eat a whole heap of pesticides, insecticides and other far-from-delicious agricultural drugs, well then we aren't going to feel just as good as we should.

The other factor will, of course, be taste. The imprimatur of the best chefs is this: start with the best product, and everything else flows naturally. Chefs understand that, and so do John and John, and that is why they have already had a big influence on your culinary life.

JOHN HOEY ●
Shandon, Mallusk
Tel: (01232) 832433

JOHN McCORMICK ●
Seaview Terrace, Holywood
Tel: (01232) 423063

Bushmills Whiskey

"Bushmills looks more like a Scottish distillery than many found these days in the Highlands", writes Jim Murray in his "Irish Whiskey Almanac". "Its lines are classically those of distilleries built in the boom years of Scotch whisky in the late 19th century, and are on a very grand scale".

The grandness of the buildings and the grandness of their product makes the distillery a busy tourist trap, but it really should be visited. If you can't make it, however, then transport yourself there via a glass of their brilliant varieties.

The taste for white Bushmills, as the basic brand is known, tends to be confined to locals, though it is subtle and ultimately persuasive.

But the 10 year-old Single Malt, the thunderous blend that is Black Bush, and the duty free-sold 1608 – described by Jim Murray as "one of Ireland's best whiskeys" – are marvellous, bewitching whiskeys, diverse, dedicated, full of fleeting notes of flavour that drum a merry dance around your head.

OLD BUSHMILLS DISTILLERY
Bushmills
Tel: (012657) 31521

● **OPEN:** 10am-noon, 2pm-4pm Mon-Thur, 10am-noon Fri.
Reservations necessary for groups.

JOURDAN'S ℝ
Alastair Fullerton
50 Main St, Connor, Kells
Tel: (01266) 892878

Alaistair Fullerton cut a swathe with his imaginative cooking when in the kitchen of Roscoff, and whilst he must cater to a more conservative clientele out here in north Antrim, his work is still suffused with flair and his cooking with flavour.

● **OPEN:** GRILL/STEAK BAR - 12.15pm-2.30pm, 5.15pm-9.30pm.
RESTAURANT - 6.30pm-10pm Tue-Sat, Sun lunch.
● **AVERAGE PRICE:** Lunch under £15. Dinner under £20. Access, Visa/Master.
At the junction with Parkgate Road.

THE GINGER TREE ℝ
Shotaro Obana
29 Ballyrobert Road
Newtownabbey
Tel: (01232) 848176

A minimalist dining room in a substantial farmer's house is home to an engaging Japanese restaurant, where the cooking is user friendly and enjoyable.

● **OPEN:** Noon-2.30pm Mon-Fri, 7pm-10pm Mon-Sat
● **AVERAGE PRICE:** Lunch under £15. Dinner under £20. Access, Visa/Master.
Take signs for Corrs Corner at the Glengormley Junction of the M2, then signs for Ballyclare, the restaurant is two miles on.

Antrim holidays

Whilst all around them have dwindled and declined, the north Antrim coastal towns where holidaymakers head to mop up a mixture of sunshine and rain endure and persist.

The golfers head for Portrush, droves of caravanners head for Portstewart and Ballycastle continues to exert a charm which some find intoxicating and others find amorphous.

Partly, these Victorian relics endure because of the strong sense of tradition which filters through the generations. And it is also a classless thing, this movement to the far north at holidaytime, with the bourgeoisie also having their favoured haunts and their holiday homes here and there.

And one of those favoured haunts is George McAlpin's Ramore restaurant and wine bar, right on the harbour at Portrush. This is not merely one of the best places to eat in the North, it is also one of the most seriously, calmly stylish places you will find to eat in Ireland.

George McAlpin's cooking nowadays has shaken off that French chapeau which dominated his style, in favour of a more easy-going, effective meld of influences. Wines are great, and on the right sort of balmy night, this is a mighty place.

The crack is also mighty in Rosemary White's Maddybenny Farmhouse, only a few miles away.

Tumultuous breakfasts are the speciality, and it is a cosy, welcoming place which now has some self-catering cottages.

MADDYBENNY FARM HOUSE Ⓐ
Rosemary White
18 Maddybenny Park
Portrush
Tel: (01265) 823394

● **OPEN:** All year except Xmas.
● **AVERAGE PRICE:**
B&B under £25.
No Credit Cards.
Off the A29, on the outskirts of Portrush.

RAMORE Ⓡ
George McAlpin
The Harbour
Portrush
Restaurant Tel: (01265) 824313
Wine Bar Tel: (01265) 823444

● **OPEN:**
RESTAURANT – 6.30pm-10.30pm Tue-Sat,
WINE BAR – 12.30pm-2.15pm, 5.30pm-9.15pm Mon-Sat.
● **AVERAGE PRICE:**
WINE BAR – under £10.
RESTAURANT – under £30.
WINE BAR – no cards
RESTAURANT – Visa, Access/Master
On the harbour in Portrush.

COUNTY DOWN

WINDSOR HOME BAKERY ⑤
36-38 Newry Street
Banbridge
Tel: (018206) 23666

This fine big shop has a greater
ambition than many of the
domestically-inclined bakeries of the
town and there are thoughtful extra
elements here which would not be
out of place in a French trâiteur:
good stuffed tomatoes and other
standby dishes which are so helpful
to the harassed cook.

The baking – whether their
celebrated fruit loaves or simple
things like farls and sticky buns – is
well executed, but the skill which is
so obvious is nevertheless quietly
focused around that comforting
homeliness which is so pleasing.

● **OPEN:** 8am-5.30pm Mon-Sat. Town
Centre.

THE AVA ⑤
The Hillen Brothers
132 Main Street
Bangor
Tel: (01247) 465490

One of the best independent off-
licences you will find, with a
smashing range of plonk, booze and
beers and staff who are endlessly
delightful and helpful.

● **OPEN:** 9.30am-9pm Mon-Sat.
Bangor town centre, opposite Post Office.

SHANKS Ⓡ
Richard Gibson
Robbie & Shirley Millar
The Blackwood
Crawfordsburn Road
Clandeboye, nr Bangor
Tel: (01247) 853313

Robbie Millar's cooking isn't quite
like anyone else's. He seems to work
a seam all of his own, drawing in
ideas with a freshness of conception
that makes his work very special.

If there are consistent themes
found in his work, then it may be the
fact that he utilises a sweetness in his
cooking which makes it friendly and
approachable, found in dishes like
pumpkin ravioli with a tomato and
sage butter, or tapenade crusted
goat's cheese with yellow sundried
tomatoes. This is food that you can't
help falling in love with, and any
intellectual doubts about its
unlikeliness are swept away the very
second you taste this cooking.

He works his magic in Shanks, a
lean, cool place where Shirley Millar
shows the sort of skills at front of
house which you can only be born
with. The design goes against the
grain of Northern Ireland suburban
– like Roscoff it is a place many folk

dislike due to its plainness and ergonomic efficiency – but Shanks has proven to be a huge success. Partly this is also due to the skills of the decisively enigmatic Richard Gibson, the general manager of the complex. Do give notice when you are booking that you want to eat vegetarian dishes, as the menus actually contain few non-meat dishes.

● **OPEN:** Bar food: 12.30pm-2pm Tue-Fri & Sun. Restaurant: 7.30pm-10pm Tue-Sat
● **AVERAGE PRICE:** Lunch under £10. Dinner over £20. Visa, Access/Master. Signposted from the A2, Bangor to Belfast Road at the Newtownards turn off.

CROSSGAR

JAMES NICHOLSON ⓢ
Jim & Elspeth Nicholson
27A Killyleagh Street
Crossgar
Tel: (01396) 830091, Fax: 830028

James Nicholson's profound skill as a wine merchant puts everyone else in the business in Ireland into second place. His selectivity and savvy means that his list is continually evolving and improving, always pitching up new surprises that can be so confoundedly delicious you wonder how everyone else can have missed them.

How does he do it? Well, for one thing, Nicholson successfully straddles the divide between the old school of wine merchant - the claret class, with their waistcoats and their sad posturing – and the new school – those eager souls with their mouths

as full of over-emphasised adjectives as they are of oaky Aussie chardonnay.

Residing comfortably somewhere in between is where Jim and Elspeth Nicholson have marked out their space. Nicholson is neither a snob nor an opportunist, and he is likely quite stubborn. Refusing to align himself with either camp has gifted him with a clear vision of his business which is gamely unclichéd, and which determines his work finding and selling great wines.

And here are the great wines. The choicest selections of the great growths and the grand crus: the benchmark-making oenologists from Australia and New Zealand; the most dynamic creators from the new bits of the old world.

But in addition to the classic producers and the new pretenders, Nicholson has assembled a fine list of the deeply unfashionable wines of Germany, stocks excellent sherries, and sells the best malts, Cognacs and ports. In short, if he has it, you want to drink it. He is the wine merchant's wine merchant, and all the other wine merchants know it.

Nicholson's now also operate a delivery service for the south, with free delivery on cases of wine. This operates out of a bonded warehouse in Dublin, and orders should be placed with Charles O'Reilly on (045) 483767.

● **OPEN:** 10am-7pm (shop), 9am-5pm (office). Delivery free throughout the north and south for a minimum order of one case. Killyleagh Street runs off the centre of Crossgar.

MARYBROOK MILLS
ABBEYCORN ORGANICS Ⓕ
John Lewis Crosby
Ralragh Road
Crossgar
Tel: (01396) 830173/574

"We give the flour an extra grind to flatten the bran, and I think this gives us a distinctive product", says John Lewis Crosby.

Indeed, but even without that extra grinding, Marybrook Stoneground Flour would be distinctive, for not only are the grinding stones powered by the water of the Ballynahinch River, but Marybrook Mills is actually the last combined corn and flax mill still intact.

John Lewis Crosby has been working Marybrook mill since 1987, though the history of the mill stretches back to the beginning of the eighteenth century. Recently, he has taken on the milling of Abbeycorn Organic Wholemeal, formerly produced by the monks in Portglenone.

Marybrook has that nice, toasty, subdued aroma which suggests it could be properly described as wholesome, as well as wholemeal. It makes a joyfully complex and zesty soda bread, rampant with flavour. The Abbeycorn Organics, meanwhile, is slightly rounder, denser, its flavours more compacted than the more open Marybrook flour.

● **OPEN:** The flours can be found in good shops and delis, and some Stewart's supermarkets.

THE CABIN Ⓢ
32 New Street, Donaghadee
Tel: (01247) 883598

A lovable little sweetie shop straight from the pages of a kiddie's book, where you head to for vanilla ice cream.

● **OPEN:** 11am-6.30pm Mon-Wed, 11am-9pm Fri-Sun. (Closed Thur).

THE BUCK'S HEAD INN Ⓟ
Craig & Maureen Griffith
Dundrum Village
Tel: (0139675) 868/859

A beer garden and conservatory are part of the attraction of the Buck's Head. More so is the extensive, imaginative full menu of vegetarian-food – a delightful surprise that is unusual in Irish pub food.

● **OPEN:** 12.30pm-2.30pm, 5.30pm-9pm Mon-Sat. 12.30pm-2.30pm, 5.30pm-8.30pm Sun.
● **AVERAGE PRICE:** Meals under £10. Visa, Access.
In the centre of Dundrum village.

DEANE'S ON THE SQUARE Ⓡ
Michael Deane
Station Square, Helen's Bay
Tel: (01247) 852841/273155

Michael Deane is a dazzlingly fine cook, and a man devoted to the business of being a chef. Indeed, his work can oftentimes seem like a map of current obsessions and attractions within the business of cooking, with his talent allowing him to select whatever fashions he chooses, and make them work.

Give them some notice that you are vegetarian and they can do delightful things such as casserole of lentils and potatoes, lovely tian of aubergine. Service is sometimes a little hesitant, and tends to work best when the restaurant is busy.

● **OPEN:** 7pm-10pm Tue-Sat,
12.30pm-3pm Sun.
● **AVERAGE PRICE:** Lunch under £20.
Dinner under £30.
Visa, Access/Master.
Top of Station Square.

HOLYWOOD

THE BAY TREE ®
Rosalind MacNeice
Audley Court
Holywood
Tel: (01232) 426414

Sue Farmer's cooking is the secret strength of The Bay Tree, her professionalism and culinary ambition the factor which lifts this attractive pottery shop and tea rooms out of the ordinary, and into the realms of something special.

The lunchtime standards are always well done – soups and bakes, excellent vegetarian dishes, scrumptious baking – but her ambition is best seen at the First Friday dinners, when her fluency with seeds and nuts is at its best in

creations such as a smart salad of rocket, beetroot, pear and hazelnuts. It is very relaxed food, quietly inventive, but its greatest asset may be the fact that it is just so thoughtful and considerate.

● **OPEN:** 10am-4.30pm, Mon-Sat.
First Fri in the month evenings by reservation only. Set back from the street amidst a courtyard of shops.

THE IONA Ⓢ Ⓡ ⊕
Heidi Brave
27 Church Road
Holywood
Tel: (01232) 428597

Heidi Brave's shop is not just the finest wholefood shop in the north, it is one of the finest shops in the North, a trove of good things chosen with great care. It manages to sell wholefoods without feeling wholefoody, and to sell gourmet things without being precious.

This is the result of Ms Brave's excellent connections: we have found farmhouse cheeses for sale in here that we didn't even know existed, and the affiliations with the organic and, especially, the bio-dynamic associations means that fine foods beat a path to her door.

Upstairs, the Iona Bistro sails along in its ever popular, BYO style, with assured cooking and relaxed ambience.

● **OPEN:** 9.15am-5.30pm Mon-Sat.
BISTRO – 12.30pm-2.30pm.
6.30-late Mon-Sat.
Holywood town centre.

PANINI ⓢ

Tony McNeil
25 Church Road
Holywood
Tel: (01232) 427774

Tony McNeil's shop has good Irish farmhouse and continental cheeses, the oils and pastas and other accoutrements from Carluccio, and lots of other vital deli items including the ubiquitous Cottage Pride preserves and freshly baked Continental frozen doughs.

● OPEN:
7am-6pm Mon-Sat.
Holywood town centre.

HOLYWOOD ORGANIC FOODS ⓢ

John McCormick
23 Seaview Terrace
Holywood
Tel: (01232) 423068

John McCormick is one of the most important and influential growers in the North, and in addition to supplying many restaurants, he has a stall in the Old Bell's Bakery, just a stone's throw from the crossroads in the centre of Holywood, each Saturday morning where you can buy his splendiferous vegetables, and ask his advice – John refers to the shop as his consulting rooms.

It is hoped, during the year, to develop the building, in association with the Camphill community at Glencraig, so watch that space.

● OPEN: 9am-5.30pm Sat.

SULLIVAN'S ⓡ

Simon Shaw
Sullivan Place
Holywood
Tel: (01232) 421000

Sullivan's is a modest space, where Simon Shaw prepares modest, soulful food, at modest prices. He has never bothered to secure a wine licence – this is a b.y.o. place – the ambience has remained informal, and has never lost track of the simplicity which is the true strength of his food.

It is not grandiose, or glamourous, but its democratic air and code of service makes it someplace which has, almost unwittingly, become someplace special.

● OPEN: 10am-4pm Mon-Sat,
6.30pm-10pm Tue-Sat.
● AVERAGE PRICE:
Lunch under £10.
Dinner under £20.
Visa, Access/Master.
Top of Sullivan Place, just off the main strip.

NEWTOWNARDS

HOMEGROWN ⓢ

Trevor & Margaret White
66B East Street
Newtownards
Tel: (01247) 818318

Good varieties of spuds, salad leaves, fresh fruits and berries, home-cooked meats.

● OPEN: 8am-5.30pm Mon-Sat.
At the top end of the town, and hard to find.

RECIPES

CLASSIC
contemporary

VEGETARIAN
combinations
from
IRELAND's

greatest chefs

SWEET SUMMER CHILL-OUT

Simon Connor's cooking often seems to perplex people. He loves simplicity and directness of flavour so much that the standard ballast of a dinner menu, those bits and pieces which conventionally surround the main item, hold little interest for him.

Instead, he prefers the very pure, almost Zen-like dedication of a single, simple thing, and this summer pea soup shows exactly what he tries to achieve. It is not merely a soup, but a soulful pillow of sweet summer tastes, with all that yearning greenness caught up in a bowl which is gorgeously refreshing and satisfying.

Indeed, the beauty of this dish is not just its flavour, but its ability to represent something more than itself, to offer us an elemental echo of natural flavours. And, like any splendid dish, it needs no more than some good company – this is a great summer dinner dish, thanks to its ease of preparation – and some good, chilled white wine.

SIMON CONNOR'S CHILLED MINTED PEA SOUP

SERVES SIX

50ml (2 fl oz) olive oil

1 small onion, peeled and diced

1 small leek, washed and sliced

2 sticks celery, chopped

2 cloves of garlic, peeled and minced

1.2 litres (2 pints) vegetable stock

900g (2 lbs) peas

2 tablespoons fresh mint leaves

salt and freshly ground black pepper

50ml (2 fl oz) yogurt

Method: Heat the olive oil in a saucepan and add the onion, leek, celery, garlic and cook, stirring for 4-5 minutes, or until the vegetables are softened.
● Add the stock, bring to the boil and simmer for twenty five minutes. Stir in the peas and mint and simmer for fifteen minutes. Purée the mixture until smooth. Pass through a sieve. Taste for seasoning.
● Chill in the refrigerator.
● Serve in individual bowls with a spoonful of the yogurt.

MAKING THE MIGHTY MISO

"The number of ways to prepare a good miso soup are perhaps as many as there are cooks. Miso soup can change in flavour as you change or vary the combination of vegetables. However, it is better to use strong flavoured vegetables, especially root vegetables."

Claudia Meister's directions for superb miso soup correctly point out that miso can be all things to all cooks, but this miso is very distinctly hers, showcasing her love of direct

but thunderously pure and revitalising flavours.

Here is a soup to make you feel reborn, a scintillating romp of tastes which Ms Meister's work seems devoted to capturing, whatever ingredients or ideas she has to hand.

Mugi miso is a dark, fermented barley & soya bean paste, and contributes a powerful complexity and richness to the final concoction.

This is a an unforgettable invention, goodness itself.

LISS ARD LAKE LODGE MISO SOUP

SERVES FOUR

sesame oil

4 onions, quartered

3 carrots, thickly sliced

2 leeks in slices (white parts only)

3 shallots, unpeeled in quarters

1 large piece ginger, broken & crushed

1 bulb garlic

2 bay leaves

dried shiitake mushrooms (and/or porcini, champignons)

mixed fresh sage, parsley stalks, rosemary, coriander & Sichuan pepper corns, to taste

red wine vinegar

soya sauce

generous 1 litre (2 pints) vegetable stock

mugi miso

Garnish of one or more of the following: chives, sliced spring onions, crispy seaweed, hijiki

Method: Brown all the vegetables in a large pan with some sesame oil. Let them get really brown as this adds to the dark colour and the main taste of the miso soup later. Add a little red wine vinegar and a little soya sauce. Cover the vegetables with vegetable stock and bring to a simmer. Leave simmering for one hour.

● Put the liquid through a very fine sieve and heat again.

● Take away from the stove and mix in mugi miso (1-2 rounded teaspoons per person, or more to taste). Do not boil miso!

● Serve with some chives or spring onions or crispy seaweed or hijiki.

THE WILDNESS OF MILDNESS

The sublime subtlety of this dish is mesmerising. Where so much modern cooking tends towards the overt and the overstated, this meld of mellifluity shows the confidence and modesty of Stefan Matz's work. Rather than assail you with the power of its respective ingredients, the garlic, ricotta and rosemary are used with astute restraint, and flavours which with other cooks would attack like a steel claw, are here harnessed to behave like a silk glove. The keynote is the word "mild", which does not mean bland, but rather poised, seductive, a dish which calls for a wine of equal merit, like a fine, achingly cool Riesling.

STEFAN MATZ'S PASTA WITH MILD GARLIC, RICOTTA AND FRESH ROSEMARY

SERVES FOUR

4 large shallots, roughly chopped

3 cloves garlic, roughly chopped, seedling taken out

butter

6 sprigs fresh rosemary, chopped

100ml (3 fl oz) dry white wine

400ml ($^3/_4$ pint) vegetable stock

150ml ($^1/_4$ pint) fresh cream

salt, pepper, lemon juice

100g (2oz) crumbly ricotta cheese

50g (1oz) butter

Pasta for four people (tagliatelli or spaghetti are recommended)

Method: Sweat the shallots and garlic in butter until soft. Add the rosemary. Add the white wine, boil to evaporate. Add the vegetable stock and cream and let simmer for 20 minutes, stirring occasionally. Purée the sauce in a food processor and strain through a sieve.

● Bring the sauce to the boil, adjust the seasoning with salt, pepper and some lemon juice. Add a few cubes of ice cold butter. Cook pasta to al dente, strain and add to the sauce. Mix thoroughly. Serve in a bowl and crumble the ricotta cheese over the pasta. Garnish with finely chopped rosemary and some chopped tomatoes.

● If desired the butter can be replaced with olive oil, and the cream is optional. When cooking the sauce without cream it is recommended to thicken the sauce slightly with flour to give the sauce a coating consistency.

POLITICS AND PUMPKINS

Conrad Gallagher's true gift is to prepare food which is not merely artistically and architecturally impressive, but also mesmerisingly delicious. In this masterpiece the sweetness of the pumpkin is embraced by the fire of the chilli and the grilled vegetables crown a monumental dish. For Conrad Gallagher, there is no difficulty in reconciling these elements – he should have been a politician.

CONRAD GALLAGHER'S PUMPKIN RISOTTO WITH GRILLED VEGETABLES AND CHILLI AIOLI

SERVES FOUR

Chilli Aiöli:
100ml (3 fl oz) olive oil
1 garlic clove, crushed
3 red chillies, sliced
1 tablespoon tomato purée
2 tomatoes, chopped
fresh rosemary

Grilled Vegetables:
1 red pepper
1 green pepper
1 small aubergine
2 field mushrooms
2 red onions
olive oil
lemon juice, salt and pepper

Pumpkin Risotto
1 tablespoon olive oil
1 garlic clove, crushed
1 shallot, diced
3 sprigs fresh rosemary, chopped
stripped leaves from 3-5 sprigs fresh thyme
1.2 litres (2 pints) vegetable stock
225g (8oz) arborio rice
25g (1oz) mascapone cheese
55g (2oz) natural yogurt
25g (1oz) grated parmesan
55g (2oz) puréed pumpkin
salt and pepper
3 tablespoons extra virgin olive oil

Method: Make the chilli aiöli 24 hours in advance. Sauté the garlic, chilli and rosemary in the olive oil. Add the tomato purée and tomatoes. Gently cook until the chilli softens. Remove from the heat and allow to cool and infuse overnight. Sieve, pushing through the tomato pulp and the oil. Stir before using.

● One hour before cooking, marinate the sliced vegetables in the olive oil, lemon juice and seasonings. To make the risotto combine the garlic, shallot, rosemary and thyme and olive oil in a large pan. Sweat over low heat for approximately 10-15 minutes until shallot is soft. Do not allow to colour.

● Meanwhile heat the vegetable stock in a separate pan. Increase the heat and add the rice to the garlic mixture. Sauté for 2-3 minutes or until the rice starts to turn golden.

Stir continuously.

● Add the hot vegetable stock a few ladlefulls at a time, continuing to stir, allowing each ladlefull to be absorbed before adding the rest. Continue to add stock until you reach the desired consistency, the rice should be al dente.

● Add the mascapone cheese and natural yogurt and the pumpkin purée. Season and add some extra-virgin olive oil to taste. Mix well.

● Grill the vegetables, turning occasionally.

● To serve: place a layer of risotto into a large warmed bowl. Season with more black pepper and layer the grilled vegetables on top. Sprinkle with grated Parmesan and drizzle with chilli aioli.

● Serve immediately.

GOODNESS GRACIOUS GREATNESS

If this great dish of Gerry Galvin's shows one single thing above all its many qualities, it is the intellectual liberation which this great chef enjoys. Who else would spice the risotto with dried fruit, and spice that fruit? Who else would think of a simple, zingy compote as the perfect foil for the rice balls? Gerry Galvin doesn't so much invent dishes as dream them, and he is fortunate, then, in having the technical gifts to bring them to realisation, delicious realisation. There are no frontiers in his work, either as a chef or as a restaurateur, in which guise he has long been the most radical, inventive personality in the country.

GERRY GALVIN'S RICE BALLS WITH PEPPER COMPOTE
SERVES SIX

The Rice:

1 tablespoon vegetable oil
25g (1oz) butter
1 shallot, finely chopped
1 clove garlic, chopped
40g (1$^1/_2$ oz) mixed dried apricots, finely diced
1 teaspoon ground coriander
1 level dessertspoon cumin seeds
pinch ground ginger
176g (6oz) Arborio rice
1 litre (1$^3/_4$ pints) vegetable stock
a handful of finely shredded coriander leaves
salt, pepper, flour,
oil for deep frying

Pepper Compote:

1 red, yellow and green pepper (seeded and sliced thinly)
2 medium onions (sliced thinly)
1 tablespoon olive oil
1 tablespoon white wine
1 tablespoon honey
1 tablespoon white wine vinegar
Salt and white pepper.

Method: To make the Compote – In a heavy-based saucepan cook all ingredients, covered, for 3 minutes. Uncover and simmer for 10 minutes. Stir now and then, season to taste.

● Cook the rice as if you were making a risotto. In a large pan sauté the onion and garlic in the butter and vegetable oil. As they begin to colour add the finely chopped dried apricots, the spices and the rice. Stir until all the grains of rice are coated, and then little by little, add the boiling stock, only adding more as the stock becomes absorbed in the rice. The risotto should be just sticky – not too liquid. Season with salt and pepper and the finely shredded coriander leaves. Allow to cool.

● To make the rice balls heat the oil until a grain of rice sizzles the second it touches it. Form the rice into balls with floured hands. Deep fry until just crispy. Drain and serve with the compote.

THE MODERN BAKE

Some cooks just create goodness with all the things they do, and Margaret Duffy's cooking just creates goodness, day in, day out. It makes not merely for delicious, lip-smacking eating, but for the sort of food which is a balm for the soul, which seems almost to have healing powers.

This bake is typical of her work. Generous with flavour, it is a dish which is generosity itself, a complete meal, achieved with prudent consideration. The freshness of the vegetables is delightfully counterpointed by the rich savour of the blue cheese.

But there is more, of course, to being a great cook than just appreciating what ingredients work together. The blend here, and the accumulation of textures, shows how a clever cook can make a dish in which the absence of meat is never a consideraion. This is the sort of modern vegetarian cooking which blows out of the water that moribund rubbish which sets out to imitate meat and meat flavours, and thus fatally compromises itself.

Ms Duffy shows that a clever cook simply sets out on a different path, and achieves something much more accessible, much more delicious. It's a typical 101 Talbot invention, but, alas!, cooking it at home means that one cannot enjoy the handsome company of Ms Duffy's partner, Pascal Bradley, and his elegant witticisms.

MARGARET DUFFY'S BROCCOLI, FENNEL, FLAT MUSHROOM & POTATOES BAKED WITH CHEESE

SERVES FOUR

4 cloves garlic, crushed

4 potatoes, peeled & sliced

2 heads fennel, sliced

350g (12oz) broccoli, well trimmed

6 large flat mushrooms, thinly sliced

Glass white wine

175ml (6 fl oz) cream

225g (8oz) Cashel Blue cheese, cubed

115g (4oz) grated mozzarella

olive oil

Method: Heat the oven to its hottest temperature. Heat oil in the baking tray and cook potatoes and garlic in it. Remove from the oven.

● Place in layers in this order: cooked potato, fennel, broccoli, Cashel Blue and mushrooms.

Pour white wine, cream, a little salt and a good pinch of ground black pepper. Cover with tin foil and bake in the oven for 45 minutes, approx. Remove tin foil.

● Top with mozzarella and brown under the grill. Serve with tossed green salad.

I DREAM OF AUBERGINE, MUNG BEAN, AND THEE

Mung bean and aubergine has the sort of sweet internal rhymes which would appeal to a great wordsmith like Lorenz Hart, and you might very well find yourself scripting an ode to joy after you cook Tim Boland's effortlessly delicious dish.

As you would expect from a cook who worked alongside Margaret Duffy in Dublin's 101 Talbot restaurant, Mr Boland carries a torch for flavour, the sort of flavours which attach themselves to the raft of good things which is this casserole.

The combination of ingredients comes together brilliantly here to sing with one voice, as you yourself may well do...

"I dream of an auberge, serving aubergine and mung bean, as made by Tim...". Well, your version will scan better.

TIM BOLAND'S MUNG BEAN AND AUBERGINE CASSEROLE

SERVES FOUR

2 large aubergines, cubed	6-8 cloves garlic, minced
4 breakfast flat mushrooms	115g (4oz) mung beans, soaked and cooked
sunflower and sesame oil	1 teaspoon ground coriander
1 onion, chopped	1 teaspoon Chinese five-spice powder
2 bulbs fennel, diced	15g ($^1/_2$ oz) dillisk, chopped into bite size
2 inches ginger, grated	pieces
juice and zest of 1 lemon	1 sprig carageen moss, crumbled
1 or 2 chillies, seeds removed, slivered	salt & soya sauce

Method: Toss the aubergines in some sunflower and sesame oil and roast in a hot oven for approximately 20 minutes. After about 10 minutes add the garlic and toss before returning to the oven. Roast the mushrooms also, whole, for approximately 15 minutes.

● Sweat the onion, chilli and ginger in sunflower oil. Add the fennel, spices and seaweed, and when these have softened add the lemon and 1 pint water. Simmer for 20 minutes. Take the aubergines and mushrooms from the oven, chop the mushrooms and add both to the fennel mixture. Finally stir in the cooked beans. Simmer the lot for about 5 minutes.

● The best condiment for this dish is Japanese wasabi sauce.

CONVINCING THE CRITICS

We brought a friend to Avoca Handweavers one day for lunch. A food writer, with an international reputation, a garland of awards, and the most exacting critical disposition of anyone we know. She was the kind of person who would – and should – give you much pause when deciding where to bring her for lunch.

But when you think of Joanna Hill's cooking at Avoca, and its elegance and trueness, its confidence and its fluid embrace of and command of flavour, you wonder why you would consider going anywhere else. So we went to Avoca.

The sun shone, we sat on the verandah, and lunch was stunning, full of the simple gestures and tastes which are to be found in this demon piperade tart, abetted by good things such as real lemonade, real biscuits, soft, sweet bread.

Our friend was, of course, bowled over, for nothing is so impressive, to the critic with the hyperactive critical faculty, than simplicity, than knowing when something is just right, than knowing when something is perfect. This tart is one of those just right, just perfect things which they do in Avoca Handweavers.

JOANNA HILL'S PIPERADE TART

SERVES FOUR TO SIX

Pastry:
225g (8oz) flour
115g (4oz) butter, cold
salt and pepper
1 tablespoon olive oil
iced water
1 egg

Filling:
1 Spanish onion
3 red peppers
3 yellow peppers
olive oil
225g (8oz) soft goat's cheese
4 beef/plum tomatoes
large bunch of basil

Method: Rub the butter into the seasoned flour. Beat together the egg and olive oil. Add to the flour with enough water to bring the pastry together. Wrap in cling film and leave to rest in the fridge for 1 hour. Roll out and line a 12-inch tart tin (with a remomvable base). Bake blind.
● Cut the onion into half rings and cut the peppers into strips. Heat about 2 tablespoons of olive oil in a saucepan. Cook the onions and the peppers on a high heat for about 10 minutes and then turn the heat down and cook, uncovered, turning occasionally, for about an hour until the mixture resembles marmalade. Season after about half an hour.
● Slice the goat's cheese and crumble over the pastry base. Spread the pepper mixture (piperade) on top. Slice the tomatoes and arrange on top. Bake at 200C/400F for approximately 20 minutes. Tear up the basil and mix with 2 tablespoons olive oil. Spread over the top of the tart. Serve warm.

A SYMPHONY OF SMALL DETAILS

Sheila Keiro's cooking has something of a musical element, a factor perhaps emphasised by her fondness for working themes and variations on a set of given ingredients, just as a musician might improvise over basic themes to create something new.

But like a good musician, she likes to spice things up a little, to create her own signature. The use here of the nuts and seeds, of the tarragon and the apricots, sets this apart from a conventional salad, with these added elements contributing contrast, surprise. They represent small gestures with the dish, but vital ones, the sort of grace notes one would expect from such an intuitive cook.

Freshness of flavour and trueness of taste are her aims, something which this simple salad captures perfectly. It is a classic party salad dish, inasmuch as simplicity of preparation and its guarantee of solid satisfaction make it a failsafe, a future staple of your repertoire.

SHEILA KEIRO'S BISTRO CARROT & APPLE SALAD

MAKES ONE LARGE BOWL

The Dressing:
juice of 1 lemon
$1^1/_2$ tablespoons chopped tarragon
125ml ($4^1/_2$ fl oz) olive oil
salt and freshly ground black pepper

The Salad:
700g ($1^1/_2$ lbs) carrots, washed, peeled
3 Granny Smith apples, peeled, cored and quartered
115g (4oz) dried apricots, chopped
3 tablespoons each of pinenuts, green pumpkin seeds, sunflower seeds
parsley

Method: Blend all the Dressing ingredients together in a processor or whisk together to make a dressing.

● Coarsely grate the carrot and apple and mix together.

● Add apricots, pinenuts, pumpkin seeds and sunflower seeds and mix well together.

● Add dressing and toss through ingredients to coat.

● Put into a salad bowl and garnish with freshly chopped parsley.

THE KNOCK-OUT MONSTER MASH

The Elephant & Castle has built its enormous success, and its enormous influence, on the fundamental things.

Ambience, service, value, all are things you can take for granted when you walk through the doors in the E&C. And, of course, the thing you can most take for granted is the respect and patience which they show to simple, staple foods. Like good mash. Like a knockout mash with sun-dried tomatoes and basil, this splendid idea from prep chef Joe O'Brien.

For this dish shows the sort of alchemy they can achieve in the E&C. It is extremely simple, and yet its success depends on perfect balance, on a determination to get each detail right. A nice, dry, floury spud, all the better to make a smooth, light mash. Good tomatoes; fresh basil; fine butter. And plenty of elbow grease, to whip it to a froth of perfection.

Simple, of course. And yet, you will strain to do it just as well as they do it in the E&C. Don't let this put you off making it at home, for it is indubitably delicious, and if you live in Newport, let's say, it's quite a hack to Temple Bar to try Joe's mash. That's Newport, Rhode Island, by the way.

Their ability to get these simple things perfect floods one with admiration for Liz Mee and her team. There is a driven quality about their work which has never dimmed throughout their time in business, and today they burn, burn, burn as brightly as ever.

JOE O'BRIEN'S MASHED POTATO WITH BASIL AND SUNDRIED TOMATO

SERVES FOUR

900g (2lbs) potatoes

25g (1oz) butter

75ml (2-3 fl oz) cream

Half cup fresh basil leaves, julienned

1 cup sundried tomatoes (in oil, drained), julienned

1 clove garlic, minced

Salt and Pepper

Method: Boil potatoes in salted water until soft. Drain (reserving a little of the cooking water) and dry over a low heat.

● Heat the butter and cream, and add the potatoes and mash very well. Season well with salt and pepper.

● Add remaining ingredients, stirring, not mashing. Check seasoning.

● Do remember to make loads of the purée, as leftovers make the most delicious potato cakes for breakfast, brunch or lunch.

UP TO THE MINUTE AND AGELESS

On the face of it, Denis Cotter's work seems as voguish as all get out. Just look at this casserole, with its olives and goat's cheese complementing the basic staples. And look at the potato cake, with its crinkling of trendy rocket leaves. Up to the minute stuff.

Yet when you eat Denis Cotter's food it is the almost age-old style of his work, its respect for seasonality and freshness, its intellectual rigour which impresses. This completeness is vital, for he has evolved a very personal style of cooking which has all the comfort and the succulence which so much vegetarian cookery lacks. Nothing is missing in a dish like this. It has everything it needs, and no more. But if it is perfect, it is also soulful, and fun to cook. Truth be told, this cooking is beyond fashion, just as you would expect from the foremost vegetarian cook in Ireland.

DENIS COTTER'S LEEK, FENNEL & BUTTERBEAN CASSEROLE WITH OLIVES, HERBS AND GOAT'S CHEESE. SERVED WITH POTATO-ROCKET CAKES

SERVES SIX

Sauce:
1 onion, thinly sliced in rounds
10 garlic cloves, sliced
1 tablespoon olive oil
6-8 tomatoes, sliced in rounds
1 tablespoon tomato passata
150mls (5 fl oz) white wine
3 bay leaves
100g (4oz) black olives, halved

Casserole:
3-4 fennel bulbs, halved, cored and sliced
4 good sized leeks, chopped
100g (4oz) dry butterbeans – soaked, cooked
100g (4oz) goat's cheese log

olive oil
salt, pepper
handful of fresh seasonal herbs

Potato/Rocket Cakes:
700g (1lb 8oz) floury potatoes, steamed, mashed
small bunch scallions, finely chopped
punch nutmeg
1 teaspoon Dijon mustard
50g (2oz) cream cheese
1 tablespoon butter
1 egg
two handfuls chopped rocket leaves
salt and pepper
breadcrumbs
olive oil for frying

Method: Sauté onion and garlic in the oil until softened. Add wine and reduce. Add the rest of the sauce ingredients and stew until tomatoes are beginning to break up. Set aside.
● Stew the fennel in 2 tablespoons oil in a covered heavy-based pan until beginning to soften, adding a splash of water if necessary (about 10 mins). Add a further tablespoon of oil with the leeks and repeat until the leeks are softening, Then add the beans, the tomato sauce, seasoning and add herbs. Cook, uncovered until the sauce thickens. Tip into a serving dish, or onto individual plates. Crumble the cheese over and melt it under a hot grill.
● To make the potato cakes: Cook the potatoes and mash with the rest of the ingredients. Shape and coat with the breadcrumbs. Chill, then shallow fry over a medium heat.

SUSTAINING THE FATE OF NATIONS

This is such a great dish that it could sustain the fate of nations. A true flavour raver, it nevertheless has that element of comfort and lushness which is a hallmark of Denis Cotter's work, the pillows of pumpkin and almond snuggling in amidst the feta custard, with the terrific torchy taste of a brilliant coriander and chilli pesto to send everything skywards. If any one dish amongst these recipes shows the bend and amend discipline at the root of modern Irish vegetarian cookery, then perhaps this is it. Ingredients are altered from the classics, techniques are assimilated and adapted, and all in the service of making something truly delicious.

DENIS COTTER'S PUMPKIN & ALMOND CABBAGE DOLMA IN FETA CUSTARD WITH CORIANDER & CHILLI PESTO

SERVES FOUR

The Dolma:
12 leaves Savoy or Spring cabbage, stalks trimmed and boiled for 5 mins
1 onion, diced
6 cloves garlic, crushed
1 teaspoon cumin seeds
2 small chillies, chopped
$1/_4$ teaspoon nutmeg
juice of half a lime
$1/_4$ teaspoon cinnamon
2 tablespoons parsley, chopped
$1/_4$ teaspoon salt
115g (4oz) whole skinned almonds, toasted and chopped
1 small pumpkin (about 900g/2lbs)
1 egg

55g (2oz) breadcrumbs
The Custard:
100g (4oz) feta
2 cloves garlic
400mls (14 fl oz)yogurt
1 egg
pinch cayenne pepper

Coriander & Chilli Pesto
4 small green chillies
100g (4oz) fresh coriander
25g (1 oz) almonds, blanched & peeled
2 cloves garlic
juice 1 lime
pinch of salt
olive oil (about 300ml/$1/_2$pint)

Method: Combine the custard ingredients in the food processor and reserve. Make the Pesto by combining all ingredients except the olive oil in the processor and grind until smooth. Add the olive oil as you go until you achieve a thick pouring consistency.

● To make the Dolma peel, seed and chop the pumpkin. Steam until it softens then mash roughly with a fork. Cook the onion and spices in a little oil until soft, then combine with the other ingredients. Allow to cool. Place about a tablespoon of pumpkin mixture at the base of a cabbage leaf, and roll up fairly tightly, tucking in the sides to make a secure parcel.
● Repeat and arrange all the parcels in an oven dish. Pour the feta custard over and bake at a medium heat until custard is browned a little and set softly.
● Serve with the pesto poured over.

INDEX

OTHER TITLES FROM ESTRAGON PRESS

WRITTEN BY
JOHN & SALLY McKENNA

THE BRIDGESTONE IRISH FOOD GUIDE

THE BRIDGESTONE 100 BEST SERIES:

THE BRIDGESTONE 100 BEST RESTAURANTS IN IRELAND

THE BRIDGESTONE 100 BEST PLACES TO STAY IN IRELAND

THE BRIDGESTONE 100 BEST PLACES TO EAT IN DUBLIN

**THE BRIDGESTONE TITLES ARE AVAILABLE
FROM ALL GOOD BOOK SHOPS**